HUMAN
NONVERBAL
BEHAVIOR

HUMAN NONVERBAL BEHAVIOR

an annotated bibliography

COMPILED BY
CONSTANCE E. OBUDHO

GP GREENWOOD PRESS
Westport, Connecticut • London, England

178234

R

016.00156
0 12

Library of Congress Cataloging in Publication Data

Obudho, Constance E.
    Human nonverbal behavior.

    Includes indexes.
    1. Nonverbal communication—Bibliography.
I. Title
Z7204.C59025 [BF637.C45]   016.00156   79-7586
ISBN 0-313-21094-2

Library of Congress Catalog Card Number: 79-7586
ISBN: 0-313-21094-2

First published in 1979

Greenwood Press, Inc.
51 Riverside Avenue, Westport, Connecticut 06880

Printed in the United States of America

10 9 8 7 6 5 4 3 2 1

To Our Beloved Children:
Leslie Dianne Ayier
Christopher James Odare

Contents

Preface

This bibliography presents articles and books about human non-verbal behavior written between 1940 and 1978. This particular time span was chosen partially to control for the vast number of works which would have been included without this limitation and also because many of the works which were done prior to 1940 were published in foreign languages whose translations were not readily available. The bulk of nonverbal behavior studies has been done in the 1950s, 1960s, and 1970s. Including works from the 1940s, this bibliography provides the necessary background sources for many of the topics studied and the approaches used today.

Each work is accompanied by a brief and uncritical description of the purpose, procedure, and results of the study or book where applicable. An annotation is not provided for works which were not directly available or when a secondary source was unavailable. In addition, some annotations are summaries of abstracts from *Psychological Abstracts* when the original source could not be secured. A phrase indicating "Summary of Abstract" follows these annotations in parentheses. The works are divided into two sections: Studies with Normal Individuals and Studies with Psychiatric Subjects. At times, the subject sample included both types of individuals. In such cases the work has been put into the psychiatric subject section. Each section is alphabetized according to author's name or title of the work, and each author's name or title is preceded by an entry number. These numbers run consecutively, from the first to the last section. There are also an Author Index and a Subject Index.

Hopefully, this book will serve as a convenient source of references for individuals who are interested in nonverbal communication. However, it is a fact that any bibliography is subject to errors and omissions. I would appreciate hearing from readers who can supply corrections or additions.

I would like to express my gratitude to my husband Robert who was patient with me and looked after our children during those times when the work was hectic. I would also like to thank Mrs. Cecilia Harbester who did another wonderful job in typing my manuscript.

Introduction

THE STUDY OF NONVERBAL BEHAVIOR

Nonverbal communication in humans provides an interesting and exciting area of investigation. The disciplines which have undertaken the study of this phenomenon are quite diverse. Investigations have been done by biologists, ethologists, sociologists, clinical psychologists, anthropologists, social psychologists, and even a pastor. Although there has been some controversy over the definition of nonverbal behavior, most researchers have assumed that if words are not spoken or written, the behavior involved is nonverbal in nature (Knapp, 1972, p. 4).

There are numerous studies concerning the ways in which people communicate without words. Birdwhistell has asserted that communication is a continuous interaction process containing multileveled, overlapping, discontinuous segments of behavior. Research with visible body motion is beginning to show that this behavior is as ordered and coded as verbal language (Argyle, 1973, p. 93). In referring to language, Birdwhistell said:

> Who knows how any human internalizes the conventional understanding of his social group to the extent that his social behavior becomes by and large predictable to other members of his group? . . . There is little solace in a so-called "Learning Theory" although one is impressed with [how subjects can be trained]. The fact remains that infants from every society in the world can and do internalize the communication system of that society in approximately the same amount of time so that the "normal" 6-year-old is able to move smoothly within the communication system of his society. (Argyle, 1973, p. 6)

Investigators are attempting to determine whether or not similar statements can be made about nonverbal communication.

Just as there are subdivisions of linguistic study, there are subdivisions of nonverbal behavior research. *Kinesics,* which is defined as the systematic study of those patterned and learned aspects of body motions that can be demonstrated to have communicational value (Knapp, 1963, p. 125), is one subdivision. Birdwhistell (1970), an outstanding researcher in this area, has conducted a number of experiments on the communicational effect of body motion. He has also devised a notational system for recording such behavior. Other researchers have noted these behavior patterns in terms of the space used during social interactions. This spatial usage is considered another form of nonverbal behavior or communication. The expression *personal space,* coined by Katz (1937), has been used to describe this phenomenon. An extensive study of personal space was made by Hall (1955 and 1966) who discovered cultural differences in the use of space as a form of nonverbal communication. Hall chose to call the phenomenon *proxemics.* From interviews and observations of middle-class, healthy, adult American males and females, usually coming from the northeastern United States, Hall characterized four interaction distances—intimate, personal, social, and public. His terms were chosen to describe the activities and relationships associated with each distance. In his research on cultural differences in the usage of space, Hall found that Germans used larger areas of personal space and were less flexible in their spatial behavior than Americans. Arabs, the French, and Latin Americans, on the other hand, were much more tolerant of close quarters and had smaller personal distances than Americans. Finally, certain sex differences were found. Hall observed that American males preferred to stand 18-20 inches from each other during face-to-face interactions, but about 22-24 inches from a female under the same conditions.

Sommer (1969) also studied the characteristics of personal space behavior and presented an interesting review of the ways people behave and are expected to behave according to the dynamics of this phenomenon. For example, he noted that during police interrogations, one police textbook recommended that the interrogator sit close to the suspect with no desk or table between them because an obstruction of any sort would give the suspect a degree of confidence and relief. At the beginning of the interrogation the officer's chair could be two or three feet away, but after the session had begun, the officer should move his chair closer so that ultimately one of the suspect's knees would be just about in between the interrogator's two knees. Another example told of a theater owner who noticed how crowds arranged themselves in his lobby before each picture. The lobby was designed to hold about 200 people who would wait behind a roped area for the theater to clear. According to the owner, when a family picture like

Mary Poppins or *Born Free* was showing, only about 100 to 125 people could be lined up because they tended to stand about one foot apart and did not touch the person in front or behind them. However, when a sex comedy such as *Tom Jones* or *Irma la Douce* was playing, he could get 300 to 350 people in the same space. The patrons tended to stand so close to each other that the theater owner jokingly remarked, "You'd think they were all going to the same home at the end of the show" (p. 29). These two anecdotes suggest some of the powers and processes of nonverbal behavior.

Another aspect of behavior treated in nonverbal research is the expression of emotion in the face of man. This particular type of behavior has been studied for some time. In 1872, Darwin published *The Expression of Emotion in Man and Animals*. His purpose was to determine which human expressive movements were innate and universal and which were learned and, consequently, culturally specific. More recent interest in facial expressions of affect has been taken over by such researchers as Tomkins and McCarter (1964) and Ekman, Friesen, and Tomkins (1971), to mention but a few. It is generally felt that certain facial expressions of emotion are universal, but that they may be influenced by such things as culture and age.

The relationship between body type or physique and personality is yet another subdivision within nonverbal behavior research. The relationship has been a source of interest for researchers since the late eighteenth century when John Lavater, a pastor, published *Essays on Physiognomy*. His was the first systematic study of the perceived reflection of personality traits in the face and body of an individual. Much later, Kretschmer (1925) devised a catalogue of three body builds and correlated them with certain temperaments. More recently, studies of relationships between body type and personality have shown that people tend to stereotype the kinds of characteristics associated with certain physiques (Sleet, 1969).

A final subdivision to be discussed concerns the body postures and gestures which are investigated in psychoanalytic research. According to Krout (1935), the clinical observation of expressive behavior began in the late nineteenth century when Freud observed the various chance actions exhibited by his patients. Unfortunately Freud did not attempt to classify these behaviors systematically or to relate them to specific disorders. Consequently, the field is still open to questions concerning the meaning of the various behaviors exhibited by psychiatric patients. Some recent research has shown that a method can be devised for accurately recording and interpreting nonverbal behavior observed in psychotherapeutic interviews. Scheflen (1963) used a content analysis of communication and illustrated his method by analyzing, in detail, therapy sessions with a schizophrenic patient, her mother, and two psychiatrists. Many therapists believe that by attending to the non-verbal expressions of patients (as well as to their verbal expressions) they can understand the patient's underlying problem better.

SOME NONVERBAL BEHAVIOR HYPOTHESES

Researchers have not been satisfied simply to observe and record nonverbal behavior. They have also advanced some hypotheses to explain certain aspects of it. For example, in an essay on territoriality Lyman and Scott (1967) argued that the maintenance of body territory between humans is a fundamental activity which provides them with space to maintain their identities and indulge in idiosyncratic behaviors (p. 55). Horowitz, Duff, and Stratton (1964) also have attempted to explain personal space and suggested that it acts as a body buffer zone which protects the individual against threats to his self-esteem and bodily harm. Finally, in discussing several types of nonverbal behaviors, Argyle and Dean (1965) have suggested a theory of behavioral equilibrium. They have suggested approach and avoidance factors which produce an equilibrium level among such behaviors as eye contact, body lean, gestures, facial expressions, touching, and distance. When the appropriate level of one of these factors is disturbed, compensatory changes are believed to occur in the other factors to restore equilibrium. These few examples of some of the hypotheses which have been suggested to explain nonverbal behavior are interesting and have helped to generate further research.

To reiterate, the field of nonverbal behavior is large and offers a wealth of information for those who are interested in doing research or for those who are simply interested in understanding more about others.

REFERENCES

Argyle, M. (Ed.) *Social Encounters.* Chicago, Illinois: Aldine Publishing Co., 1973.
——, and Dean, J. Eye-contact, distance, and affiliation. *Sociometry*, 1965, 28, 289-304.
Birdwhistell, R. *Kinesics and Context: Essays on Body Motion Communication.* Philadelphia, Pennsylvania: University of Pennsylvania Press, 1970.
Dosey, M.A., and Meisels, M. Personal space and self-protection. *Journal of Personality and Social Psychology*, 1969, 11, 93-97.
Ekman, P., Friesen, W.V., and Tomkins, S.S. Facial affect scoring technique: a first validity study. *Semiotica*, 1971, 3, 37-58.
Hall, E.T. The anthropology of manners. *Scientific American*, 1955, 192, 85-89.
——. *The Hidden Dimension.* Garden City, New York: Doubleday and Co., Inc., 1966.

Horowitz, M.J., Duff, D., and Stratton, L. The body-buffer zone: an exploration of personal space. *Archives of General Psychiatry*, 1964, 11, 651-656.

Katz, N. *Animals and Men.* New York: Longmans, Green, 1937.

Knapp, M.L. *Nonverbal Communication in Human Interaction.* New York: Holt, Rinehart & Winston, 1972.

Knapp, P.H. *Expression of the Emotions in Man.* New York: International Universities Press, Inc., 1963.

Kretschmer, E. *Physique and Character.* New York: Harcourt & Brace, 1925.

Krout, M.H. Autistic gestures: an experimental study in symbolic movement. *Psychological Monographs*, 1935, Whole No. 208, XLVI, 4.

Lyman, S.M., and Scott, M.B. Territoriality: a neglected sociological dimension. *Social Problems*, 1967, 15, 236-249.

Scheflen, A.E. Communication and regulation in psychotherapy. *Psychiatry*, 1963, 26, 126-236.

Sleet, D.A. Physique and social image. *Perceptual and Motor Skills*, 1969, 28, 295-299.

Sommer, R. *Personal Space.* Englewood Cliffs, New Jersey: Prentice-Hall, 1969.

Tomkins, S.S., and McCarter, R. What and where are the primary affects?: some evidence for a theory. *Perceptual and Motor Skills*, 1964, 18, 119-158.

HUMAN
NONVERBAL
BEHAVIOR

1

Studies with Normal Individuals

1. Addington, D. W. The relationship of selected vocal characteristics to personality perception. Speech Monograph,
1968, 35, 492-503.

   Addington required male and female subjects to rate the
   personalities of male and female speakers they heard on
   recordings. A passage was presented by the speakers
   which differed in rate, pitch, and voice quality. He
   discussed his results in terms of sex of the rater and
   the speaker, interrater reliability, relationship of the
   vocal characteristics to ratings given the speaker, and
   factor analysis of the responses. (Summary of abstract
   summary.)

2. Aiello, J. R. A test of equilibrium theory: Visual interaction in relation to orientation, distance, and sex of
interactants. Psychonomic Science, 1972, 27, 335-336.

   Aiello conducted a study to examine the affects of physical distance, body orientation, and sex of interactants
   on visual interaction. Male and female college students
   were subjects and interacted individually in a 12-minute
   discussion concerning a volunteer army with one of two
   male or one of two female confederates. The confederate
   assumed one of three seating distances--two, six, or 10
   feet--and one of two seating positions--directly across
   the table or at a right angle to the subject. Each subject's visual behavior was observed by judges and subject's and confederate's verbal behaviors were also measured. The results showed that (1) female subjects
   looked in the region of the confederate's eyes more than
   male subjects; (2) amount of looking and length of glance
   increased linearly with distance for male subjects, but a
   curvilinear relationship was found for female subjects;
   (3) male subjects looked more with male confederates and
   female subjects looked more with female confederates; and

(4) body orientation affected length of subject's glance so that glances were longer when subject and confederate were face-to-face.

3. Aiello, J. R. and Cooper, R. E. Use of personal space as a function of social affect. Reprinted from the Proceedings, 80th Annual Convention, American Psychological Association, 1972, pp. 207-208.

The authors explored the relationship between the degree of mutual liking in a dyad and physical distance and angle of body orientation or axis. A sociometric questionnaire was administered to junior high school students on which they were to indicate the five same-sex classmates they liked most and the five they liked least. At a later time pairs of students were unobtrusively observed as they engaged in a conversation in a room provided for the experiment. A significant relationship was found between affect and distance in that interacting dyads of individuals consisting of members who liked each other stood closer together than did those with members who did not like each other. No significant main effect was found for affect and axis, although an inspection of trial means showed that there was an increase in body angle between negatively disposed dyads over the observation period.

4. Aiello, J. R. and Jones, S. E. Field study of the proxemic behavior of young school children in three subcultural groups. Journal of Personality and Social Psychology, 1971, 19, 351-356.

The authors looked at distance and axis behavior between pairs of first- and second-grade Black, White, and Puerto Rican children interacting in same-sex, same-race pairs in school playgrounds. Observations were made by two teachers trained as judges. The results showed that middle-class White children stood farther apart than lower-class Black and Puerto Rican children supporting Hall's (1966) assertion that lower-income Blacks and Puerto Ricans are more highly involved than White middle-class Americans and therefore use a closer interaction distance (p. 352). Additionally, White males stood farther apart than did White females. The results for axis showed that Black children stood less directly than did White children, and, surprisingly, females interacted at a less direct angle than males.

5. Albert, S. and Dabbs, J. J. M. Physical distance and persuasion. Journal of Personality and Social Psychology, 1970, 15(3), 265-270.

The aim of the study was to investigate the affects of different distances between a speaker and listener on communication and persuasion. Undergraduate students were subjects and were each exposed to two 5-minute

messages delivered by a friendly or hostile communicator
seated at one-two, four-five, or 14-15 feet away. An
attitude change measure, a postexperimental questionnaire
to elicit perceptions of the speaker, a selective attention measure to determine the percentage of time each
subject spent thinking about what the speaker was saying,
and a social schemata task completed before and after the
subject heard the speaker were also given. Results showed
that the middle distance was considered to be the most
appropriate. Perception of the speaker was unaffected by
the distance at which he sat, except for perceived expert-
ness on self-disclosure which was greatest at the medium
distance. More attention was paid toward speech content
at the medium distance than at the close and far distances. Recall of a topic was highest at the medium
distance. Persuasion (attitude change) increased as the
speaker moved away. Persuasive messages were accepted
more readily from the friendly than hostile speaker.
Negative attitude change (resistance) occurred at the
close distance. Finally, for the social schemata task,
a majority of the subjects placed the figures further
apart in the close-hostile condition after meeting with
the speaker.

6. Altman, I. and Haythorn, W. W. The ecology of isolated
groups. Behavioral Science, 1967, 12, 169-182.

The experimenters examined social activity and territorial behavior for areas of a room, chairs, and beds within socially isolated and nonisolated dyads. Dyads were
composed of male volunteers matched on several personality variables. Nine dyads lived in a small room for 10
days with no outside contact for the isolation condition.
Another nine pairs served as a control, followed the same
time schedule, but had access to other people and outside
facilities. According to the results, men in isolated
groups showed a gradual increase in territorial behavior
for all objects and areas and socially isolated themselves from each other. Nonisolated groups also showed
a strong preference for particular beds, but did not display similar behavior toward areas or chairs. Additionally, at both the beginning and end of the experiment,
control subjects spent equal amounts of time in joint and
solitary activities; however, the latter activity increased and the former declined during middle days.

7. Alton, J. DeL. Kinesic signals at utterance boundaries
in preschool children. Semiotica, 1974, 11, 43-74.

Alton examined the body movements of eight preschool
children interacting in pairs in order to analyze the
behavior they engaged in during the transition from
speaker to listener. Eight basic body movements over
eight parts of the body were scored. Alton found that
the amount of kinesic activity was not distributed uni-
formly across the length of utterances. Kinesic behavior

increased with the final segment of verbal utterances. Another finding was that liftward and downward kinesic activity was used to signal the intention to end verbalization.

8. Anderson, D. R.   Eye contact, topic intimacy, and equilibrium theory.   Journal of Social Psychology, 1976, 100, 313-314.

Anderson had 36 same-sex dyads (males and females) composed of people with varying degrees of willingness to disclose. Each dyad discussed three topics, one of high, one of medium, and the final one of low intimacy. No main effect for topic intimacy was found. He reported, however, that the nonsignificant trend suggested a curvilinear relationship between eye contact and topic intimacy such that eye contact increased from the low to the medium intimacy topic and decreased between the medium to the high intimacy topic. His finding did not support the equilibrium theory. Anderson suggested the need for further study and the diversification of nonverbal variables before general support is given to the theory.

9. Archer, D. and Akert, R. M.   Words and everything else: Verbal and nonverbal cues in social interpretation.   Journal of Personality and Social Psychology, 1977, 35(6), 443-449.

Archer and Akert introduced a new technique for studying the process of interpreting nonverbal cues. Brief sequences of unposed behavior in various simultaneous nonverbal modes as well as in a verbal channel were presented to college students. They were required to answer questions about each sequence. It was found that when subjects were shown the videotape and read a transcript which described the behavior, they were more accurate than subjects who only read the transcript. In fact, the transcript sample of subjects performed significantly below the chance level.

10. Argyle, M.   Bodily communication.   New York: International Universities Press, 1975.

Argyle stated that his book intended to examine the cultural and biological roots of nonverbal communication, why this type of communication is used, differences in body cues, and various theoretical and practical implications involved in the study of the phenomena. His book was divided into four parts covering such things as nonverbal behavior among animals, the expression of emotion and personality in humans, spatial behavior, eye behavior, gestures, and the effects of clothes, physique, and other factors of one's appearance.

11. Argyle, M.   Eye contact and distance: A reply to Stephenson and Rutter.   British Journal of Psychology, 1970, 61(3), 395-396.

Argyle criticized Stephenson and Rutter's (1970) assumption and methodology when they replicated his experiment on eye contact and distance between pairs of people. They concluded that the eye contact/distance effect was not real, while Argyle asserted that it was genuine. Argyle concluded that the artificial laboratory experiment (as used by Stephenson and Rutter) runs the risk of creating situations which do not exist in the real world and of therefore generating misleading results.

12. Argyle, M. (Ed.). Social encounters. Chicago, Ill.: Aldine Publishing Co., 1973.

13. Argyle, M. Social interaction. New York: Atherton, 1969.

14. Argyle, M., Alkema, F., and Gilmour, R. The communication of friendly and hostile attitudes by verbal and non-verbal signals. European Journal of Social Psychology, 1971, 1, 385-402.

15. Argyle, M. and Dean, J. Eye contact, distance, and affiliation. Sociometry, 1965, 28, 289-304.

The authors conducted an experiment which suggested that people move towards an equilibrium distance and adopt a particular level of eye contact. As predicted, there was less eye contact and glances were shorter the closer two subjects were placed together (where one member of each pair was a confederate who gazed continuously at the other). The effect was greatest for opposite sex pairs. In another experiment it was found that subjects would stand closer to a second person when his eyes were shut, also as predicted by the theory.

16. Argyle, M. and Kendon, A. The experimental analysis of human performance. In L. Berkowitz (Ed.), Advances in experimental psychology (Vol. 3). New York: Academic Press, 1967.

17. Argyle, M., Lalljee, M., and Cook, M. Effects of visibility on interaction in a dyad. Human Relations, 1968, 2, 3-17.

The authors reported a series of experiments in which one or both members of a dyad were partly or completely visible to each other. Results indicated that when one member was partly visible, the member with more visual information tended to become dominant, felt more comfortable, and became the observer. When vision was reduced, speech was less synchronized and there were more interruptions and pauses. Visual feedback of the other's reaction was probably needed with the face being the most useful area for this. Finally, sex differences were found in that females were less comfortable without visual information, males tended to dominate even under conditions of reduced visibility, and in mixed dyads females assumed the role of observer.

18. Argyle, M., Satter, V., Nicholson, H., Williams, M., and
Burgess, P. The communication of inferior and superior atti-
tudes by verbal and nonverbal signals. British Journal of
Social and Clinical Psychology, 1970, 9, 222-231.

Argyle et al. hypothesized that (1) nonverbal cues for
interpersonal attitudes would have more impact than verbal cues, (2) conflict between these two types of cues is
disturbing, and (3) individuals differ in the weight they
give to each type of cue. They also questioned whether
each type of cue could operate alone. Male and female
college students were subjects. They were required to
indicate their impressions of people they saw on videotapes several times. The subjects were also given some
personality tests. Argyle et al. found that nonverbal
cues had more impact than verbal ones. Hypothesis 2
was not supported. Females were more responsive to nonverbal than verbal cues. Finally, personality affected
the subjects' responses.

19. Aronovitch, C. D. The voice of personality: Stereotyped
judgments and their relation to voice quality and sex of
speaker. Journal of Social Psychology, 1976, 99, 207-220.

Aronovitch was concerned with the judgments people make
from voice cues and how the judgments are related to
vocal parameters. Taped voices of 57 American college
students were played to other college students to be
rated on various personality characteristics. The researcher found that the subjects attributed certain personality characteristics to the speakers on the basis of
voice samples. The cue used commonly for male and female
speakers was speech rate. Pitch and loudness, however,
were used differently between male and female speakers.
Lastly, male and female raters seemed to judge the male
and female voices similarly.

20. Ashear, V. and Snortum, J. R. Eye contact in children as
a function of age, sex, and social and intellectual variables.
Developmental Psychology, 1971, 4, 479.

Male and female preschool, kindergarten, and second-,
fifth-, and eighth-grade children were interviewed by a
female experimenter. A significant sex difference (more
so for females) was found concerning eye contact while
speaking and overall contact, but not for listening.
The eye contact by grade level interaction was significant for speaking, listening, and overall contact; and
more so for younger subjects.

21. Bailey, K. G., Hartnett, J., and Glover, H. W. Modeling
and personal space behavior in children. Journal of Psychology, 1973, 85, 143-150.

An approach versus being approached behavioral measure of
personal space was taken on fifth and sixth graders in

three conditions--modeling close, modeling far, and a
control. A male peer served as model and a female adult
served as target. Results showed strong modeling effects
with both sexes of subjects tending to respond as the
model did. However, girls used more space in the control
condition. It was concluded that modeling theory was a
viable conceptual tool for use in personal space research.

22. Barefoot, J. C., Hoople, H., and McClay, D. Avoidance of
an act which would violate personal space. Psychonomic Science, 1972, 28, 205-206.

Male and female experimenters were seated at one of three
distances from a water fountain in a public building.
Male passersby were less likely to drink when the experimenter was near (one foot) the fountain than when the
experimenter was seated at the less proximate positions
(five and 10 feet). This finding supported previous research on reactions to spatial invasions.

23. Bartels, B. D. Nonverbal immediacy in dyads as a function of degree of acquaintance and locus of control. Dissertation Abstracts International, 1977(Jul), Vol. 38(1-B), 387.

Bartels studied distance, gaze, and body orientation as a
function of degree of acquaintanceship and internal-
external locus of control in a live interaction setting.
Female subjects categorized as high on internal-external
locus of control engaged in standing interactions with
females categorized as friends or strangers. The nonverbal behaviors were monitored by judges. Bartels found
that friends did not stand more immediately than strangers, locus of control was not more important in interactions with strangers, and immediacy behaviors did not
show more changes over time with strangers, contrary to
what had been expected.

24. Bass, B. M. and Klubeck, S. Effects of seating arrangement on leaderless group discussion. Journal of Abnormal and
Social Psychology, 1952, 47, 724-727.

The authors studied the relationship between the particular seat a participant had during an initially leaderless
discussion and the leadership status he attained, as estimated by two observers. Male and female college students
were observed in groups of eight. The authors found that
the particular seat a person occupied was of negligible
importance in determining a participant's tendencies to
attain leadership status during the course of the discussion because of the great variations among individuals
occupying a seat of a given type. However, in the rectangular arrangement persons occupying end positions
attained a mean status significantly more than double
that of persons occupying middle seats.

25. Bass, M. H. and Weinstein, M. S.   Early development of interpersonal distance in children. Canadian Journal of Behavioral Science, 1971, 3, 368-376.

The purpose of the study was to determine whether or not interpersonal distance behaviors would be shown by children aged five to nine and how certain factors (sex, grade, setting, and degree of acquaintance) influenced these behaviors. It was hypothesized that sex differences would be greater for nine-year-olds than for younger children, interfigure distances in an informal setting would be less than in a more formal setting, and that the children would stand farther from strangers than from friends in all settings. White middle-class Canadian children attending a small semirural public school were subjects. The results were that, contrary to the hypothesis, sex differences did not reach significance. For grades, it was found that kindergarten children had the lowest mean spatial distances in all settings and for all degrees of acquaintance. The tendency to use smaller distances continued until the second grade where there was a sharp increase in the distances the children kept from their friends. Additionally, inappropriate figure placements were found for kindergartners to second graders. Setting results showed that for all grades except grade one, mean spatial distances were higher in the living room than in the office. And, lastly, for acquaintance it was found that distances were greater for strangers than friends at all grade levels.

26. Baxter, J. C.   Interpersonal spacing in natural settings. Sociometry, 1970, 33, 444-456.

Baxter conducted a study in order to examine the distances at which people interacted in several natural settings. Two-person groups of White, Black, and Mexican-Americans were observed at the Houston zoo in three sex combinations --male-male, male-female, and female-female--and three age levels--children, adolescents, and adults. It was found that the Mexican groups stood closest, Whites were intermediate, and Blacks stood farthest. According to the analysis by age, children interacted most proximally, adolescents intermediately, and adults at the greatest distance; and this ordering remained constant across ethnic origin and sex. In regard to sex, opposite sex pairs interacted at a closer distance than same-sex pairs, with male-male dyads interacting at the greatest distance. Several interactions were also found.

27. Bayard, R. T.   Nonverbal communication between spouses. Dissertation Abstracts International, 1975(Oct), Vol. 36(4-B), 1959.

Bayard measured marital communication using (a) a self-report measure of verbal and nonverbal communication, (b) videotapes and ratings of facial cues sent by a sender to

a receiver, and (c) ratings of nonverbal performances.
He also measured marital adjustment using (a) the subject's desire to take part or not in marital counseling,
and (b) a self-report measure. He predicted that the
three measures of marital communication would be related
positively with the two measures of adjustment. Fifty-
four individuals from a family therapy clinic and from
the general community were used as subjects. The results
showed that only measures (a) and (c) were positively
related to marital adjustment. Measure (b) was found
to be negatively related to marital adjustment.

28. Beck, S. B. and Ward-Hull, C. I. Variables related to
women's somatic preferences of the male and female body.
Journal of Personality and Social Psychology, 1976, 34(6),
1200-1210.

   Beck and Ward-Hull wanted to determine which sizes of
   certain parts of the body were desirable to female subjects, which personality variables of the subjects were
   related to their preferences, and the extent to which the
   preferences of their subjects were different from or similar to the preferences of subjects in previous studies.
   One hundred and fifteen female undergraduates were subjects. The subjects were to choose from 15 male and 15
   female silhouette figures the ones (for each sex) they
   liked best. Chest/breast, buttock, and leg sizes were
   varied. It was found that the subjects preferred males
   with a small buttock and of moderate overall body size.
   They preferred females of moderate size and small but-
   tocks as well. No definite trend was found in regard to
   size of leg. Results for personality variables in
   regard to previous findings were discussed.

29. Benoist, I. R. and Butcher, J. N. Nonverbal cues to sex-
role attitudes. Journal of Research in Personality, 1977,
11, 431-442.

   Benoist and Butcher explored how self-reports of masculinity and femininity would be related to nonverbal behaviors as viewed by peers. Male and female college students
   were given the Minnesota Attitude Survey (MAS) and based
   upon their responses were categorized into a high-feminine
   (male) group, a high-feminine (female) group, a low-feminine (male) group, and a low-feminine (female) group.
   These subjects were videotaped while they were interviewed. The subjects were rated on an adjective checklist by other students who viewed the videotapes. Audio
   was not included. The results showed that 91 out of the
   170 adjectives used discriminated between the sexes.
   Differences were also found for sex by high or low feminine grouping. The researchers suggested that further
   research needed to be done to explore fully the issue.

30. Bergman, B. A. The effects of group size, personal
space, and success-failure upon physiological arousal, test

performance, and questionnaire response. Dissertation Abstracts International, 1971(Dec), Vol. 32(6-A), 3419-3420.

Bergman wanted to determine the affects of group size, personal space, and success-failure on physiological arousal (measured by the Palmer Sweat Index); test performance; and questionnaire responses. Male college students were subjects. For the success-failure condition, one-third of the subjects in each of 28 groups was told that their performance on an intellectual task was outstanding and that they would receive $4 for their effort. A second third of the subjects was told that their performance on the same task was average and that they would receive $2. The remaining third was told that they had failed on the task and would receive no money. For the low-density condition, subjects in half of the groups sat in a circle with one yard between each person on either side. In the high-density condition, the other subjects sat in chairs with the front legs two inches apart. Test performance was measured by six different tests and scales. Some of the results were that high-density subjects showed more autonomic response than low-density subjects. Success-failure instructions interacted with test performance. Subjects in the high-density condition felt their group atmosphere was warmer and friendlier than those in the low-density groups, and they also reported greater discomfort and unhappiness than low-density subjects.

31. Berman, A. L. Social schemas: An investigation of age and socialization variables. Psychological Reports, 1971, 28, 343-348.

Berman conducted a study to examine whether some developmental factor such as latency was operative so that clear-cut social schemas did not emerge until some point between the ages sampled by Weinstein and Kuethe in studies with normal subjects. Additionally, the experimenter wanted to examine the affect of differences in perceptions of maternal attributes on the formation of social schemas. Male Catholic White children were subjects. They were divided into three age groups: 5.5-6.5, 9.5-10.5, and 15.5-16.5. Group 2 was used to test the second hypothesis. Kuethe's figure placement technique was used, and four sets of stimuli were employed. Group 2 subjects were given the Perceived Maternal Warmth Questionnaire (PMWQ). Results showed that there was no significant difference between the replacements of human versus nonhuman figures for Groups 1 and 3. For Group 2, differences in the replacement of the mother-child pair were significant but in the direction opposite to that predicted. Also, for Group 2 (which was subdivided into those who perceived their mothers as warm, affectionate, and nurturant; and those who saw their mothers as punitive and controlling) it was discovered that neither group replaced human figures closer than

pairs of rectangles. The experimenter concluded that
the felt figure replacement task was a perceptual-
maturation task and that Gestalt laws such as closure
and proximity to which schemas ascribe seemed to operate
and were more prominent with older subjects.

32. Birdwhistell, R. L. Kinesics and context: Essays on
body motion communication. Philadelphia, Pa.: University
of Pennsylvania Press, 1970.

Birdwhistell's book contained essays on the ordered system of the isolable elements of body motion. He noted
that the material was not intended to be a kinesic textbook or a manual of instruction. He hoped his effort
would introduce the reader to the notion that the study
of human communication was relevant and desirable. The
book was divided into five basic parts with various segments within each. In Appendix I, Birdwhistell presented
his notational system for body motions. He divided the
body into eight arbitrary sections and noted that these
could be abandoned should more appropriate ones be developed. The eight sections he used were the head; face;
trunk; shoulder, arm, and wrist; hand and fingers; hips,
legs, and ankles; feet and walking; and neck. He also
presents drawings which provide examples of movements
within each section.

33. Birdwhistell, R. L. The language of the body: The
natural environment of words. In A. Silverstein (Ed.),
Human communication: Theoretical explorations, pp. 203-
220. Hillsdale, N. J.: Lawrence Erlbaum Associates, 1974.

Birdwhistell discussed the fact that human communication
was more than merely an exchange of words in discrete
messages, but that it involved the entire body. Included
in his article was material from a lecture concerning how
the body communicates. The discipline of kinesics which
covers the study of body motions which communicate and
may be used to substitute for speech was discussed. In
addition, a brief review of the kinemes (body motions)
used by middle-class Americans was also presented.

34. Bishop, G. D. The effects of perceived similarity on
interracial attitudes and behaviors. Dissertation Abstracts
International, 1976(Dec), Vol. 37(6-B), 3142-3143.

Bishop examined the influence of similarity or dissimilarity of dialect style (Black and White) on interracial
perceptions. Specifically, he looked at the effects of
belief similarity-dissimilarity and dialect on the attitudes and nonverbal behaviors of White subjects toward a
Black or a White person during a face-to-face interaction.
Female college students interacted with a Black or White
female assistant using standard English or Black English.
Videotapes were made of the interactions. There was a
dialect effect such that subjects were more favorable

toward the Black assistant who used White English. White assistants were rated more favorably than Black assistants. Finally, there were no significant effects for nonverbal behaviors.

35. Blalock, M. B. The use of kinesics in establishing and determining means in superior-subordinate communications. Dissertation Abstracts International, 1974(Aug), Vol. 35(2-A), 645-646.

Blalock conducted her study to identify and to analyze positive and negative body movements. She also wanted to determine the effects they had on message perception. She presented three hypotheses. Two hundred and ninety-two employees of large companies were used as subjects. They were divided into nine groups and were given different message forms. After receiving the messages, they responded to a semantic differential which required them to indicate their perceptions of seven message concepts. Blalock found that there were differences in message perceptions but that these were not generally due to personality or demographic variables. She also found that the effect of body language on message perception was not very great when positive vocalization was used. Another finding was that positive body movements increased the credibility of messages. Other results were also reported.

36. Blass, T., Freedman, N., and Steingart, J. Body movement and verbal encoding in the congenitally blind. Perceptual and Motor Skills, 1974, 39, 279-293.

Blass et al. were interested in examining the prevalence of object- and body-focused hand gestures of congenitally blind subjects involved in an encoding task. They also wanted to determine the relationship between the gestures and verbal performance. Ten subjects were videotaped as they engaged in a five-minute monologue. The results showed that they used only body-focused movements. This result was compared with results of sighted subjects in another experiment, and it was found that the blind subjects used more of such gestures than the sighted subjects. Another finding was that a correlation of .51 to .53 existed between body touching and verbal fluency. Finally, skill at encoding certain complex sentences was dependent upon the prevalence of certain types of gestures.

37. Block, J. A study of affective responsiveness in a lie-detection situation. Journal of Abnormal and Social Psychology, 1957, 55, 11-15.

Block wanted to verify and extend the results of a study done by Jones (1935) in which overt behaviors were investigated in relation to GSR reactivity among adolescents. Block used 70 male applicants to a medical school as

subjects. Each subject was observed in various personality revealing situations. In addition, each subject participated in a bogus lie-detection test and was told that
his skill as a liar was being measured. The 20 most
highly reactive and the 20 least reactive subjects according to GSR ratings were compared in terms of the personality observations and on intelligence. No significant
differences were found for intelligence. On personality
measures, reactors were seen as, for example, withdrawn
and worrying. Nonreactors, on the other hand, were seen
as independent and nonconforming, for example. Other
findings comparing the two groups were also reported.

38. Bloom, R. W. Structural referents of kinesic behavior:
A reliability study and dimensional analysis. Dissertation
Abstracts International, 1976(Aug), Vol. 37(2-B), 999.

Bloom found certain methodological deficiencies in studies inferring meaning from kinesic behavior. This
prompted his research. College students rated the
Lightfoot facial expressions with five to 10 structural
referents. The subjects also completed the Chapin Social
Insight test because Bloom felt social insight may be an
intervening variable in structural perception. He tested
two hypotheses: (1) statiscally reliable judgments of
structural referents from kinesic cues would be obtained,
and (2) high social-insight subjects would be more accurate than low social-insight subjects at inferring structural referents from kinesic cues. Hypothesis 1 was
supported; however, high- and low-insight subjects did
not differ in the values they ascribed to structural
referents, that is, on Form A and Form B, for most of
the facial expressions used.

39. Bloom, R. W., Harvey, H., and Howells, G. The development of interpersonal distance in children and adolescents.
Paper presented at a session on Spatial and Nonverbal Behavior at the 53rd Annual Convention of the Western Psychological Association, Anaheim, Calif., April 11-14, 1973.

The authors noted that much research has not been done
to determine when personal space develops. They used a
modification of an approach technique employed by Horowitz et al. (1964) to investigate how children and adolescents use interpersonal space at various ages, when
the behavior is first displayed, and what changes in
interpersonal space usage occur with maturation. Subjects from kindergarten, third, sixth, and ninth grades
were used with equal numbers of males and females from
each grade level. Each subject was required to approach
a music stand and two confederates (one with a White surname and one with a Spanish surname) from the front,
side, and rear. Results showed that kindergarten and
ninth-grade subjects maintained greater distances between themselves and people or objects than did third-
and sixth-grade subjects. All subjects approached the

music stand closer than they did the confederates. Sex
differences were found. Approach by sex interactions
showed that boys approached both Spanish surname and
White confederates more closely than did females.

40. Blurton-Jones, N. G. Criteria for use in describing
facial expressions of children. Human Biology, 1971, 43,
365-413.

Blurton-Jones wanted to develop precise descriptions for
the facial expressions she wanted to study. She divided
the face into eight segments called components. Her aim
was to describe each component, not to categorize whole
facial expressions. Five hundred photographs were taken
of normal children between the ages of two and five.
The eight segments were: brow position, mouth shape,
lip position, eye openness, tongue position, eye direction, lip separation, teeth, and miscellaneous. Her
article gives descriptions of each of the components
within a segment. She also included comments on the
way facial muscles produce the components and the situations in which they might occur.

41. Bonfanti, B. H. The evaluation of nonverbal and verbal
traits and behaviors of blind adults and the effect of training upon these behaviors. Dissertation Abstracts International, 1977(Jul), Vol. 38(1-A), 23.

Bonfanti wanted to determine the effects of a training
program designed to modify deviant behavior patterns on
the congenitally blind individual's performance during a
social interaction. Eight congenitally blind and 19
adventitiously blinded adults were subjects. Each subject was observed during a conversation in a triad and
was rated on 52 communication behaviors and traits.
Four of the congenitally blind subjects participated in
the training program. The remaining four were controls.
The results showed that the nonverbal and verbal behaviors of congenitally blind and adventitiously blinded
adults differed. Training changed the behavior of the
congenitally blind subjects such that it resembled the
behavior of the adventitiously blinded subjects. Lastly,
the changes in behavior among congenitally blind subjects affected their social performance.

42. Bonoma, T. V. and Felder, L. Nonverbal communication and
marketing: Toward a communicational analysis. Journal of
Marketing Research, 1977, 14, 169-180.

Bonoma and Felder reviewed various research on measurement and theory of nonverbal components of interactive
behavior. It was noted that although nonverbal behaviors
may be difficult to manage, they can be used as checks
on the validity of verbal measures of consumption behavior. The authors identified three major types of nonverbal behavior studies and suggested that the cognitive

igan and Humphries were concerned with how facial
ssions and body gestures were used by children as
ls of communication. They perused the research on
rbal behavior, especially with children, and dis-
d the various methods of observation and the find-
.   In addition, they pointed out common pitfalls
untered when describing nonverbal expression. They
 discussed the need to study the development of non-
al expression from birth onward. Finally, they sug-
ed the relevance of nonverbal expression in psychi-

ekman, N. C. and Moller, A. T.   Preferred seating
n and distance in various situations. Journal of
ing Psychology, 1973, 20, 504-508.

 authors looked at the preference of college students
 four seating positions in counseling, formal, home,
 two social situations and the preferred distance be-
en chairs in the various positions. Subjects were to
dicate preferences from pictures. Results showed pref-
ences in some situations, although similarities occurred
 others. The conclusion was that individuals tend to
refer a relatively formal position under unfamiliar cir-
mstances, whereas a more informal position is preferred
der more familiar circumstances. In terms of distance,
lthough the middle distance was preferred most often,
rrespective of seating position, subjects who were sub-
issive and dependent and displayed correct social behav-
or, self-control, and consideration for others tended to
refer the greater distance between chairs. Subjects who
ere dominant, self-assured, and independent-minded and
ho showed less social correctness, self-control, and
onsideration tended to prefer the middle and near
distances.

Brown, C. J.   The role of face and voice cues in the dis-
ination of mother from stranger in early infancy. Dis-
ation Abstracts International, 1976(Apr), Vol. 36(10-B),
.

Brown tested 18 male infants and 18 female infants on
their ability to discriminate their mother from a female
stranger on the basis of the availability of face and
voice cues. Three conditions were devised: one in which
the infants saw four repeated presentations of the mother's face and voice as well as four presentations of the
stranger's face and voice. A second group saw presentations of the stranger's and mother's face only. Finally,
a third group heard the mother's and stranger's voice
only. Duration of visual fixation, vocalization, and
smiling were measured. Some of the results were that in
the face-only condition, the infants decreased vocalization over presentations of the mother's face, but increased them with the stranger's face. Lastly, in the
voice-only condition, the person presented first

approach would be of great
porated into marketing ana
findings from the cognitive
observations by marketers c
ponents. (Summary of journ

43. Borges, G. and Rizzeri, D.
published paper, University of L

44. Bossom, J. and Moslow, A. H.
factor in impressions of warmth i
normal and Social Psychology, 195

The investigators were interes
ation among judges in their fi
people. The judges were under
equal groups of secure and inse
upon their responses to a paper
individuals to be judged were i
from college yearbooks. Two hu
They were of the same racial, so
gious backgrounds. The judges r
gories labeled Very Warm, Warm,
comparison of the secure, insecu
judges showed that the secure gro
gory more than the neutral and in
result was that when only the Ver
categories were examined, there wa
ference between the secure and ins

45. Bourget, L. G. C. Delight and info
as elements of positive interpersonal f
Abstracts International, 1977(Oct), Vol

Bourget conducted a study to determi
different types of positive feedback
feedback included smiling, a pleased
maximum eye contact, and a pleased to
condition providing statements about
the subject was also included. Subje
ally interviewed. They also filled o
concerning a relationship they were pr
with a friend. Bourget found that the
back was influential, although the info
was not. Those subjects who had been i
condition felt more positively toward t
had better feelings about themselves, a
terested in trying to make changes in th
with their friend than those in the "low
tion. These feelings were generally als
sist one week after the feedback session

46. Brannigan, C. R. and Humphries, D. A. Hu
behavior: A means of communication. In N. G
(Ed.), Ethological studies of child behavior.
England: Cambridge University Press, 1972.

Bran
expr
sign
nonv
cuss
ings
enc
als
verl
ges
atr

47. Bro
positio
Counsel

The
fo
an
tw
in
er
in
p
c
u
a
i
m

48.
cri
ser
529

determined the total amount of vocalization during the presentations.

49. Brown, C. T. and Keller, P. W. Monologue to dialogue: An exploration of interpersonal communication. Englewood Cliffs, N. J.: Prentice-Hall, 1973.

Brown and Keller discussed various aspects of communication including how people transmit and interpret verbal and nonverbal communications. Their Chapter Four was specifically concerned with how others make decisions about the verbal language of others by using nonverbal cues. In this chapter they presented information about how various parts of the body communicate. Chapter Five discussed the role of emotion in communication. Each of their 10 chapters ended with a list of objectives and discussion questions.

50. Bruning, J. L. and Liebert, D. M. Name and facial feature stereotyping. Perceptual and Motor Skills, 1973, 37, 889-890.

Male and female college students rated pictures of other college students on a nine-point scale in regard to degree of masculinity or femininity. The pictures were then shown to another sample of college students who were to match 25 names derived from the Buchanan and Bruning (1971) lists concerning masculinity-femininity with the pictures. It was found that there was a tendency to identify each picture from among a small number of names which were very similar in degree of associated masculinity-femininity.

51. Bryan, T. H. Learning disabled children's comprehension of nonverbal communication. Journal of Learning Disabilities, 1977, 10, 501-506.

Bryan looked at the differences between the ability of Black and White learning disabled and normal children to understand nonverbal communication. The children were shown a film of an adult female displaying positive or negative emotions combined with dominant or submissive expressions in various scenarios (the children's PONS). Each child was required to choose an item which best described the scene. Bryan found that the learning disabled children got lower mean accuracy scores on the test than the normal children. There was no difference due to race or its interaction with learning disability. No significant difference between groups was found due to type of scenario.

52. Buchanan, D. R., Goldman, M., and Juhnke, R. Eye contact, sex, and the violation of personal space. Journal of Social Psychology, 1977, 103, 19-25.

Buchanan et al. investigated the relationship among degrees of eye contact, violations of personal space,

and sex of participants in three studies conducted in a
public elevator in an office building. In Study I, male
and female subjects had to violate the personal space of
two male or two female assistants who either directed
their gazes toward the subjects or diverted their gazes
as the subjects entered the elevator. The results showed
that males and females avoided violation of the personal
space of the directly gazing male assistant. With the
female assistants, a majority of the female subjects
chose to violate the personal space of the directly gazing female. In Study II, two same-sex confederates were
used. One avoided gazing, the other diverted his gaze.
The male and female subjects violated the personal space
of the former assistant. In the final study, a male and
a female assistant directed their gazes toward entering
subjects. Male subjects did not show preference by sex
in violating personal space. Females, on the other hand,
violated the space of the female assistant.

53. Buck, R. Nonverbal communication of affect in children.
Journal of Personality and Social Psychology, 1975, 31, 644-
653.

The study was designed to develop a paradigm for measuring the nonverbal behavior of young children. Male and
female preschool children were subjects. Videotapes were
made to show the subjects for each of four content categories. The children were videotaped while they watched
a series of slides. Buck found that nonverbal expressions could be determined from children and that there
were individual differences in the ability to relate
affect between children. He also found that there was
no significant sex difference for this ability. The
ability to send affect messages nonverbally was related
to various personality variables.

54. Buck, R. Nonverbal communication of affect in preschool
children: Relationships with personality and skin conductance. Journal of Personality and Social Psychology, 1977,
35, 225-236.

Buck investigated the relationship between communication
accuracy and skin conductance among preschool children.
As the children watched 16 emotional color slides, their
mothers watched their spontaneous facial expressions and
gestures via television and judged the kind of slide the
child was seeing. The children were also required to
rate how each slide made them feel. In this regard, it
was found that more familiar people made them feel more
positive than less familiar people. Unpleasant slides
were rated as making them feel the least positive. Skin
conductance had also been monitored while the children
watched the slides, and results showed that high communication accuracy was related to low skin conductance
responding. There was no sex difference in communication accuracy.

55. Buck, R., Miller, R. E., and Caul, W. F. Sex personality and physiological variables in the communication of affect via facial expression. Journal of Personality and Social Psychology, 1974, 30, 587-596.

The study investigated whether or not there were relationships between sex and personality variables and communication accuracy among 32 female and 32 male undergraduates. Mixed-sex and same-sex pairs of senders and observers were used. Senders watched slides of various contents, and observers were to interpret their facial expressions and also indicate the content of the slide being watched. It was found that females were more accurate in sending nonverbal communications (of the face) than were males. Certain physiological and personality variable findings were also reported.

56. Buck, R., Savin, V. J., Miller, R. E., and Caul, W. F. Nonverbal communication of affect in humans. Proceedings of the 77th Annual Convention of the American Psychological Association, 1969, 4, 367-368.

The experiment was conducted to determine whether people can communicate information relevant to their emotional state through facial expressions, whether a person's physiological responses are influenced by the reception of facial information from another, and personality factors which are relevant to the ability to send and receive this information. Male and female subjects were used. Each was compared with a same-sex partner. One member of a paper acted as the sender, the other as the decoder. Senders were shown slides and their facial expressions in response to the slides were transmitted to a screen where the observer judged the nature of the slide the other was viewing, and whether or not the other's emotional response was pleasant or unpleasant. Results showed that 10 of the 12 female pairs categorized the slides correctly, while only three of the nine male pairs did so. All of the female pairs showed a positive correlation between the sender's and the observer's ratings of pleasantness-unpleasantness. Only three pairs of males had a significant correlation between these ratings. Results about physiological ratings were looked at for females only, and it was found that correlations between the sender's and observer's changes from the preslide to the slide period were low and seemed to be unrelated to communication accuracy.

57. Buck, R., Worthington, J., and Schiffman, T. Nonverbal communication of affect in preschool children. Proceedings of the 81st Annual Convention of the American Psychological Association, 1973, 8, 103-104.

The researchers tested the ability of preschool children to send signals to others by means of spontaneous facial expressions and gestures. Male and female preschool

children acted as senders. Their mothers were primary
observers along with undergraduates. The children were
videotaped, and the resulting films were used as stimuli.
Each child viewed a series of 16 slides and was required
to indicate how each made him feel by pointing to one of
a series of faces. The slides presented showed him in
certain situations as well as other events. The mothers
and the undergraduate observers rated the facial expressions of the children (taken while they viewed the slides)
as to how pleasant or unpleasant the slide made him feel.
Results showed significant communication when the mothers
were observers and there was no sex difference for the
children. For the undergraduate observers, 13 of the 29
children showed significant communication. The researchers also explored further their findings concerning individual differences among the children.

58. Bunge, M. M. Using hand motions to stimulate visual
imagery in a physical science classroom. Dissertation Abstracts International, 1977(Mar), Vol. 37(9-A), 5691-5692.

Bunge used the thought model method which involves tracing imaginary figures in the air using the hand, accompanied by verbal descriptions, to teach lessons to junior
college students. One group of students watched, while
another group listened to weekly lessons. The results
showed no significant difference between the means for
the two groups. Results when students were shifted from
one mode to another and when different students were put
into the two modes were also presented.

59. Burroughs, W., Schultz, W., and Autrey, S. Quality of
argument, leadership votes, and eye contact in three person
leaderless groups. Journal of Social Psychology, 1973, 90,
89-93.

Burroughs et al. wanted to examine the relationship between eye contact, leadership voting, and quality of performance. Groups of two females, consisting of one subject and one confederate, were formed. The subject's
duration of speech and amount of eye contact were measured. It was found that when the confederate gave high
quality arguments she received more eye contact and more
leadership votes from naive group members. She was also
ranked significantly higher on a leadership questionnaire
in the high quality condition. The correlation between
eye contact and leadership votes across quality conditions was .69.

60. Burruss, J. A. Evaluating therapists' effectiveness.
Dissertation Abstracts International, 1977(Sep), Vol. 38(3-B),
1394.

Burruss looked at the relationship between a therapist's
sensitivity to nonverbal cues and his or her effectiveness. Fifty alcoholism counselors were shown a film

showing various real-life situations. The counselors
also rated themselves and were rated by others on certain
personal characteristics including such things as, for
example, warmth, empathetic understanding, objectivity,
dependability, directness, and genuineness. Data on
their effectiveness were collected. Burruss found a
relationship between the ability to detect positive-
submissive affect in particular and certain of the rated
characteristics. He noted the significance of his results for the selection and training of therapists.

61. Byrne, D., Baskett, G. D., and Hodges, L. Behavioral
indications of interpersonal attraction. Journal of Applied
Social Psychology, 1971, 1, 137-149.

    The researchers conducted two experiments in which they
    manipulated attitude similarity and looked at the affects
    of congruent and incongruent attitudes on a subject's
    seating choice in regard to a confederate. In Experiment
    I, 20 male and 20 female college students were subjects.
    Two male and two female students were confederates. Sub-
    jects were also required to fill out a paper-and-pencil
    measure of attraction. Higher attraction scores were
    received by agreeing than by disagreeing confederates.
    Females sat closer to agreeing than disagreeing confeder-
    ates. In Experiment II, as in Experiment I, higher
    attraction scores were given to agreeing confederates.
    Also, the hypothesis that males would choose to sit
    across from agreeing confederates was confirmed. The
    females' responses did not differ from chance.

62. Campbell, D. T., Kruskal, W. H., and Wallace, W. P.
Seating aggregation as an index of attitude. Sociometry,
1966, 29, 1-15.

    The researchers looked at seating aggregations as an
    index of racial attitudes among Black and White college
    students in a classroom setting. Data in 1951 and 1963-
    1964 were collected. The students were observed in two
    colleges separately composed of least prejudiced and most
    prejudiced individuals, according to an unpublished study.
    The researchers found that there were fewer Black-White
    seating adjacencies than would be expected by chance.
    The two schools also differed in seating aggregations
    in the expected direction. Aggregation was also found
    by sex of student. Campbell et al. suggested that their
    index of seating aggregation was worthy of more research.

63. Campbell, W. W. Interpersonal orientation correlates of
nonverbal behavior in conversational interaction. Dissertation Abstracts International, 1977(Aug), Vol. 38(2-B), 959.

    Campbell examined the relationship between nonverbal
    behavior and interpersonal orientation. Male and female
    college students engaged in conversations which were
    videotaped. Five types of nonverbal behaviors were

recorded: hand movement, facing, turn length, head tilts,
and body touching. Various interpersonal orientation measures were also taken. Campbell found that there was a
significant relationship between interpersonal orientation
and nonverbal behavior. Other hypotheses which predicted
associations between certain of the nonverbal behaviors
were also supported. Personality types emerged and were
associated with some of the nonverbal behaviors studied.

64. Cantor, J. R. Imitation of aggression as a function of
exposure to a model's emotional expressions contingent upon
his performance of aggressive acts. Dissertation Abstracts
International, 1975(Jan), Vol. 35(7-B), 3643.

Cantor wanted to determine the effects of a model's expressions of emotion on the tendency of subjects to imi-
tate the emotions. One of three videotapes of an individual behaving euphorically, neutrally, or dysphorically
while shocking a rat and also behaving kindly toward the
rat was shown to each subject. The subjects were fifth-
and sixth-grade boys. After seeing a videotape the subject was required to stimulate the rat using the same
equipment as the model. The subjects were allowed to
choose the type, intensity, and duration of stimulation
to the rat. Cantor found that some of the subjects had
not perceived the emotions as they had been expected.
However, she also found that the boys who had seen the
euphoric-shock or dysphoric-shock conditions used more
shock than those who had seen the neutral condition.
Other results were reported.

65. Caputo, J. S. An investigation of nonverbal behavior
research and its applicability to the study of classroom
interaction. Dissertation Abstracts International, 1977
(Aug), Vol. 38(2-A), 553-554.

Caputo presented what he felt was the necessary information for incorporating nonverbal behavior into studies
examining classroom interactions. He reviewed the major
researches within the field of nonverbal behavior and
delineated the methodology of each study. He also suggested the application of language function theory to
nonverbal research. Finally, he included an extensive
bibliography to help in the further research of the
phenomenon.

66. Carlson, R. and Price, M. A. Generality of social
schemas. Journal of Personality and Social Psychology, 1966,
3(5), 589-592.

The experimenters investigated the generality of the
social schemas described by Kuethe in a broader population representing subjects differing in age, sex, and
social experience. It was predicted that social schemas
would be better established and more preemptive at suc-
cessive age levels, that adolescents would differ from

preadolescents and adults in responding to stimuli representing a parent and child, that sex differences would
be found, and that responses of delinquent adolescents
with backgrounds of family disorganization would differ
from community adolescents. Male and female subjects
were divided into four subgroups: preadolescents, community adolescents, delinquent adolescents, and adults.
Following Kuethe's techniques, nine sets of stimuli were
used. Findings showed that the nodal schemas described
by Kuethe were stable ways of organizing perceptions,
and in only one set (man-woman-dog) did the subjects
deviate from the mode. Age differences were observed
such that adults grouped human figures more often than
did adolescents who grouped them more than preadolescents. An age by sex interaction was found in placement of man-child and woman-child figures. Adolescent
males placed the child closer to the mother. Little of
the variation in social schemas was found to be attrib-
utable to differences in social experiences, specifically between community and delinquent adolescents.
The experimenters concluded that while the findings
supported Kuethe's general hypothesis, sex and level
of development limited the generality of specific
social schemas.

67. Cartwright-Smith, J. D. Some determinants and consequences of control over the nonverbal expression of emotion.
Dissertation Abstracts International, 1975(Oct), Vol. 36
(4-B), 1961.

Cartwright-Smith conducted two experiments to determine
the influence of social context on nonverbal emotional
expression. The study was also devised to determine
the effects of changes in nonverbal expression on the
emotional state. For Study I, male undergraduates received painful electric shocks while believing themselves to be alone or while being observed by another
male or female. Cartwright-Smith predicted that nonverbal expressions of discomfort would be less when the
subject felt he was being observed and that the reduction in overt expression would lead to an actual reduction in distress as measured by self-reports. His predictions were conformed. He also found that the sex of
the observer did not affect the magnitude of the observation effects. For Study II, the subjects were asked
to pose nonverbal displays. One group was told they
were being videotaped and that the viewers would be
deceived by their performance. The second group prac-
ticed their displays while being unwittingly videotaped. A control group did not pose. Similar findings
in the self-reports and autonomic measures were found
for this study as had been found in the other one. It
was concluded that whether the nonverbal expressions
were manipulated by social contexts or posed, their
modification led to changes in subjective and autonomic
measures of emotion states.

68. Cash, T. F., Begley, P. J., McCown, D. A., and Weise, B. C. When counselors are heard but not seen: Initial impact of physical attractiveness. Journal of Counseling Psychology, 1975, 22, 273-279.

Cash et al. wanted to assess the influence of a counselor's physical attractiveness on a client's initial impressions and expectations about therapeutic gains. Male and female college students viewed videotapes of an actor posing as a college student counselor. In one tape the actor appeared as an attractive man--a mesomorph with dark hair and stylishly dressed. In the other film he appeared as an unattractive man--an endomorph with shadows under his eyes, less stylishly dressed, etc. In each videotape the actor read a self-introduction indicating his counseling experiences. The subjects were to indicate their impressions of the "counselors." Results showed that the attractive counselor was considered to be more intelligent, assertive, trustworthy, warm, likeable, and friendlier than the unattractive counselor. Both, however, were seen as similarly sincere, courteous, relaxed, professional, and interested. No sex differences were found between the subjects in their impressions.

69. Chaikin, A. L., Derlega, V. J., Yoder, J., and Phillips, D. The effects of appearance on compliance. Journal of Social Psychology, 1974, 92, 199-200.

The researchers tested whether or not the physical appearance of a solicitor effected compliance to his request when the request was altruistic. A 20-year-old male, dressed conservatively with tie and jacket or like a hippie, approached individuals over 30 at a shopping center to donate to a charity or sign a petition. Members of both sexes were approached. Chaikin et al. found that, contrary to their prediction, there was a main effect for dress. Fewer people complied to the hippie than to the conservative solicitor. People also complied more to the request for a signature than for money.

70. Chaikin, A. L., Sigler, E., and Derlega, V. J. Nonverbal mediators of teacher expectancy effects. Journal of Personality and Social Psychology, 1974, 30, 144-149.

The study was done to investigate the transmission of teacher expectancy effects on certain nonverbal dimensions. Male and female undergraduates served as "teacher" subjects. Two 10-year-old males acted as "pupils." The pupils were described as either bright or dull. A control group of subjects received no information about the child's intelligence. The teaching session between the subject and confederate was videotaped. It was found that teachers smiled more, leaned forward, nodded their heads, and gave more direct gazes when they believed the child to be bright. There were no significant differences between the nonverbal responses by subjects with the "dull" child or control subjects.

71. Champness, B. G.   Mutual glance and the significance of look. Advancement of Science, 1970, pp. 309-312.

72. Cheyne, J. A.   Development of forms and functions of smiling in preschoolers. Child Development, 1976, 47, 820-823.

Cheyne wanted to determine whether or not there were differences in the relations of forms and functions of smiling among preschool children of different ages. Male and female nursery school children were observed during their normal play periods. Ratings were made of the types of smiles used by the children and the people in whose presence they occurred. The results were that the social form of smiling increased with age, especially with same-sex peers. As to other forms of smiles, more upper smiles were used than closed or broad smiles, and the frequency of use of upper smiles increased with age.

73. Cheyne, J. A. and Efran, M. G.   The effect of spatial and interpersonal variables on the invasion of group controlled territories. Sociometry, 1972, 35(3), 477-489.

Cheyne and Efran conducted two studies to determine whether or not individuals would intrude upon the personal space of others. Study I looked at the intrusion behavior of college students who had to walk between or around two confederates standing in a corridor. It was found that intrusion was influenced by the activity of the confederates, the sex composition of the pair, and an interaction between these two factors. Study II further investigated sex differences and was conducted in a large shopping center. The researchers found that when the confederates stood between 40 and 46 inches apart, intrusion was reduced (as opposed to when they stood 52 inches apart). In addition, male-female pairs of confederates were most effective at reducing intrusion, while male-male pairs were least effective.

74. Clark, B. M.   A study of participants' versus nonparticipants' perception of teacher nonverbal behavior in the natural classroom setting. Dissertation Abstracts International, 1977(Feb), Vol. 37(8-A), 4815-4816.

Clark designed her study to answer the following questions: (1) Do participant and nonparticipant observers perceive similar nonverbal teacher behaviors in assessing the affective quality of teacher nonverbal behavior? (2) What cues are identified by these observers in assessing the affective quality of teacher nonverbal behavior? (3) To what extent do the cues identified by these observers predict the variance in their assessment of nonverbal behavior? Videotapes were made of five ninth-grade

teachers in a classroom situation. Seven students acted
as participant observers, and seven doctoral students
acted as nonparticipant observers. The results indicated
that the students rated their teacher's nonverbal behavior in a higher degree than did the nonparticipant observers. In addition, the teachers' nonverbal behaviors had
different qualitative aspects for the two groups of
observers.

75. Clements, J. E. and Tracy, D. B. Effects of touch and
verbal reinforcement on the classroom behavior of emotionally
disturbed boys. Exceptional Children, 1977, 43, 453-454.

Clements and Tracy examined the effects of touching and
verbal reinforcement and a combination of the two on
accuracy of performance and attention to an arithmetic
task. Normally, intelligent nine-year-old males were
subjects. The researchers found that touching was valuable as a reinforcer, particularly when it was combined
with verbal praise. (Summary of abstract reference.)

76. Cline, M. G. The perception of where a person is looking.
American Journal of Psychology, 1967, 80, 41-50.

Cline attempted to replicate results by Gibson and Pick
(1963) concerning a subject's ability to determine whether
or not he was being looked at by another and also considered acuity for targets other than those located between
the subject's eyes. Using the Gibson and Pick hypothesis
that the proximal stimulus for the perception of direction of gaze was the invariant resultant of eye-head positions, Cline required a looking person (L) to fixate her
eyes on various targets while maintaining a passive facial
expression. Each subject was to report where L was looking in regard to dots on a response board. Accuracy for
being looked at was high, and the Gibson and Pick hypothesis was generally supported.

77. Coleman, J. C. Facial expressions of emotion. Psychological Monographs, 1949, 63(1, Whole No. 296).

Coleman elicited and recorded facial expressions of emotion as well as identifying the influence of the eye,
mouth, and full face in these emotions. Photographs of
one male and one female were shown to college students.
The judges were divided into four groups. Groups I and
II saw photos of the female. Groups III and IV saw
photos of the male. Portions of the pictures showing
mouth, eyes, and then full face were presented. Some
of the findings were that for three of the groups of
judges, identifications of emotion were made more reliably from the full face than from the eye or mouth
regions. The percentage of correct identifications of
emotions varied with region of face and the circumstances
under which the emotional expression had been elicited
from the male and female targets. Finally, no sex differences in judgments of emotion were found.

78. Collett, P. and Marsh, P.   Patterns of public behavior.
Semiotica, 1974, 12, 281-300.

    Collett and Marsh conducted a study to determine the
    relationship between collision avoidance by pedestrians
    and the processes of monitoring and externalization.
    They observed pedestrians on a controlled crossing at
    Oxford Circus in London. Videotapes were made of the
    behavior. They categorized the behavior into such
    things as line of approach, approach overlap, direction
    of pass, shoulder orientation, head orientation, and
    position. They found sex differences for the various
    behaviors. They also found the tendency for people to
    walk on the right. When passing, however, the decision
    to go right or left depended upon the degree of overlap
    in terms of the two approaching people.

79. Conroy, J., III and Sundstrom, E.   Territorial dominance
in a dyadic conversation as a function of similarity of
opinion. Journal of Personality and Social Psychology,
1977, 35, 570-576.

    Conroy and Sundstrom hypothesized that territorial domi-
    nance would emerge in a cooperative situation when a
    resident and a visitor had dissimilar opinions but not
    when they had similar opinions. Pairs of male college
    students met in the residences or dorm rooms of one mem-
    ber of the pair. Sixteen pairs of similar opinion sub-
    jects and 16 pairs of dissimilar opinion subjects were
    formed. The subjects met and were to construct a skit
    concerning whether the university should grant formal
    recognition to a gay liberation organization on campus.
    The results were that in dissimilar pairs, the residents
    spent more time talking, while in similar pairs the
    visitor spent the most time talking. The results con-
    firmed the hypothesis.

80. Considine, J.   Observation of reaction to eye contact
with a male. Unpublished paper, University of Lowell, 1975.

81. Cook, M.   Gaze and mutual gaze in social encounters.
American Scientist, 1977, 65, 328-333.

    Cook reviewed some of the studies on eye-contact behavior
    among individuals during social interactions. He pre-
    sented works on such facets of this behavior as amount
    of looking time and when gazing is displayed. He also
    discussed some of the techniques which have been used to
    measure and record eye-contact behavior.

82. Cooke, B. G.   Nonverbal communication among Afro-Ameri-
cans: An initial classification. In Thomas Kochman (Ed.),
Rappin' and stylin' out: Communication in urban Black America. Urbana: University of Illinois Press, 1972.

Cooke presented an article which discussed various
aspects of nonverbal behavior which are relevant to Afro-
Americans. He presented verbal examples and pictures of
some of the gestures and postures which are common to
Afro-American culture. He covered such things as standing and walking which are handled differently by males
and females under various circumstances, "getting" and
"giving skin," and the effects of hair and clothing on
nonverbal communication.

83. Cooke, T. P. Increasing levels of positive social-emotional behavior through the use of behavior analytic teaching
tactics. Dissertation Abstracts International, 1975(Oct),
Vol. 36(4-A), 2133.

Cooke wanted to teach children four social-emotional behaviors: smiling, sharing, positive physical contact,
and verbal complimenting. He approached this through
instructing or modeling and through social praise. He
found that these social-emotional behaviors could be increased and that smiling, sharing, and positive physical
contact could be generalized to a free-play situation,
and that the trained behavior persisted even in the presence of naive subjects when an adult trainer was not
around. Cooke indicated that his results were discussed
in terms of providing accountable procedures for social-
emotional education and also in terms of how they related
to broadening the scope of behavior analytic research.

84. Cooper, J. B. and Pollock, D. The identification of
prejudicial attitudes by the galvanic skin response. Journal
of Psychology, 1959, 50, 241-245.

Cooper and Pollock wanted to determine whether or not a
person's large GSRs to complimentary statements about a
group indicated a negative attitude toward the group.
Male and female college students were subjects. Galvanic
skin responses were recorded first and then ratings and
rankings of the stimulus group were taken. Complimentary
statements were read about nine national groups as GSRs
were measured. The prediction that high and low psychological responses would be predictive of attitudes toward
particular groups was supported.

85. Cooper, J. B. and Siegel, H. E. The galvanic skin response as a measure of emotion in prejudice. Journal of
Psychology, 1956, 42, 149-155.

Cooper and Siegel investigated whether or not prejudicial
attitudes were accompanied by higher levels of GSRs than
nonprejudicial attitudes. College students were given
an attitude questionnaire concerning 20 ethnic groups.
Only those students who rated a group as disliking it
very much or intensely and then ranked that group at the
bottom position were subjects. Galvanic skin responses
were recorded for each subject as he listened to four

positive statements which were read by an experimenter about the groups he had rated in neutral and negative positions. It was found that 20 of the 23 subjects had greater GSRs to the statements directed toward groups for which they had indicated negative attitudes.

86. Coutts, L. M. and Ledden, M. Nonverbal compensatory reactions to changes in interpersonal proximity. Journal of Social Psychology, 1977, 102, 283-290.

Coutts and Ledden tested Argyle and Dean's equilibrium hypothesis concerning nonverbal behaviors. Female college students were interviewed by a female assistant who increased, maintained, or decreased her seating distance from the subject across different sessions. A female observer recorded the subject's smiling, interpersonal gaze, body lean, and body orientation. The results showed that as had been predicted, subjects in the close condition decreased smiles and gazes in relation to the assistant. Those in the far condition increased all of the nonverbal behaviors recorded.

87. Credell, C. F. Nonverbal behavior in teaching: Another dimension to classroom communication. Dissertation Abstracts International, 1977(Oct), Vol. 38(4-A), 1843.

Credell wanted to determine whether teachers who had been rated positively on various criteria of nonverbal behavior by pupils, parents, and principals were able to recognize more positive and more negative nonverbal behaviors among other teachers than teachers who had been rated more negatively. Some of the nonverbal behaviors which were rated were physical appearance, gestures, facial expressions, and proxemics. Credell found that positive teachers observed more positive responses among the teachers they rated than negative teachers. There was a significant difference among the overall negative responses for the positive and negative teachers. Credell suggested that because the teachers who were being rated knew they were being videotaped, this may have effected their classroom behavior.

88. Cross, J. F., Cross, J., and Daly, J. Sex, race, age, and beauty as factors in recognition of faces. Perception and Psychophysics, 1971, 10, 393-396.

Cross et al. were concerned with the ability of Black and White children and adults from racially segregated and racially integrated backgrounds to recognize a variety of facial types. Three hundred subjects were shown 12 photographed faces collected from high school yearbooks and school portraits of grade school children and their teachers. They found that female subjects recognized female faces more often than male faces. Males recognized both sexes' faces more frequently than Black faces. Black subjects recognized both races with equal

facility. In terms of misidentification, the researchers found that Black faces and male faces were misiden-
tified more often than White faces and female faces.
Misidentification decreased with age. Lastly, perceived
beauty of a face facilitated recognition.

89. Dabbs, J. M. Physical closeness and negative feelings.
Psychonomic Science, 1971, 23, 141-143.

Pairs of male subjects argued or talked for 20 minutes
in two different sized rooms. Proximity in the small
room was expected to increase arousal which, in turn,
would intensify either hostile feelings associated with
arguing or friendly feelings associated with talking.
However, verbal reports and Palmar Sweat Measures suggested an affinity between proximity and arguing. Arguing is congruent with negative feelings aroused by proximity, and arguing may also allow individuals to focus
upon intellectual content and thereby escape from an unpleasant interpersonal situation. According to questionnaire responses, subjects in the small room disa-
greed more with partners, but tended not to get into
open disagreements.

90. Dabbs, J. M., Fuller, J. P. H., and Carr, T. S. Personal space when 'cornered': College students and prison inmates. Proceedings of the 81st Annual Convention of the
American Psychological Association, 1973, 8, 213-214.

The investigators studied personal space within two different social and physical settings. Study I was done
with college students. The subjects approached or were
approached by another person while standing in the center of the room or with shoulders against the wall.
Dabbs et al. found that the subjects stayed farther away
from their partners in the corner of the room whether or
not the subject was approaching or being approached.
Study II was done with prison inmates. The findings
were replicated; however, the difference between center
of room and corner was more marked with the inmates.

91. Danziger, K. Interpersonal communication. New York:
Pergamon Press, 1976.

Danziger discussed various aspects of nonverbal communication including such topics as manipulation, dual
aspects of communication, the function of nonverbal communication, and cultural differences in communication.
His book is divided into 10 chapters. He also included
an Appendix which presented a system for analyzing
rhetorical codes in various conflict situations.

92. Darley, J. M. and Cooper, J. The 'clean for Gene' phenomenon: The effects of student appearance on political
campaigning. Journal of Applied Social Psychology, 1972,
2, 24-33.

Darley and Cooper conducted field experiments to determine the effects of a political campaigner's dress on his
effectiveness. Two experiments were conducted. In Experiment I, male college students acted as campaigners. Half
were dressed conventionally in sports clothing and wore
their hair short. The other three were dressed in hippie
fashion with long hair, beads, and dungarees. The campaigners attempted to distribute leaflets at a shopping
center. It was found that regardless of their own age,
sex, or dress shoppers accepted more leaflets from the
conventionally dressed campaigners than from the deviantly dressed campaigners. In Experiment II, the campaigners sat at tables purportedly supporting one of two
political candidates. Again, they were dressed conventionally or deviantly. A result of this experiment was
that the subjects were willing to ascribe more radical
opinions to the candidate of the deviant campaigners than
to the other candidate. Other results were discussed.

93. Darwin, C. The expression of the emotions in man and
animals. Chicago: University of Chicago Press, 1965.

Darwin discussed the principles he felt accounted for the
expression of emotions and gestures used by man and animals. He collected data on affect expression from various parts of the world in an effort to make cross-cultural
comparisons. His book was divided into 14 chapters, many
of which discussed various specific expressions or expression groups. He concluded by urging physiologists to
pursue further the study of expressions of emotion.

94. Davis, M. Understanding body movement: An annotated
bibliography. New York: Arno Press, 1972.

95. Deaux, K. The behavior of women and men. Monterey,
Calif.: Brooks/Cole Publishing Co., 1976.

Deaux had a section in her book on certain aspects of
nonverbal behavior and differences in use by men and
women. She discussed visual behavior, touch, and personal space usage differences between males and females.

96. DeLong, A. J. Seating position and perceived characteristics of members of a small group. Cornell Journal of
Social Relations, 1970, 5, 134-151.

DeLong found that seating position in regard to territorial propinquity to the leader of a group possessed a
wide range of communicative value such that those seated
closer to the leader were rated higher across all scales,
while those seated farther away were rated lower.

97. Deutsch, F. Female preschoolers' perceptions of affective responses and interpersonal behavior in video-taped
episodes. Developmental Psychology, 1974, 10, 733-740.

Eight filmed episodes were shown to White female nursery school children. Four episodes had contradictory interpersonal behavior and affect, and four had congruent behavior and affect. The youngsters were divided into an average mental-age group and a high mental-age group. They were required to tell the story about each episode. The episodes contained adult female actors. Deutsch found that the subjects scored higher on the congruous than on the incongruous episodes. Age did not affect the responses. Lastly, responses to various aspects of the two main types of episodes were affected by mental age.

98. Deutsch, R. D.   The behavioral ecology of interactional space. Dissertation Abstracts International, 1976(May), Vol. 36(11-B), 5757.

Deutsch favored a transactional interpretation or description of the relationship between behavior and environment over a stimulus response account. Levels of behavioral interdependency were discussed. One of these levels was called Face Formation. It described how interactants in a face-to-face situation interrelated their distance, posture, and orientation in space over time to maintain their separate integrity and identity within the interactional space. Films of unmanipulated social behavior were analyzed. Deutsch found that such behaviors as boundary synchrony, behavioral format, and compensatory spatiality were part of the maintenance of interactional space.

99. Dibiase, W. J. and Hjelle, L. A.   Body image stereotypes and body-type preferences among male college students. Perceptual and Motor Skills, 1968, 27, 1143-1146.

Male college students rated three male silhouettes representing extreme examples of endomorphy and ectomorphy as well as mesomorphy on a temperament scale. The subjects were either overweight, underweight, or of normal weight themselves. The experimenters were interested in determining further data on social stereotypes of body images. They found that the mesomorph type was rated as more energetic, active, and dominant, while the two other types were rated as more shy, withdrawn, and dependent. Dibiase and Hjelle did not find a relationship between the subject's body weight and body preference. They concluded that cultural influences may have played a role in the choices.

100. Dinges, N. G.   Interaction distance anxiety. Dissertation Abstracts International, 1971(Jun), Vol. 31(12-B), 7593.

The study was done to investigate anxiety regarding interaction distance as it related to a systematic theory of interpersonal behavior. Male and female subjects rated anxiety toward five interpersonal distances as shown in photographs. A curvilinear relationship was suggested, i.e., short and long distances were least preferred. Those who had extreme responses on the Fundamental Interpersonal Relationships Orientation-Behavior scale (FIRO-B) showed differential anxiety responses to interpersonal distance consistent with predictions derived from the theory of fundamental interpersonal relationships.

101. Dinges, N. G. and Oetting, E. R.   Interaction distance anxiety in the counseling dyad. Journal of Counseling Psychology, 1972, 19(2), 146-149.

The experimenters extended Haase's (1970) investigation of the relationship between subject's sex and academic versus personal counseling set with reference to reactions to five interpersonal distances in two ways. An instructional set for personal counseling versus no instruction set was used to clarify differences under these conditions, and an anxiety measure was used to elicit reactions to the interaction distances. Male and female undergraduates were subjects. They were shown pictures of a male and female seated at varying distances. In each picture the armchairs were maintained at a 45 degree angle to each other with body orientation kept constant. Subjects were asked to respond to the photos in terms of how they would feel if they were in the picture. Additionally, half of the subjects were instructed to respond as if they had come to a counseling center or other mental health agency for help with a personal problem. Results were that distances of 30 and 88 inches were rated higher in anxiety than the three intermediate distances. Sex differences showed that females rated all five distances higher in anxiety than males. Lastly, personal counseling-set subjects rated the five distances higher in anxiety than no-set subjects.

102. Dosey, M. A. and Meisels, M. Personal space and self-protection. Journal of Personality and Social Psychology, 1969, 11, 93-97.

Conceptualizing personal space as a means of protection against external threat, the authors predicted that more personal space would be used under conditions of stress than nonstress. Subjects were given the Rorshach to determine body image boundary and anxiety. Groups consisting of five or six individuals were tested. For an approach condition, each subject in turn approached the other members of the groups until he or she wanted to stop. For a silhouette task, each subject was required to trace a silhouette representing himself in relation to a printed one. For a seating condition the subject was asked to choose from among two seats at a table occupied by the experimenter. Results showed that for the approach measure, those in the stress condition stayed at farther distances than those in the nonstress condition. However, because of the group nature of this task,

modeling was suggested to have influenced the results.
For the silhouette condition the stress effect was highly
significant. However, for the seating condition there
was no significant stress effect.

103. Dreyer, S. F. Affective influences on nonverbal immediacy. Dissertation Abstracts International, 1977(Jul), Vol.
38(1-B), 353.

Dreyer hypothesized that increased closeness or proximity
would decrease gradients along the dimensions of lean,
gaze, and orientation when there was negative affect.
Female college students were subjects. They were required to sit at various distances from a female confederate who interviewed them under conditions of positive
or negative affect. Observers behind a one-way mirror
monitored the gaze direction, body orientation, forward
lean, and speech duration of the subjects. The hypothesis was not supported. Contrary to what was expected,
immediacy was not greater during positive affect conditions than negative ones. One finding was that the subjects leaned forward more when the interviewer was negative than when she was positive. Dreyer suggested that
researchers get independent evidence that the nonverbal
behaviors they use to index intimacy are actually doing
so.

104. Duke, M. P. and Nowicki, S. A new measure and social
learning model for interpersonal distance. Journal of Experimental Research in Personality, 1972, 6, 119-132.

The authors presented a criticism of measurement methods
for the concepts of personal space-interpersonal distance
and presented their own instrument (the Comfortable Interpersonal Distance scale--CID) along with support for its
validity and reliability.

105. Duncan, S. Floor apportionment in a dyad. Proceedings
of the 78th Annual Convention of the American Psychological
Association, 1970, 5, 383-384.

Duncan was interested in the behavioral and verbal cues
used by members of an interacting dyad to regulate the
smooth exchange of speaker and auditor roles. An interview between two previously unacquainted male and female
was recorded on videotape. The first 19 minutes of the
interaction was studied. Three classes of cues were observed: (a) regular floor-yielding cues, (b) superordi-
nate floor-yielding cues, and (c) floor-retaining cues.
He found that there were similarities between the kinds
of cues used by the client and the interviewer, although
certain differences were also observed. Duncan discussed
the role of these cues in interactions.

106. Duncan, S. Nonverbal communication. Psychological
Bulletin, 1969, 72, 118-137.

Research efforts to specify and understand the communicative function to voice quality, body motion, touch, and
the use of personal space were reviewed. Two distinctions
were drawn between two broad research strategies in the
area: (a) the structural approach in which an underlying
system or set of rules somewhat analogous to those for
languages is sought for nonverbal behavior, and (b) the
external variable approach.

107. Duncan, S., Rosenberg, M. J., and Finkelstein, J. Nonverbal communication of experimenter bias. Proceedings of
the 77th Annual Convention of the American Psychological
Association, 1969, 4, 369-370.

The research was done to verify the significance of an
experimenter's nonverbal cues in affecting a subject's
interpretation of a message. Three male experimenters
made tape recordings of instructions for the experiment.
These recordings differed in voice intensity, pitch level,
voice openness, tempo, pitch range, and drawl clipping.
The subjects were 212 female undergraduates. Each subject received her instructions over earphones. Prior to
this, apprehension about the evaluation task was manipulated. Then subjects were shown pictures of the person
who had delivered the instructions, and they were required to rate the photographs. Duncan et al. found that
shifts in intonation and paralanguage under various eval-
uation-apprehension conditions produced differing responses by the subjects under different evaluation-appre-
hension conditions.

108. Edney, J. J., Walker, C. A., and Jordan, N. L. Is there
reactance in personal space? Journal of Social Psychology,
1976, 100, 207-217.

Edney et al. conducted two studies to determine whether
or not people would react to the close proximity of
others by claiming more personal space. They also wanted
to investigate whether or not the mediating variable for
this behavior was loss of control or security rather than
loss of freedom. Study I was conducted at a public beach
over six days. Assistants approached individuals who
were alone and interviewed them about the use of the
beach for recreation. As part of this interview, a front
and side approach technique was used to measure their personal space preference. Distance between them and their
nearest neighbors was also measured. It was found that
the average personal space a subject claimed was little
effected by the available space around him or her. There
was no significant relationship between interpersonal
distance and freedom. Study II was conducted in a laboratory with male and female college students. Subjects
answered questions about how they felt in a situation
during which they were required to stand and face another
individual at varying distances. They were also asked
questions about feelings of control and security in the

situation. Finally, each subject used string to mark
his personal space. Smaller personal space was claimed
as interpersonal distance reduced until it reached the
smallest distance at which point larger areas of personal
space were claimed. Other results concerning control and
security were presented.

109. Efran, J. S. Affective concomitants of the invasion of
shared space: Behavioral, physiological, and verbal indicators. Journal of Personality and Social Psychology, 1974,
29(2), 219-226.

The experimenter recorded nonverbal acts, physiological
reactions, and subjective moods for subjects who were
asked to either walk between two conversing confederates,
past two conversants, or down a vacant corridor. He hypothesized that subjects who violated the shared space
of the conversants would show more negative affect, as
reflected in physiological arousal, nonverbal signs of
agonistic behavior, and lower subjective mood ratings,
than would subjects who walked down the vacant corridor.
Subjects who walked past (but not between) the two confederates were predicted to show an intermediate level
of affective arousal. The subjects were male college
students. A motion picture camera recorded the subject's
expressive behavior and scales from the semantic differential were used to obtain ratings of mood. It was found
that for expressive behavior a greater incidence of agonistic mouth gestures were used by the violation subjects.
Heart rate increases (measured during the walk) were
found for all subjects. For the mood scale, as hypothesized, subjects in the violation group expressed the
least positive mood evaluations, those in the minimum
violation group had mood ratings of intermediate value,
and subjects in the no violation group had the most
positive moods.

110. Efran, J. S. Looking for approval: Effects of visual
behavior of approbation from persons differing in importance.
Journal of Personality and Social Psychology, 1968, 10, 21-26.

As freshmen met with two confederates to talk, they were
observed through a one-way mirror by the experimenter.
Confederates were either both seniors, both freshmen, or
one of each. In all conditions one of the two smiled
and was more approving than the other toward the subject.
Results showed that visual interaction was influenced by
subjects' expectations for approval and by the relative
importance they attached to receiving approval from individuals of different status. Subjects looked more at
individuals toward whom they had developed higher expectations for approval when the individuals were portrayed
as seniors than when portrayed as freshmen. The positive
relationship between scores on the Marlowe-Crowne Social
Desirability scale and amount of time the individual
spent looking at others was reported in an earlier study,
but not replicated here.

STUDIES WITH NORMAL INDIVIDUALS   39

111. Efran, J. S. and Broughton, A.   Effect of expectancies for social approval on visual behavior. Journal of Personality and Social Psychology, 1966, 4, 103-107.

The authors investigated the relationship between expectation for social approval and visual behavior using male college students as subjects. Each subject was required to talk about himself for five minutes in front of two confederates. Results showed that, in confirmation of the hypothesis derived from Rotter's social learning theory approach, subjects maintained more eye contact with individuals toward whom they had developed higher expectancies for social approval.

112. Efran, J. S. and Cheyne, J. A.   Shared space: The cooperative control of spatial areas by two interacting individuals. Canadian Journal of Behavioral Science, 1973, 5, 201-210.

The authors were interested in the amount of space small groups of individuals could cooperatively control. Two male confederates stood at several distances from each other and conducted conversations in public halls. The number of people who walked between and around them at each distance was noted. As was hypothesized, when the confederates stood at Hall's (1966) personal distance, significantly fewer people walked between them; and as distance approached Hall's social distance, more people walked between the two conversing confederates. The experimenters discussed the results in relation to human territorial behavior and the social-regulative function served by cues implicit in the distance used by interactants.

113. Efran, M. G. and Cheyne, J. A.   Affective concomitants of the invasion of shared space: Behavioral, physiological, and verbal indicators. Journal of Personality and Social Psychology, 1974, 29, 219-226.

Male college students were subjects in this study. They were told that their heart rate would be measured as they visually tracked a light stimulus and responded to an auditory stimulus as well. Each subject was tested alone. The electrocardiogram manipulation was used to provide a context in which physiological reactions could later be measured while the subject either walked between two conversants, past two conversants (not between), or down a vacant corridor. Other nonverbal responses were also noted as the subject intruded or did not intrude upon the space of the conversants. The researchers found that as they had predicted, more agonistic facial expressions were used by subjects who passed between and by the conversants than by those who did not. However, no differences were found for cardiovascular activity. The findings were discussed in terms of territorial behavior, stress, and high population density.

114. Efron, D. Gesture and environment. New York: King's
Crown Press, 1941.

Efron looked at cultural differences in gestures among
traditional and assimilated Italians and among traditional and assimilated Jews of Polish and Lithuanian descent
in New York City. He found differences among traditional
Italians and Jews; however, traditional gestures disappeared due to assimilation. (Summary of abstract
summary.)

115. Efron, D. Gesture, race and culture. The Hague:
Mouton Publishers, 1972.

116. Egolf, D. B. and Chester, S. L. Nonverbal communication
and the disorders of speech and language. Asha, 1973, 15,
511-518.

117. Ekman, P. Body position, facial expression, and verbal
behavior during interviews. Journal of Abnormal and Social
Psychology, 1964, 68, 295-301.

The communicative value of body position and facial
expression was evaluated by measuring an observer's
ability to detect a relationship between verbal and nonverbal behaviors which had been emitted at the same time.
The verbal and nonverbal stimuli were collected during
two standardized stress interviews. Observers were required to pick a picture which matched a verbal response.
In four separate experiments with different groups of
observers, accurate judgments were obtained. Evidence
for a relationship between nonverbal and verbal behavior simultaneously emitted was replicated across two
different samples of interview behavior and under three
conditions.

118. Ekman, P. Differential communication of affect by head
and body cues. Journal of Personality and Social Psychology,
1965, 2, 725-735.

119. Ekman, P. and Friesen, W. V. Detecting deception from
body or face. Journal of Personality and Social Psychology,
1974, 29, 288-298.

Ekman and Friesen tested the following two hypotheses:
(1) individuals who have just participated in a deceptive
interaction will mention the face more than the body when
asked what behavior they would use or not use in simulation; and (2) more accurate judgments will be made from
the face when deceptive behavior is judged, and there
will be little difference between judgments of the body
and face when judging honesty. Female nursing students
were subjects. They were required to be honest in
one interview when describing their feelings about a
pleasant film. In another interview they were required

to be deceptive and simulate pleasant feelings about a
negative film. The first hypothesis was supported. The
second hypothesis was partially supported.

120. Ekman, P. and Friesen, W. V. Head and body cues in the
judgment of emotion: A reformation. Perceptual and Motor
Skills, 1967, 24, 711-724.

The researchers were interested in investigating the
ability of observers to perceive the nature of an affect
using Woodworth's (1938) scale of emotions. They also
wanted to explore whether or not there was a distinction
between body arts and body positions in conveying information about an emotion. It was hypothesized that they
would agree more about an emotion when using cues from
the face or head only than when viewing cues from the
body only. Furthermore, it was expected that body acts
rather than body positions would be more influential in
the perceptions. College students viewed still photographs of other individuals showing either the head only
or the body up to the neck only. The results supported
the hypothesis. In addition, as expected, higher agreement on body acts as compared to body positions was
determined.

121. Ekman, P., Friesen, W. V., and Tomkins, S. S. Facial
affect scoring technique: A first validity study. Semiotica,
1971, 3, 37-58.

Ekman et al. developed a tool to measure facial behavior
which predicted observers' judgments and distinguished
emotional states as shown by environmental conditions or
self-reports. They also provided a description of the
facial components which distinguished emotions to facil-
itate development of a theory. They discussed the development of the facial affect scoring technique (FAST).
The face was divided into three basic areas: brows-
forehead; eyes-lids-bridge of nose; and lower face, consisting of jaw-chin-mouth-nose-cheek. Three scores were
trained to respond to the FAST items. The scoring technique predicted the emotions judged by the scores correctly for most of the faces. The combined areas were
able to provide more information for correct scores than
were individual components. Further findings from the
study were presented.

122. Ellis, H. D., Shephard, J., and Bruce, A. The effects
of age and sex upon adolescents' recognition of faces. Journal of Genetic Psychology, 1973, 123, 173-174.

Ellis et al. conducted a study in which 12- and 17-year-
old males and females were required to view 60 color
slides of adult males and females to determine their
ability to remember faces. After the initial viewing,
a four-hour interval passed before the subjects saw the
slides again. This time the original 60 were mixed with

40 others. The results showed that the older subjects
remembered more faces than the younger ones. In addition, females were better at remembering female faces
than were males. Males and females did not differ in
remembering male faces.

123. Ellsworth, P. C. and Carlsmith, J. M. Effects of eye
contact and verbal content on affective response to a dyadic
interaction. Journal of Personality and Social Psychology,
1968, 10, 15-20.

The effects of frequency of eye contact and positiveness
of verbal content were studied using female subjects.
Results showed that with positive verbal content, frequent eye contact produced more positive evaluations;
and with negative verbal content, frequent eye content
produced negative evaluation. Alternative hypotheses
for these results were also presented.

124. Ellsworth, P. C., Carlsmith, J. M., and Henson, A. The
stare as a stimulus to flight in human subjects: A series
of field experiments. Journal of Personality and Social
Psychology, 1972, 21, 302-311.

Male and female experimenters were used in a series of
field experiments designed to test the hypothesis that
avoidance behavior was elicited in human subjects by
staring. In each experiment the experimenter stared or
did not stare at people stopped at a traffic light and
measured their speed across the intersection when the
light changed. Subjects were drivers ranging in age
from about 16 to 70. Results for Experiments I and II
supported the hypothesis. There was a main effect for
sex with subjects crossing the intersection faster when
stared at by a female experimenter. The hypothesis was
also confirmed for Experiment III which used four experimenters of each sex instead of one, and no main
effect for sex was found. A fourth experiment also
confirmed the hypothesis.

125. Ellyson, S. L. Visual behavior exhibited by males differing as to interpersonal control orientation in one and two
way communication systems. Dissertation Abstracts International, 1974(Nov), Vol. 35(5-B), 2461.

Ellyson measured (using Schutz's FIRO) the control orientation of a group of individuals to determine whether or
not visual behavior differences were related to personality. Two experimental situations were conducted. In the
first experiment, mixed as well as same control-oriented
dyads were used. Ellyson found that high control-oriented subjects showed different visual interaction behavior
from low control subjects regardless of the control orientation of the partner. The results of the second experiment in which the subjects were involved in a one-way
communication system were that high control subjects
looked more at a confederate than did low control subjects.

126. Emde, R. N., Gaensbauer, T. J., and Harmon, R. J. Emotional expression in infancy. Psychological Issues, 1976, 10(1), Monograph 37.

The study was done to explore the development of emotional expression in infants. The study was a longitudinal examination of 14 infants through their first year of life. The mothers and infants were screened to meet certain criteria. Monthly visits were made to the home to conduct interviews and tests. Some of the emotional expressions which were observed and examined were smiling, fussiness, and stranger distress. The monograph is divided into four basic parts and 15 subsections. The parts contain some theoretical background for the study, discussions of sleep and wakefulness during the first year, types of affect expressions, and implications for further research.

127. Engen, T. and Levy, N. Constant-sum judgments of facial expressions. Journal of Experimental Psychology, 1956, 51, 396-398.

Engen and Levy wanted to determine the potentiality of the constant-sum method in psychometric scaling. They also wanted to compare scales of facial expressions developed by ratings provided by Schlosberg and the constant-sum method. Pictures from the Frois-Wittmann series were chosen to represent the three Schlosberg dimensions. College students were shown slides of the pictures. The subjects were to divide 100 points between pairs of pictures in terms of the amount of attention or tension or pleasantness they displayed. Three experiments using the same format were conducted. The investigators found agreement between the two methods as far as ordinal characteristics were concerned. They proposed that their results showed the constant-sum method could be extended to material more complex than weights and lines; that is, to psychometric dimensions.

128. Engen, T., Levy, N., and Schlosberg, H. A new series of facial expressions. American Psychologist, 1957, 12, 264-266.

Engen et al. secured pictures of a female model in order to obtain data on Schlosberg's third dimension which corresponds to level of activation. They asked the readers of a local newspaper to rate the 16 pictures on a nine-point scale along the dimension. One end of the scale was said to represent sleep and the other represented tension or excitment. The responses of the readers were compared with those of college students who made their judgments from projected slides. The results showed that the newspaper readers rated the level of activation lower in the middle of the scale than the students. Nevertheless, there was generally consistency of judgment between the two groups. Another aspect of their experiment had been to record skin conductance while each picture was taken, but this could not be accomplished.

44 HUMAN NONVERBAL BEHAVIOR

129. Engen, T., Levy, N., and Schlosberg, H. The dimensional analysis of a new series of facial expressions. Journal of Experimental Psychology, 1958, 55, 454-458.

In three similar experiments, college students were re-quired to rate pictures of a female displaying various facial expressions on a nine-point scale. The scale was used for each of Schlosberg's dimensions. The first ex-periment showed that the Pleasant-Unpleasant dimension was rated most consistently. In the second experiment found that subjects gave very consistent ratings (from a repeated measures format), especially for the Pleasant-Unpleasant dimension. The Attention-Rejection dimension showed the lowest reliability. In the third experiment, it was found that variability of judgment increased by restricting the range of the series of pictures judged.

130. Esser, A. H. (Ed.). Behavior and environment: The use of space by animals and men. New York: Plenum Press, 1971.

An international symposium on "The Use of Space by Ani-mals and Men" was sponsored by the Animal Behavior Soci-ety and took place at the 135th Annual Meeting of the AAAS in Dallas, Texas, in 1968. The book edited by Esser presented various papers, edited discussions, and contri-butions made by those (present and absent) who partici-pated in the symposium.

131. Evans, G. Personal space. Psychological Bulletin, 1973, 80(4), 334-344.

The author presented the major findings of personal space research from the fields of clinical psychology and per-sonality and demographic studies. Studies concerned with the effects of familiarity and affinity were also pre-sented. It was noted that the lack of consistent find-ings in the area may be attributed to the lack of experi-mental controls in many of the studies. Another criticism was in reference to the paucity of theoretical discussions about personal space. They suggested that experimenters explore personal space using multivariate techniques, and they presented a theory which suggested that personal space was "a functional, mediating, cognitive construct which allows the human organism to operate at acceptable stress levels and iads in the control of intraspecies aggression."

132. Evans, G. Personal space. Research review and bibli-ography. Man-Environment Systems, 1973, 3, 4.

Evans presented a bibliography of the many studies done in the area of personal space and summarized the major findings set forth by the researches. Additionally, brief mention was given to works which have examined methodological aspects of the area. Lastly, a critique was presented of personal space research, and an alterna-tive research strategy was suggested.

133. Evans, G. Personal space: The experimental approach.
Man-Environment Systems, 1972, 2, 3.

The author noted that most research on personal space has
relied on self-report techniques which are subject to experimenter and subject bias. His report was designed to
inform researchers about an experimental methodology which
attempts to control for subjective variation. Three measures were used to assess the behavior changes in a human
subject as a function of infringement on his personal
space: skin conductance, a four-bit reduction mode to a
two-bit classification task, and the semantic differential to compare a subjective report with the other two
measures. Results showed that with reduction in interpersonal distance the subject exhibited consistent behavioral changes which were not, however, significantly correlated with self-report shifts in feelings as expressed
on the semantic differential. Furthermore, the information processing measures were not significantly correlated with the GSR reports. The experimenter said that
a current research program was under way to determine
what variables were necessary for the appearance of personal space violation behavior.

134. Exline, R. V. Explorations in the process of person
perception: Visual interaction in relation to competition,
sex, and need for affiliation. Journal of Personality, 1963,
31, 1-20.

Sixteen groups of three men and another 16 of three women
were formed from a large number of people given a test of
n affiliation prior to the study. In the laboratory phase
each group was given the same problem to discuss but discussed it under one of two degrees of competition. Observers seated behind one-way mirrors recorded visual interaction among the members. Results showed women were
more prone to engage in visual activity than men. Highly
affiliative females looked more than low affiliative females; males showed the opposite tendency. Additionally,
women looked more overall while speaking and while listening than did men. An analysis of groups showed that high
n affiliates did not engage in more visual interaction
than lows, contrary to the hypothesis; and mutual glances
for highs were not lower in competitive than in less competitive situations.

135. Exline, R. V. and Eldridge, C. Effects of two patterns
of a speaker's visual behavior upon the perception of the
authenticity of his verbal message. Paper presented at the
Eastern Psychological Association Convention, Boston, April
1967.

136. Exline, R. V., Gottheil, E., Paredes, A., and Winkle-
meier, D. Gaze direction as a factor in the accurate judgment of nonverbal expressions of affect. Proceedings of the
76th Annual Convention of the American Psychological Association, 1968, 3, 415-416.

The investigators tested the following two hypotheses:
(1) the higher the ratio of direct glances to downcast
glances accompanying happy as compared to sad stories,
the more accurate judges will be in determining the stimulus person's affect; and (2) happy and sad stories will
be judged more accurately than angry stories. Schizophrenic and normal females were used as stimulus persons.
All were White. They recorded on film a sad, a happy,
and an angry story. The films were then shown in silence
to 34 college students who judged the affectiveness of
each presentation. Two observers who were unaware of the
purpose of the study judged gaze directions of the stimuli. Results showed that both hypotheses were supported.

137. Exline, R. V., Gray, D., and Schuette, D. Visual behavior in a dyad as affected by interview content and sex of
respondent. Journal of Personality and Social Psychology,
1965, 1, 201-209.

The authors hypothesized that mutual visual interaction
would be greater in interviews which dealt with innocuous
rather than highly personal questions, and that women subjects paired with a male or female interviewer would look
more at the interviewer than would male subjects paired
with the same interviewers. The interviewer gazed steadily at the subject while asking very personal or innocuous questions. Mutual glances were recorded and results
showed that: (a) when speaking, subjects looked at the
interviewer significantly more during innocuous questions;
(b) female subjects looked more regardless of the interviewer's sex; and (c) only sex differences were found in
postexperimental discussions such that women engaged in
significantly more mutual glances than men.

138. Exline, R. V., Thibaut, J., Brannon, C., and Gumpert, P.
Visual interaction in relation to Machiavellian and an unethical act. American Psychologist, 1961, 16, 396.

The researchers tested certain hypotheses concerning the
effects of attitudes toward others and implication in an
unethical act upon visual interaction with an interrogator. Fourty-eight pairs of individuals were tested. One
member of each pair was a confederate who was to impli-
cate the subject in cheating in a group task. The results were that there was less visual interaction under
interrogation. Additionally, high-Machiavellian subjects
decreased visual interaction less than low-Machiavellian
subjects. There were also data which showed that females
used more visual interaction than males.

139. Fair, P. LaV., Jr. Patterns of facial myoelectric activity during affective imagery. Dissertation Abstracts International, 1976(May), Vol. 36(11-B), 5829.

Fair wanted to develop a physiological index of facial
muscle patterns in the upper and lower parts of the face

during re-experiences of certain emotions and during the production of these emotions. Forty normal female adults were used as subjects. Half of this group was monitored on the upper face and the other half was monitored on the lower face. The results showed that the recordings reliably differentiated between the natural poses of the emotions based upon relative magnitude differences. Additionally, Fair found reliable differences between the imagery conditions of re-experience. However, these differences tended to depend upon the area of the face which was being monitored. For example, happiness could be discriminated from the other emotions in most of the regions which were monitored, while anger could be discriminated in fewer regions.

140. Fast, J. Excuse me, but your eyes are talking. Family Health, 1978, pp. 22-25.

Fast considered eye contact to be "the single most significant element of body language." His article discussed the use and effectiveness of this type of communication with examples of instances showing how it works. He also included a section on how to improve one's eye language.

141. Feldman, R. S. Nonverbal disclosure of teacher deception and interpersonal affect. Journal of Educational Psychology, 1976, 68(6), 807-816.

Feldman was concerned with the effect of teachers' verbal dissimulation on their nonverbal behavior. In other words, would their nonverbal behavior reveal how truthful they were being to a student and their real feelings toward the student? The "teachers" were 32 female undergraduates who were required to teach a confederate a brief lesson. After the lesson each subject heard a positive or a negative evaluation of herself. This was to manipulate liking of the confederate. Later, other tests were administered by the subjects. They were instructed to give praise to the "student" whether he did poorly or not. Their nonverbal behaviors as they were being truthful or not were recorded on videotape. Results showed that judges rated that teachers were more pleased with their students when they were telling the truth. They were also rated as more pleased when they liked the student. Lastly, displays of pleased behavior were more noticeable in the public versus the private teaching condition. Other results were also reported.

142. Felipe, N. Interpersonal distance and small group interaction. Cornell Journal of Social Relations, 1966, 1, 59-64.

Felipe presented two major approaches to the study of small group interaction with respect to spatial arrangement: (1) the influence of spatial arrangement on interactions, and (2) the effect of interactions on preferred spatial arrangements and on preferred patterns of different types of interaction.

143. Felipe, N. and Sommer, R.   Invasions of personal space. Social Problems, 1966, 14, 206-214.

In a study of the effects of norm violation, a simple staged deviation was performed in two different settings. The violation involved sitting too close to an individual, once on the grounds of a state mental hospital, and the other in the study hall of a university library.   In both instances the spatial invasion had a disruptive effect producing various accommodations on the part of the victim followed, when these failed, by flight reactions.

144. Fischer, C. T.   Social schemas: Response sets or perceptual meanings?   Journal of Personality and Social Psychology, 1968, 10(1), 8-14.

In addition to replicating Kuethe's free placement measure while using different figures, the purpose of Fischer's experiment was to obtain data on free placement of profile figures.   Male and female undergraduates were subjects.   Results supported Kuethe's free placement findings.   There were no significant sex differences. Profile findings showed that in a set of three male profiles, figures facing each other were placed farther apart than those facing outward or in the same direction. In a second study, the experimenter attempted to discover reconstruction responses of males and females.   Results showed that smaller distances were used between both geometric and human figures when these were replaced.   However, when data were analyzed with regard to sex, it appeared that each group had different perceptions of the situation.

145. Fischer, K. L.   A multidimensional scaling analysis of raters' perceptions of nonverbal and verbal behaviors occurring in same and different sex interactions.   Dissertation Abstracts International, 1977(May), Vol. 37(9-B), 4745.

Fischer looked at sex differences in person perception and the possibility that perceptions made along masculine-feminine and dominant-submissive lines might be similar. Male and female college students were subjects.   They were given tests of dominance-submission and masculinity-femininity.   High and low categories of subjects were formed.   Eight males and eight females were targets, and the remaining subjects were raters.   Two assistants interacted with the targets, and the interaction was videotaped.   Same-sex and other-sex pairs interacted.   Different raters rated the subjects on masculinity-femininity and in dominance-submission.   Fischer found that his judges differed on perception based upon their sex.   The target persons were perceived differently by each category

of raters. Voice quality was most often attended to by
the raters. Finally, the sex of the interactant affected
perceptions. Other results were also presented.

146. Forstan, R. F. and Larson, C. V. The dynamics of space:
An experimental study in proxemic behavior among Latin Americans and North Americans. Journal of Communication, 1968,
18, 109-116.

The authors hypothesized that there would be differences
between Latin Americans and North Americans in regard to
seating position, interaction distance, and amount of
touching during a dyadic conversation. Pairs of subjects
were matched according to cultural group and observed as
they discussed a problem concerning the Middle East
crisis. No significant difference was found between the
two in chosen seating positions (face-to-face with paral-
lel shoulders or face-to-face with shoulders at a 45 degree
angle). However, significant differences were found between distances used. No tests were conducted for physical contact since members of only one dyad engaged in
this--handshaking.

147. Foster, C. B. Systematic observation of teacher behavior
using the ego state categories of transactional analysis.
Dissertation Abstracts International, 1977(Oct), Vol. 38
(4-A), 2056-2057.

Foster wanted to verify two hypotheses: (1) an instrument could be developed using the ego states of transactional analysis to identify and record a teacher's verbal
and nonverbal behavior, and (2) there would be no difference between direct observation and videotape (indirect)
observation of teacher ego states. Seven teachers were
observed. Ratings were made of ego states and nonverbal
messages. Both hypotheses were supported. Foster noted
the benefits of videotape observations.

148. Fox, J. G. Self-imposed stigmata: A study of tattooing
among female inmates. Dissertation Abstracts International,
1976(Nov), Vol. 37(5-A), 3201.

Fox interviewed 120 female state prison inmates and 58
female city jail inmates to assess the social and personal significance of tattooing in confinement. He also
wanted to determine the interrelationships between tattooing and the inmate social system. Fox discovered that
the women with tattoos had longer histories of criminal
or delinquent behavior and were in for more serious of-
fenses. There was also a stronger lesbian orientation
among the women with tattoos. In addition, women who
chose the male role in the lesbian relationship tended
to be more heavily tattooed than the women assuming the
female role. In general, tattooing was used as a way of
communicating needs. Various ethnic differences were
found for the tattooed women. Finally, Fox learned that

women with tattooes encountered social and employment difficulties when released, because of their tattoos.

149. Foy, J. O'N. The interpersonal conversation: Nonverbal communication and marital interaction. Dissertation Abstracts International, 1977(Sep), Vol. 38(3-A), 1225.

Foy examined nonverbal behavior cues which were exchanged between marital partners. Videotapes of the couples were made while they engaged in two experimental tasks. Judges scored the frequencies of 13 nonverbal behaviors. Couples had been categorized as either compatible or incompatible; old or young (based upon length of marriage); and high or low on expression of inclusion, control, and affection. Some of the results were that compatible couples used more arm and hand gestures when cooperating and more eye behavior while in the conflict situation. Incompatible couples used more speech volume in the conflict situation. Older and younger couples did not differ on any of the 13 variables. Other findings were presented.

150. Frank, L. K. Tactile communication. Genetic Psychological Monographs, 1957, 56, 209-255.

Frank gave a general discussion of tactile experiences in personality development, cultural patterning, pathology, and research possibilities.

151. Frankel, S. A. and Barrett, J. Variations in personal space as a function of authoritarianism, self-esteem, and racial characteristics of a stimulus situation. Journal of Consulting and Clinical Psychology, 1971, 37(1), 95-98.

The objectives of the study were to investigate the effects of presentations of Black and White human stimuli on personal space and to study the relationship between personal space, authoritarianism, and self-esteem. White male undergraduates were subjects. Two male college students, one White and one Black, were stimuli. It was predicted that when approached by White and Black stimuli the largest area of personal space would be used by subjects high in authoritarianism and low in self-esteem, and that these subjects would also use larger areas of personal space in response to the approach of the Black stimulus than the White stimulus. Results showed that low self-esteem subjects used greater personal space distances in response to the Black stimulus than to the White stimulus. High authoritarian subjects used larger areas of space in response to the Black stimulus than to the White stimulus. The significant race by self-esteem by authoritarian interaction showed that greater personal space was used by high authoritarian, low self-esteem subjects toward the Black stimulus. Lastly, low authoritarian subjects showed a similar response toward the stimulus, while high authoritarian and self-esteem subjects used smaller areas than did high authoritarian, low self-esteem subjects.

152. Freedman, N., Blass, T., Rifkin, A., and Quitkin, F.
Body movements and the verbal encoding of aggressive affect.
Journal of Personality and Social Psychology, 1973, 26, 72-85.

Freedman et al. were concerned with the contribution
body movements made to the verbal encoding of aggressive
behavior. Twenty-four female college students were
videotaped during a structured interview. The nonverbal
behavior which was observed was hand movements (body-
focused or object-focused). It was found that subjects
high in object-focused gestures expressed aggression
overtly, and subjects high in body-focused gestures expressed aggression covertly. The researchers discussed
their results in terms of the roles of object- and body-
focused movements in encoding affect in addition to
aggression.

153. Freedman, N., O'Hanlon, J., Oltman, P., and Witkin, H. A.
The imprint of psychological differentiation on kinetic behav-
ior in varying communicative contexts. Journal of Abnormal
Psychology, 1972, 79, 239-258.

Freedman et al. hypothesized that kinetic behavior was
related to the individual's level of psychological differentiation. Their study was concerned with determining the prevalence of object- and body-focused hand
gestures as a function of communicative content and
level of psychological differentiation. Twenty-four
female subjects were divided into equal groups based upon
field independence-dependence. They were observed and
videotaped during three interview conditions: cold association, warm association, and warm interchange. It was
found that the two groups differed on gestural behavior.
Field-dependent subjects engaged in more hand-to-hand
body-focused movements during the cold and warm association interviews. Additionally, these subjects showed
more object-focused motor primacy gestures during the
warm interchange session.

154. Frisch, J. E. and Zedeck, S. Status, interest, and proximity as factors in interaction and communication channels.
Journal of Psychology, 1972, 82, 259-267.

Frisch and Zedeck studied the affects of interaction between status, physical proximity, and area of interest
upon the number of contacts in a communication system.
College students were subjects. Proximity was defined
as the distance separating each subject from another in
their offices. Status was defined in terms of the number
of years the subject had been a student. Interest was
determined by the subject's field of specialization within the department. The average number of intraoffice
contacts was greater than interoffice contacts. However,
while offices close to each other tended to have greater
amounts of communication, there was considerable fluctu-
ation. The within-group trend for communication also

held for interest and status, but there was no interaction. A replication of the study found significant main
effects as well as interactions between status and interest and status and proximity. The experimenters discussed the shortcomings of the self-report technique used
in the study.

155. Fry, A. M. and Willis, F. N. Invasion of personal space
as function of the age of the invader. Psychological Record,
1971, 21, 385-389.

The personal space of male and female adults was invaded
by children aged five, eight, and 10. Two observers recorded the reactions of the subject and the results indicated that the capacity to elicit adult-like reactions in
a spatial invasion appeared between the ages of five and
10. Five-year-old invaders received a generally positive
reaction (smiling, speaking, or turning toward) when they
approached the adults as they waited in line for a movie.
Eight-year-olds were often ignored. Ten-year-olds received a negative reaction similar to that received by
an adult--subject moved or leaned away, showed excessive
motor activity. There was some evidence to indicate that
sex of subject and invader was a factor influencing the
reactions, but age was the most important factor.

156. Fry, R. and Smith, G. F. The effects of feedback and
eye contact on performance of a digit-coding task. Journal
of Social Psychology, 1975, 96, 145-146.

Fry and Smith examined male college students' performances
on an object digit-coding task during which eye contact
was manipulated as female confederates read the instructions. Feedback to the subjects for results on the Em-
bedded Figures Test was manipulated by giving insufficient
time and then randomly assigning them to either a very
high, very low, or no score condition. The results showed
that subjects who were given no feedback on the prior test
correctly encoded fewer digits than subjects who had been
given positive or negative feedback. For nonverbal behavior, high eye-contact subjects correctly encoded more
digits than low eye-contact subjects.

157. Frijda, N. A., and Philipszoon, E. Dimensions of recognition of expression. Journal of Abnormal and Social Psychology, 1963, 66, 45-51.

Two studies were conducted. The first one analyzed the
dimensions determined (from factor analysis) in the recognition of facial expressions. The second study presented an analysis of the relationship with facial features. Six male and six female college students rated
30 pictures posed by a female actress on 27 bipolar seven-
point scales in Study I. Each subject was seen individually. The results showed four factors which accounted
for 80% of the variance. In Study II, the factor scores

on each factor were computed for each picture and then ranked according to magnitude. Measures of the facial features were also obtained. The results were that, for example, the first factor (pleasantness-unpleasantness) was positively related to smiling and laughter and inversely to frowning. The second factor (which was called naturalness and submission-artificialty and condescension was positively correlated with the subtlety of the expression and negatively related with tenseness and amount of muscular activity.

158. Fugita, S. The effects of anxiety and approval on visual interaction. <u>Dissertation Abstracts International</u>, 1970(Jul), Vol. 31(8-A), 464.

Male college juniors talked to two confederates for five minutes in an evaluative setting in order to test the affects of social approval and anxiety on visual interaction. During the talk, one confederate smiled and nodded at appropriate times to show his approval, while the other grimaced and shook his head to show disapproval. To manipulate anxiety, the subject talked to two confederates who were described as being graduate students with high grade-point averages or junior college freshmen with low grade-point averages. Topics were designed to be ego-involving and to accentuate the presence or absence of the subject's expertise as compared to that of the confederate's. Results showed that when subjects talked to higher status or expertise persons, they maintained more eye contact with the approving confederate. The hypothesis that subjects would visually interact more with a disapproving confederate when the two were of lower status than themselves was not supported. Increase in eye contact with approvers and decrease with nonapprovers occurred over time.

159. Fulcher, J. S. 'Voluntary' facial expression in blind and seeing children. <u>Archives of Psychology</u>, 1942, p. 272.

Fulcher wanted to examine two questions: (1) the nature of facial expressions displayed by children on request and whether or not they changed with age, and (2) the effect of blindness on the facial expressions displayed. Sighted and blind male and female children, teen-agers, and young adults were subjects. Motion pictures showed facial expressions while the subjects posed the emotions told to them by the experimenter. Fulcher found that the ability to form appropriate facial expressions developed early with sighted children and became more energetic and better defined with age. Decreased facial activity was found for the blind subjects. Older blind children displayed less facial activity than younger blind children. Sighted boys showed more facial activity than sighted girls. This was also true, but to a lesser extent, for blind boys and girls. Finally, sighted subjects showed marked differences in expressing different emotions,

while the blind subjects showed slighter differences.
Other results were also reported.

160. Gale, A., Lucas, B., Nissim, R., and Harpham, B. Same
EEG correlates of face-to-face contact. British Journal of
Social and Clinical Psychology, 1972, 11, 326-332.

Gale et al. predicted that EEG amplitude would vary inversely with complexity/arousal. Complexity/arousal referred to the various conditions used in which the subject
continually gazed at an experimenter who smiled, looked,
or averted his eyes. Twelve male college students were
subjects. The experimenter was a 32-year-old male. The
subject and the experimenter sat facing each other across
a table. The behavior was observed and recorded. The
EEG was also recorded. The results were that in most
instances the avert condition led to higher EEG amplitude than the look and smile conditions. In general, as
arousal increased, EEG decreased. The experimenters
noted that in future research they planned to examine
the influence of sex and personality and also to study
clinical populations.

161. Gale, A., Spratt, G., Chapman, A. J., and Smallbone, A.
EEG correlates of eye contact and interpersonal distance.
Biological Psychology, 1975, 3, 237-245.

The experimenters combined eye contact and distance variables to examine individual and interactive effects.
Eighteen adult males were subjects. The subject sat in
a chair which could be adjusted to make his eyes level
with those of the confederate who stood. Interaction
behavior was monitored at various distances. The EEG
recordings were also made. Their results were that alpha
activity increased with eyes averted and as a function of
distance. Another finding was that EEG abundance was
greater for the eyes-closed condition. Third, they found
that the subjects' EEGs were effected by direct gaze even
after they themselves had their eyes closed. Other results were also discussed.

162. Gallois, C. Turn taking: Synchrony and sex role in
conversational interaction. Dissertation Abstracts International, 1977(Apr), Vol. 37(10-B), 5434.

Gallois wanted to examine the structure of nonverbal behavior during conversation turns and the way in which
interactants in dyadic conversations synchronized their
nonverbal behavior. Males and females interacted with
same- or other-sex partners. Their conversations were
videotaped and the occurrence or nonoccurrence of certain nonverbal behaviors in each turn was recorded.
Gallois found that the subjects synchronized their behavior within one turn, but not across turns. Gaze
direction was the behavior which was found to be not
prominent in mixed as well as same-sex dyads, with the

occurrence of this behavior by one member provoking the
same behavior in the other member. Gallois discussed
his results in terms of two different models concerning
interaction. He also discussed the two structurally
different classes of turns his findings pointed out.

163. Gardin, H., Kaplan, K. J., Firestone, I. J., and Cowan,
G. Seating position, eye contact, and cooperative-competitive
tendencies in a prisoner's dilemma game. Unpublished paper,
Wayne State University, Detroit, Mich., 1973.

Gardin et al. examined the affects of side-by-side versus
across seating on cooperation in a two-person prisoner's
dilemma game under conditions where natural visual contact was allowed and where it was blocked by a barrier.
It was hypothesized that greater cooperation would occur
for the side-by-side college student subjects and more
cooperation for the greater eye contact across subjects.
A second aim of the study was to investigate the relationship between level of cooperation by subject pairs,
independent of their assigned experimental condition and
the intimacy value of chosen seating arrangements. Here
it was predicted that a direct relationship between cooperation and seating intimacy would be found. Subjects
were assigned in pairs to one of four experimental conditions: side-by-side with visual contact, across the
table with visual contact, side-by-side with no visual
contact, and across with no visual contact. After the
game, subjects were taken to another room to fill out a
questionnaire. Their chosen seat (from among eight
chairs) was recorded. Results for the game showed that
most cooperation occurred in the across-no barrier condition followed by side-by-side-barrier, the side-by-side-
no barrier, and the across-barrier conditions. A test of
the second hypothesis showed that cooperation was mildly
associated with the intimacy of subsequent seating
arrangements with tendencies toward side-by-side seating
choices occurring.

164. Gatton, M. J. and Tyler, J. D. Nonverbal interview behavior and dependency. Journal of Social Psychology, 1974,
93, 303-304.

The purpose of the study was to explore the relationship
between dependency and responsiveness to the nonverbal
cues of an interviewer. The researchers predicted that
when nonverbal cues were shifted from positive ones to
negative ones, dependent people would be more responsive
to the shift than autonomous people. College students
were subjects. They were classified as dependent or
autonomous according to scores on the Autonomy and Defer-
ence scales of the Edwards Personal Preference Schedule.
The nonverbal cues used by the interviewer were orientation toward or away from the subject, leaning, eye contact, and smiling. Gatton and Tyler found that the subjects smiled more times and maintained more eye contact

with positive cues. However, their general hypothesis
was not supported.

165. Gerber, G. L. and Kaswan, J. Expression of emotion
through family grouping schemata, distance, and interpersonal
focus. Journal of Consulting and Clinical Psychology, 1971,
36(3), 370-377.

The experimenters examined spatial differences in doll
placement as a function of affective state and explored
the possible differences among family members in the
placement of a family of dolls. Subjects were members
of 10 intact White upper middle-class families with two
children. One of the children in each family had a
learning problem. In addition, three of the second children were males and seven were females. All subjects
were given four dolls representing a mother, father, and
two children and were required to place them on a board
in accordance with a theme told to them by the experimenter. Analysis of the data showed a significant main
effort for story themes. The ordering was: loving,
happy, worried, sad, and angry families with themes of
negative emotional connotations eliciting more distant
placements than those with positive connotations. Some
other results were that family members were less likely
to be directly oriented toward each other for sad themes
than in the other themes. Lastly, parents tended to
represent the family as a close knit group more often
than children, and the child with the learning problem
had a larger number of dolls oriented away from one
another for sad and angry themes than all other family
members.

166. Gibson, J. and Pick, A. D. Perception of another person's looking behavior. American Journal of Psychology,
1963, 76, 86-94.

167. Ginsberg, H. J., Pollman, V. A., and Wauson, M. S. An
ethological analysis of nonverbal inhibitors of aggressive
behavior in male elementary school children. Developmental
Psychology, 1977, 13, 417-418.

Ginsberg et al. wanted to classify the types of behaviors
which were most effective at inhibiting aggression between children during unstructured play. They hypothesized that displays of diminished body stature would ter-
minate attack by an aggressor more than other behaviors.
Elementary school children in grades three to five were
videotaped daily for six weeks during unstructured play-
ground activities. Aggression behavior was taped. It
was defined in terms of five modes of attack. The behavior of the child under attack was analyzed. A measure
of the child's stature under attack and during termina-
tion of the encounter (prior to cessation of the attack)
was made. It was found that diminution of body posture
on the part of the child being attacked occurred prior

to cessation of the attack. Such behaviors as bowing
the head, kneeling, waxy flexibility, and slumping of
the shoulders were observed.

168. Gitter, A. G., Black, H., and Walkley, J. Nonverbal
communication and the judgment of leadership. Psychological
Reports, 1976, 39, 1117-1118.

Gitter et al. wanted to determine whether or not nonverbal communication affected judgments of leadership.
There were 55 subjects who were exposed to either a
strong or a weak nonverbal communication and either an
audio-visual presentation or an audio presentation only.
Films of an actor depicting the role of a leader or a
follower were shown to the subjects. Some of the nonverbal behaviors which were manipulated were voice,
facial contortion, and gesture. It was found that when
the actor displayed strong nonverbal communication, he
was perceived to have more structure than when he displayed weak nonverbal communication. Sex of subject and
mode of communication were not significant effects.

169. Gitter, A. G., Mostofsky, D., and Guichard, M. Some
parameters in the perception of gaze. Journal of Social
Psychology, 1972, 88, 115-121.

The authors investigated two aspects of visual interaction: whether presence of Person 2 influenced perceived
direction of gaze, focus of gaze, and expression of emotion in Person 1; and whether in a two-person situation
the perceived focus of gaze and expression of emotion
were influenced by the subject's perceiving or not perceiving Person 2 as looking at Person 1. Male and female subjects were shown photographs of either one or a
pair of White females displaying various directions of
gaze and were asked to evaluate direction of gaze, focus
of gaze, and type of emotion. Subjects who saw photographs of the pair of females were also asked to indicate
whether Person 2 was looking at Person 1. Results showed
that the presence of a second person affected the perception of Person 1 in that her eyes were perceived to look
more toward the other. She was also perceived to express
more emotion. When Person 2 was perceived as looking at
Person 1, Person 1 was perceived as expressing less emotion than when Person 2 was not perceived as looking at
her. Additionally, whether Person 2 was present or not,
women perceived more emotion in Person 1's face than did
men.

170. Gladstones, W. H. A multidimensional study of facial
expression of emotion. Australian Journal of Psychology,
1962, 14, 95-100.

The purpose of the study was to apply multidimensional
scaling to a set of 10 pictures chosen from the Lightfoot
series published by Morgan (1956) to determine whether or

not the resulting dimensions resembled those proposed by
Schlosberg (1954). College students were required to
make their judgments of the faces only on the basis of
similarities and differences in expressions and that they
were to decide for each triad of pictures which of the
lower two expressions were more like the top one. The
results were that three principal axes appeared. One
resembled Schlosberg's Pleasant-Unpleasant dimension.
Another represented his Tension-Sleep dimension. The
third was suggested to resemble an Expressionless-Mobile
factor.

171. Goffman, E. The presentation of self in everyday life.
Garden City, N. Y.: Doubleday Anchor, 1959.

172. Going, M. and Read, J. D. Effects of uniqueness, sex
of subject, and sex of photograph on facial recognition.
Perceptual and Motor Skills, 1974, 39, 109-110.

Going and Read explored the effects of facial uniqueness
on face recognition. Photos of male and female college
students who had been rated as having either a unique or
not unique face were used as stimuli. Twenty-eight photos
were shown to male and female undergraduates. A one-
minute interval lapsed and a total of 112 slides were
then shown to the subjects. They were required to indicate the faces they recognized from the original 28. It
was found that highly unique faces were identified correctly more often than low-unique faces. It was also
found that females recognized female faces more often
than male faces. Males recognized the faces of both
sexes equally as often.

173. Goldberg, G. N., Keisler, C., and Collins, B. Visual
behavior and face-to-face distance during interaction.
Sociometry, 1969, 32, 43-53.

Goldberg et al. required male college students to sit
at two different distances from a male interviewer to
determine the effects of distance on eye behavior. They
found that the subjects seated at the closer distance
spent less time looking at the interviewer's eyes. In
addition, subjects with higher factor scores on a measure
of socioemotional evaluations of the interviewer spent
more time looking at his eyes. (Summary of abstract
summary.)

174. Golding, P. The role of distance and posture in the
evaluation of interactions. Proceedings of the 75th Annual
Convention of the American Psychological Association, 1967,
2, 243-244.

175. Goldstein, H. S. Gender identity, stress and psychological differentiation in figure-drawing choice. Perceptual
and Motor Skills, 1972, 35, 127-132.

The study was done to further investigate the affects
of stress on the figure drawn just in the Draw-a-Person
test. Twenty-eight male subjects were used. After
viewing two stressful films, which were proceeded or
followed by a neutral film, the subjects were allowed
to sleep. Their figure drawings were obtained after a
postsleep inquiry during which they recounted the film
and their dreams. For the drawings, the subjects were
asked to draw a person and then to draw someone of the
opposite sex to that which had been drawn first. The
results showed that there was a tendency to draw a figure of the opposite sex first after experiencing stress.
One explanation was that drawing a figure of the opposite sex may have been a defense against revealing the
self.

176. Goldstein, J. M. Effects of duration of eye contact
on information retention and liking in mixed- and same-sex
dyads. Dissertation Abstracts International, 1977(Jul),
Vol. 38(1-B), 415.

Goldstein investigated whether various durations of eye
contact (no, short, or long) influenced a subject's
liking for an assistant and/or the subject's ability
to remember the verbal content of the assistant's communication. He hypothesized that short eye contact
would lead to the highest retention scores on tests
concerning the assistant's communication and that short
eye contact would lead to the most favorable ratings of
the assistant. College students interacted with a same-
or other-sex assistant who manipulated eye contact during what was supposed to be a learning or an ESP experiment. Goldstein found a monotonic relationship between
eye contact and liking, but no significant difference
between groups in terms of eye contact and information
retention.

177. Goldstein, M. A., Kilroy, M. C., and Van DeVoort, D.
Gaze as a function of conversation and degree of love.
Journal of Psychology, 1976, 92, 227-234.

Goldstein et al. wanted to test the possibility that
Rubin's (1970) results concerning the fact that lovers
spend more time gazing at each other than those less
in love actually reflected the fact that lovers talk
to each other more than others. As a consequence, the
gaze Rubin found may have been the result of eye contact which is found to be a concomitant of talking.
Ten couples who scored high on Rubin's love scale and
10 pairs of subjects who were unacquainted with each
other were tested. Amount of mutual eye contact during
and without conversation was recorded. The researchers
also recorded conversation time. Goldstein et al. found
that lovers spent more time talking to each other than
strangers; however, there was support for Rubin's

findings in that lovers also spent a good deal of time
gazing at each other while not talking. The researchers also noted some methodological problems which may
have affected their results.

178. Gottheil, E., Corey, J., and Paredes, A. Psychological
and physical dimensions of personal space. Journal of Psychology, 1968, 69, 7-9.

Gottheil et al. investigated the degree of correspondence which existed between the psychological distance
and the physical distance which was maintained by the
subjects in their study during an interview situation.
Female subjects were interviewed by a male interviewer.
They asked their subjects to place magnets which represented the following objects: a mother, a father, a
best male friend, God, and an interviewer. These magnets were to be placed in relation to a stationary magnet which represented the subject himself. Physical
distance (measured nose to nose) was rated from photographs which were taken during the interview as the
interactants were seated across from each other.
Gottheil et al. found a correlation between the projective measure responses and the overt behavioral
responses. When a subject felt close to an interviewer, according to the magnet placement, she maintained
less physical distance from him during the interview.

179. Gray, S. L. Eye contact as a function of sex, race,
and interpersonal need. Dissertation Abstracts International, 1971(Sep), Vol. 32(3-B), 1842.

Gray conducted an investigation for the purpose of
determining how the following factors would be effected
by amount of eye contact behavior: need for affiliation, need for dominance, the sex of the subject, and
the race of the interviewer. White male and female
college freshmen served as subjects. They were classified as high or low in their need for affiliation and
their need for dominance according to Schutz's (1958)
Fundamental Interpersonal Relations Orientation-Behavior
test. The subjects talked with a Black or with a White
male interviewer during a low stress session. During
this interview, the amount of time the subject looked
at the interviewer was recorded. The results showed
that dominant female subjects looked at the interviewer more often than did dominant male subjects.
It was found that need for affiliation was not correlated with amount of eye contact. In addition,
there was some indication that females preferred to
look at the Black interviewer more than the White
interviewer.

180. Greenbaum, P. and Rosenfeld, H. M.   Patterns of avoidance in response to interpersonal staring and proximity: Effects of bystanders on drivers at a traffic intersection. Journal of Personality and Social Psychology, 1978, 36(6), 575-587.

Greenbaum and Rosenfeld conducted their study in order to examine the effect of manipulating interpersonal distance and staring on a subject's avoidance behavior. They measured avoidance behavior by the occurrence and direction of the initial proxemic avoidance, the percentage of time the subject spent at a stoplight near a park engaged in avoidance of the confederate's gaze, the mean length of the subject's gaze, and the speed and latency of departure time by the subject. Eight hundred and forty-six drivers (both male and female) were used as subjects. Greenbaum and Rosenfeld found that the proximity of a seated confederate effected avoidant stopping positions. It was also found that for nonavoiders, proximity resulted in a significant increase in verbalization along with gazing. Finally, they found that for silent nonavoiders, staring by the confederate resulted in gaze reduction and increased departure speed. The researchers also briefly discussed their results in terms of an equilibrium theory model.

181. Greenburg, C. I. and Firestone, I. J.   Compensatory responses to crowding: Effects of personal space intrusion and privacy reduction. Journal of Personality and Social Psychology, 1977, 35(9), 637-644.

Greenburg and Firestone conducted their study to show that people who were exposed to intrusion (confrontation by an interviewer sitting close with a forward body lean and engaging in frequent gaze behavior) would experience more stress, perceive more crowdedness, and show stronger withdrawal behaviors than people who were exposed to a nonintrusive interviewer. Male college students were used as subjects and also acted as confederates and interviewers. The subjects were also exposed to a condition in which confederates intruded upon their privacy by being in the room as they spoke to the interviewer. The results showed that Greenburg and Firestone's hypothesis was supported. In addition to this, intrusion was the most potent factor in the subjects feeling crowded. Subjects in the intrusion and in the surveillance conditions (privacy was reduced because of the presence of confederates) showed more withdrawal behaviors. Finally, there were no major effects due to the seat location conditions in regard to perceptions of crowding and withdrawal behaviors.

182. Greenspan, S., Barenboim, C., and Chandler, M. J. Empathy and pseudo-empathy: The affective judgments of first- and third-graders. Journal of Genetic Psychology, 1976, 129, 77-88.

Greenspan et al. investigated possible qualitative differences in the ability of different ages of children to make empathic judgments. Two almost identical social situations were presented to the subjects. In one, the situational context and the affects expressed were consistent. In the other, they were not. The subjects were 80 male and female elementary school children. Videotapes of the social interactions were shown. Scores of the children's judgment of the target's affect state and facial expression (among other variables) were recorded. No differences in empathic responses for the unambiguous videotape were found. However, the two age groups differed in responses to the ambiguous videotape. The younger children made more incorrect judgments of facial expression than the older children. Additionally, the subjects differed in terms of their certainty about their judgments by age. Younger children were more certain of their judgments in the ambiguous condition than were older subjects.

183. Guardo, C. J. Factor structure of children's personal space schemata. Child Development, 1971, 42, 1307-1312.

Three 10-year-olds from two different schools responded to same- or other-sex silhouettes of peers by tracing a figure representing themselves in relation to the particular silhouette presentation. Factor analysis was done on the data, and factors were obtained for each of the four age groups. For example, a Heterosexual Schema factor was found for all subjects and demonstrated that children of both sexes had a broad generalized attitude toward the opposite sex. Males, seven to 10, had two heterosexual factors: one for interactions with female strangers and the other for intimate interactions with females. Another important finding was the increase in identifiable factors for older groups and the identification of the Causal Interaction factor for older groups only. (The importance of the study was the identification of a factor structure for children's schemata which adds further support to the evidence for internal spatial patterning tendencies.)

184. Guardo, C. J. Personal space in children. Child Development, 1969, 40, 143-151.

Guardo hypothesized that as the distance between members of a depicted dyad increased, the degree of acquaintance assigned to them by sixth-grade children would decrease and the degree of liking assigned would decrease. Using same-sex pairs of silhouette figures representing peers standing in profile and facing each other, subjects were required to make their judgments. In the second task, subjects were asked to trace a figure of a silhouette representing themselves in relation to a printed one which was described by the experimenter concerning degrees of acquaintance, liking, and threat. It was found that as interfigure distance increased, the degree of acquaintance and liking assigned decreased. The experimenter noted that actual use of interaction distance was not assessed because of the methodological difficulty involved; for example, defining the type of interaction taking place.

185. Guardo, C. J. and Meisels, M. Child-parent spatial patterns under praise and reproof. Developmental Psychology, 1971, 5, 365.

Male and female third and 10th graders were shown silhouettes of two adult males and two adult females described as mothers or fathers reproving or praising a child. Subjects were asked to place their self-referent silhouette in relation to these figures. In the praise condition, female subjects placed the referent closer to parental figures than did male subjects, younger subjects placed the referent closer than older subjects, and subjects placed the self closer to the father figure. However, in the reproof condition, subjects placed the self farther from the father than the mother. It was suggested from the results shown that habitual reproof may cause psychological distance between child and parents, that the father's approval and disapproval have more affect than mother's, and that children move farther away (psychologically) from parents with age.

186. Gubar, G. Recognition of human facial expressions judged live in a laboratory setting. Journal of Personality and Social Psychology, 1966, 4, 108-111.

Gubar wanted to develop a method for the study of live expressions of emotion within the laboratory. Fifty-four female and 15 male college students were used as subjects. The facial expressions of subjects involved in a discrimination task producing reward or punishment (in the form of shocks) were observed by either naive or experienced observers. Experienced observers were those who had previously participated in the discrimination task. The study found that previous experience in the task led to better recognition of the expression on the other person's face than did mere verbal knowledge of the situation (as with the naive observer). Gubar noted that the study did not help to clarify which part of the face was used as a cue. The eyes and the mouth seemed to receive similar weights in this judgment.

187. Gullahorn, J. T. Distance and friendship in the gross interaction matrix. Sociometry, 1952, 15, 123-134.

Gullahorn used a matrix to present a visual picture of
the interactions between female clerical workers in an
office setting. He found that even when the working conditions did not require cooperative effort, the gross
interaction rate among employees was determined by distance between individuals to a great extent. For example, interaction within rows was greater than between
rows, interaction between adjacent rows was greater than
between those separated by another row, and the women
interacted more frequently within rows with those closer
to them.

188. Guthrie, R. D. Body hot spots: The anatomy of human
social organs and behavior. New York: Van Nostrand Reinhold
Co., 1976.

Guthrie discussed the role of "social organs" in communicating things about individuals to each other. Social
organs are those parts of the human body which are emotionally loaded and whose communicative impact are influenced by cultural factors. Guthrie discussed why these
social organs are important and how they have evolved to
be so. The book was divided into six parts.

189. Haase, R. The relationship of sex and instructional set
to the regulation of interpersonal interaction distance in a
counseling analogue. Journal of Counseling Psychology, 1970,
17(3), 233-236.

Haase examined the affect of different topics of discussion within a dyad on preference for interpersonal attraction distance within the counseling setting. Male and
female undergraduates and graduates viewed slides of male-
female dyads in five different seating distances. Subjects responded to the pictures on the semantic differential. It was found that subjects preferred closer interaction distances as opposed to greater distances. No sex
differences were found and the suggested explanation was
that the projective technique may have masked the importance of sex differences. Alternatively, the nature of
the counseling session may be such that these differences
were overridden by other factors in the situation. The
experimenter questioned the existence of a functional relationship between the use of the spatial environment by
client and therapist and the nature of the outcome of the
encounter.

190. Haase, R. and DiMattia, D. J. Proxemic behavior: Counselor, administrator, and client preference for seating arrangement in dyadic interaction. Journal of Counseling
Psychology, 1970, 17(4), 319-325.

Subjects were counselors, clients, and administrators who
responded on a semantic differential to photographs of
male-female dyads in four seating arrangements common to
counseling. Differences were found in terms of seating

preferences between the three groups; however, the most preferred position was the across-the-corner-of-the-table arrangement. The experimenters noted that since these three groups had different views of physical space and its impact on the nature of the interaction, it was important to specify the relationship which might exist between spatial arrangements and counseling outcomes.

191. Haase, R. and Markley, M. S. A methodological note on the study of personal space. Journal of Consulting and Clin-ical Psychology, 1973, 40, 122-125.

The authors noted that while a great deal of research has been devoted to the concept of personal space, a direct comparison of results has been hampered by the many meth-odologies which have been used. Twenty-eight adult males and eight adult females were subjects. They participated in four experimental tasks: an approach task, a ranking of preferences for interpersonal distances portrayed by a live male and female, figure placement, and rankings of photographs showing males and females at various inter-personal distances. The investigators found that the observation of live interactions was the most reflective of subject's actual behavior. The next most valid ap-proach was the figure placement technique. The least valid measure was found to be the use of photographs. The authors noted that their results were encouraging for methods which did not require actual subject par-ticipation.

192. Hall, E. T. A system for the notation of proxemic be-havior. American Anthropologist, 1963, 65, 1003-1026.

Hall presented a notation system designed to provide a way of talking about observation concerning how man ori-ents himself in space and in relation to others. He de-scribed proxemic behavior as a function of eight differ-ent dimensions with appropriate scales. The dimensions were: (1) postural-sex identifiers, (2) sociofugal-sociopetal orientation (SFP axis), (3) kinesthetic fac-tors, (4) touch code, (5) retinal combinations, (6) thermal code, (7) olfaction code, and (8) voice loudness scale. Each dimension was presented with a number coding system.

193. Hall, E. T. Environmental communication. In A. H. Esser (Ed.), Behavior and environment: The use of space by animals and men. New York: Plenum Press, 1971.

Hall looked at the relationship between informal culture patterns and architectural spaces within Black and White cultures in the United States. He discussed the impor-tance for architects to remember the cultural needs and habits of those they designed and built for, with special reference to high-rise apartments. When such buildings are designed for Blacks they should be designed in

congruence with the informal, social, and territorial
realities of that culture (p. 247). He also stressed the
fact that cultural norms and territorial control are
eroded due to urban renewal when friends, families, club
members, and the like are scattered.

194. Hall, E. T.   Listening behavior: Some cultural differences. Phi Delta Kappan, 1969, 50, 379-380.

195. Hall, E. T.   Proxemics. Current Anthropology, 1968,
9(2-3), 83-108.

Hall believed that almost everything man is and does is
associated with space. His sense of space is a synthe-
sis of many sensory inputs: visual, auditory, kinesthetic, olfactory, and thermal. Each of these is molded and
patterned by culture. As a result, people reared in different cultures live in different sensory worlds, and
they are generally unaware of the degree to which the
worlds differ. He felt that proxemics was more concerned
with how than why, and more concerned with structure than
content.

196. Hall, E. T.   The hidden dimension. Garden City, N. Y.:
Doubleday and Co., 1966.

Hall discovered cultural differences in the use of personal space as a form of nonverbal communication. From
interviews and observations of middle-class healthy adult
American males and females, usually coming from the Northeastern United States, he characterized four interaction
distances--intimate, personal, social, and public. Concerning cultural differences, he found that American
males preferred to stand 18-20 inches from another male
during a face-to-face interaction, and about 22-24 inches
from a female under the same conditions. In cross-cultural investigations, Germans were found to have larger areas
of personal space and were less flexible in their spatial
behavior than Americans. Arabs, the French, and Latin
Americans, on the other hand, were much more tolerant of
close quarters and had smaller personal distances than
Americans.

197. Hall, E. T.   The silent language. New York: Fawcett,
1959.

198. Hamid, P. N.   Changes in person perception as a function
of dress. Perceptual and Motor Skills, 1969, 29, 191-194.

Hamid was concerned with the effects of clothes in impression formation. Eight color photographs of male and
female high school students in four modes of dress were
shown to male and female college students. The subjects
rated the stimuli on 10 polar concepts. Hamid found that
the ratings on the concepts tended to be more extreme
(higher or lower) when the stimulus was female. In

regard to style of dress, the ratings were low when the
stimulus wore a high school uniform and high when he or
she wore casual or evening clothes. Interaction findings
were also reported. Hamid noted that the effects of
dress reported in his study were not considered as complete explanations of the presence or magnitude of stereotyped changes between and across sex groups. Other
factors may have been of equal or greater importance.

199. Hamid, P. N. Style of dress as a perceptual cue in impression formation. Perceptual and Motor Skills, 1968, 26,
904-906.

Hamid wanted to determine whether or not there were consistent stereotypes based upon style of dress. Eight
color photos of females expressing neutral facial expressions and with similar physiques were used as stimuli.
These were shown to male and female college students.
They were required to arrange the eight figures in the
order which most suited each of 10 concepts to that which
least suited each concept. The results showed consistent
stereotypes based upon style of dress. For example, for
figures wearing glasses, the concepts intelligent, reli-
gious, conventional, and unimaginative were more frequently attributed. There were also sex differences for
the judges on various concepts.

200. Hammes, J. A. The personal distance effects as a function of esthetic stimulus, anxiety, and sex. Journal of
Clinical Psychology, 1964, 20, 353-354.

Hammes applied the personal distance effect defined by
Smith (1954) to the field of esthetics using subjects
differing in degrees of manifest anxiety. It was predicted that since high-anxious individuals tend to project threat into environmental stimuli, they would show
greater personal distance effects than low-anxious individuals and would additionally evaluate the stimulus objects less esthetically pleasing than low-anxious subjects. Fourteen slide photos of sculptured heads and
face masks from various cultures were the stimuli. A
projection of the slide was varied in seven sizes simulating a continuum for largest personal distance effect
to smallest effect. Esthetically pleasing slides produced smaller personal distances than unpleasant ones and
were also judged to be more pleasant. Additionally, high-
anxious subjects and female subjects gave higher esthetic
ratings than low-anxious and male subjects.

201. Hanawalt, N. G. The role of the upper and lower parts
of the face as a basis for judging facial expressions. I.
In painting and sculpture. Journal of General Psychology,
1942, 27, 331-346.

Hanawalt compared judgments of the face by subjects seeing either the entire face or the upper or lower parts

of the face. Color paintings and black and white photographs were used as stimuli. Names for each facial expression of each picture were determined from a group of
college students. College students were subjects. Each
subject was required to underline the one term (from
among six) which he or she felt best described the expression in the picture. Hanawalt found that the subjects were better at judging expressions from the paintings when the entire face was shown. The same type of
result occurred for pictures of sculptures.

202. Hanawalt, N. G. The role of the upper and lower parts
of the face as a basis for judging facial expressions. II.
In posed expressions and 'candid-camera' pictures. Journal
of General Psychology, 1944, 31, 23-36.

Hanawalt wanted to determine the role of the upper and
lower parts of the face in providing cues for making
judgments of facial expressions in poses and candid-
camera pictures. Female college students saw pictures
of either the entire face, the upper part of the face,
or the lower part of the face. He found that for some
poses, a half-face view was somewhat superior to a full-
face view. However, in general, the entire face enabled
the subjects to make better judgments. This was also
found for the candid-camera pictures. Another finding
was that there was consistent confusion for judgments of
happy and pain suffering on the upper part of the face.
The lower part of the face was better at providing cues
for judging happy expressions, while the upper part was
superior for fear and surprise. Lastly, happy expressions were most easily identified. Other results were
discussed.

203. Hardee, B. B. Interpersonal distance, eye contact, and
stigmatization: A test of the equilibrium model. Dissertation Abstracts International, 1976(Oct), Vol. 37(4-B), 1970-
1971.

Hardee conducted two field experiments to examine the
effects of potential for eye contact and stigmatization
on nonverbal behaviors, especially spatial invasion.
Male and female assistants acted in each of four conditions: a person without a handicap and with eyes visible, a person with dark glasses, a blind person with cane
and dark glasses, and a person on crutches. The experiment took place on benches in a shopping center. Results
showed that the crutch condition was significant. People
sat farther from the assistant in that condition. Hardee
also found that people sat closer to the assistant when
he or she wore dark glasses than when he or she did not.
Lastly, the distance maintained from the "blind" assistants was less than from the "normal" assistants. A
second study replicated these results.

204. Hare, A. P. and Bales, R. F. Seating position and small group interaction. Sociometry, 1963, 26, 480-486.

Hare and Bales analyzed data from several studies using five-man laboratory groups to test the hypothesis that centrality of seating position and distance between members could be used to predict the interaction pattern. In these studies, group members were seated on three sides of a rectangular table with the open side toward an observation mirror. Analysis of the various results showed that the interaction pattern only appeared in task sessions. In social sessions for the same type of group, members tended to talk more to the person next to them as they turned away from the group for a more intimate conversation. Personality variables were also related to seating choice and to interaction rate. More dominant subjects tended to choose the central seats and to do the most talking.

205. Harnett, J. J., Bailey, K. G., and Gibson, F. W., Jr. Personal space as influenced by sex and type of movement. Journal of Psychology, 1970, 76, 139-144.

The authors attempted to analyze human distance behavior using approach as the technique. In one instance, the experimenter approached the subject, and in the other the subject approached the experimenter. The subject sample consisted of males and females, and one male and one female served as the experimenters. It was found that the subjects generally allowed the experimenters to come closer to them than they came to the experimenters. Additionally, according to responses on a heterosexuality scale, male subjects high on this variable tended to allow the female experimenter to walk closer to them than did males low on this variable.

206. Harper, R. G., Wiens, A. N., and Matarazzo, J. D. Nonverbal communication: The state of the art. New York: John Wiley & Sons, 1978.

Harper et al. stated that the purpose of their book was to review the current state of works on nonverbal behavior and to present the most important methodological principles in the area to date. The works they reviewed were categorized into six basic sections, among which were articles on the formal characteristics of speech and paralanguage, facial expressions, eye behavior, proxemics, and kinesics. Their introductory chapter included many of the definitions and classification systems used for nonverbal behavior.

207. Hastorf, A. H., Osgood, C. E., and Ono, H. The semantics of facial expressions and the prediction of the meanings of stereoscopically fused facial expressions. Scandinavian Journal of Psychology, 1966, 7, 179-188.

The researchers conducted two experiments. Experiment I examined clustering of various poses for the same intention and the dimensional structure of affective system. Thirty-five poses were presented to male and female college students who rated them on a semantic differential. The aim of the second experiment was to determine the extent to which facial expressions, which had been fused in a stereoscope, could be predicted from the meanings of component expressions presented independently to the two eyes. Five poses from Experiment I were used. Male and female students were used over three sessions. In the first session, meanings of the five poses were determined. In the second and third sessions, the meanings of the fused poses were measured. The results of both experiments suggested that there may be three dimensions. Furthermore, it was concluded that the findings indicated that predictions based on a congruity principle were no better than those based on an algebraic mean of the components.

208. Hayduk, L. A. Personal space: An evaluative and orienting overview. Psychological Bulletin, 1978, 85(1), 117-134.

The article was done to define personal space as a phenomenon separate from its companion research areas. Hayduk also reviewed and evaluated current theories and measurement techniques for studying personal space. In addition, he suggested the need for further theory construction and more research on specific techniques and aspects of the phenomenon.

209. Hayes, F. C. Should we have a dictionary of gestures? Southern Folk-Lore Quarterly, 1940, 4, 239-245.

210. Hearn, G. Leadership and the spatial factor in small groups. Journal of Abnormal and Social Psychology, 1957, 54, 269-272.

Hearn used male subjects interacting in groups with the investigator acting as leader and constituting the sixth member. His purpose was to test the relative effectiveness of two training methods in improving group productivity--a self-motivated method and a trainer-induced method. The results were that people tended to interact more with those sitting farther away from them than with those next to them in the self-motivated group, while those in the trainer-induced group did just the opposite. Since subjects were randomly assigned to these groups, it was suggested that the opposite effects may have been due to the way the groups were led.

211. Heckel, R. W. Leadership and voluntary seating choice. Psychological Reports, 1973, 32, 142.

Heckel determined to find the relationship between leadership and voluntary seating at the head position during
mealtimes. Professionals in the mental health field were
subjects. The study was conducted during a week-long
workshop on experimental learning and community mental
health. Data on seating arrangements were obtained by
observing dining room behavior during the week. Additional data were obtained by asking each subject to list
the six people he felt were the true leaders during the
week. The correlation between the groups' rating of
leadership and observed seating was low; however, there
were individuals who consistently avoided using the head
or foot positions. Additionally, five individuals who
played major or leadership roles sat at the head or foot
of the table for at least one-half of the meals.

212. Hedstrom, J. E. Effects of a nonverbal communication
training model in counseling practicum upon counselor-
trainees' facilitative functioning skills. Dissertation
Abstracts International, 1975(Feb), Vol. 35(8-A), 5022-5023.

The study was done to develop and validate the Nonverbal
Communication Training Model (NCTM) and to investigate its
effects on the facilitative skills of counselor-trainees.
Graduate students in counseling were used as subjects and
the effects of the NCTM in counseling practicum were incon-
clusive. No significant differences between counselor trainees and controls were found in terms of their ability to
identify their own and clients' nonverbal behavior, their
sensitivity to affective communication, their effectiveness
as rated by their clients during and after training, and
their perceptions of the overall counseling practicum and
the practicum instructional requirements. Hedstrom planned
to investigate his measure further.

213. Heinig, R. M. A descriptive study of teacher-pupil
tactile communication in grades four through six. Dissertation Abstracts International, 1976(Jun), Vol. 36(12-A), 7948.

Heinig videotaped five elementary teachers and then students in grades four through six during a summer school
reading program. Tactile behaviors were divided into
eight categories developed by the investigator. She
found that teachers used the categories called Positive,
Close Work, and Guidance, while the children used the
category called Get Attention most frequently. Boys received more Discipline and Guidance types of touches than
did girls, and girls did not receive more Positive touch
than boys, as had been expected. A race difference was
found such that non-White children touched the teachers
more than did White children. In addition, an age effect
showed that teachers touched younger children more than
older children. Other results were reported.

214. Henley, N. M. Body politics: Power, sex, and nonverbal
communication. Englewood Cliffs, N. J.: Prentice-Hall, 1977.

Henley discussed the power motive behind nonverbal communication. She suggested that nonverbal communication
is the vertical dimension of human relations since it
can represent status, dominance, superiority, and power.
The book contained 11 sections concerning such topics
as spatial use, language, touch, facial expressions, and
eye contact.

215. Heshka, S. and Nelson, Y. Interpersonal speaking distance as a function of age, sex, and relationship. Sociom-
metry, 1972, 35(4), 491-498.

Heshka and Nelson took photographs of interacting dyads
in outdoor settings in London, England, in order to determine the affects of age, sex, and relationship on interpersonal speaking distance. A comparison was made
between the category of acquaintance, friend, relative,
and stranger with the results similar to those reported
by Little (1965) and Willis (1966). Strangers stood
farther apart than acquaintances, relatives, or friends.
However, male-male dyads were found to stand at approxi-
mately the same distance regardless of relationship,
while for female-female and male-female dyads, relationship had an affect. Age affects were only analyzed for
acquaintances, friends, and relatives.

216. Hewes, G. W. The anthropology of posture. Scientific
American, 1957, 196, 122-132.

Hewes presented an article which discussed cultural differences in the body positions used by people in different parts of the world. Photographs, paintings, and
sculpture provide sources of information about these
behaviors. Hewes presented a "map" showing the distribution of various static postures throughout the world.

217. Hewes, G. W. World distribution of certain postural
habits. American Anthropologist, 1955, 57, 231-234.

218. Hiat, A. B. Explorations in personal space. Dissertation Abstracts International, 1971(Jun), Vol. 31(12-B), 7572.

The author examined the test-retest reliability of individual distance. He also looked at the individual consistency of relative size of the relationship between
individual distance to physical size and sex, the degree
of familiarity of subject with the person approached, and
to drawing test measures. Male and female subjects were
put in approach conditions. Toe-to-toe distance between
subject and target was measured. Subjects were also required to draw themselves standing in front of a target
represented as a stick figure. Results were that subjects showed significant individual consistency in size
of individual distance relative to other subjects across
targets, although actual size of distance varied with
target. There were also differences in distance based

upon feelings and the relationship with the target.   No
significant relationship between sex of subject or target
and distance was found.   Physical measurements were not
correlated with distance.   The difference in patterns of
spatial behavior seen in the distant group versus the
average and close groups was discussed in terms of the
possible relationship between maturity and distance.
Further research was suggested.

219. Higgins, J., Peterson, J. C., and Dolby, L. L.   Social
adjustment and familial schema.   Journal of Abnormal Psychology, 1969, 74(3), 296-299.

The experimenters determined to account for typical
familial schemata within the "normal" range of functioning.   It was predicted that normal well-adjusted males
would place a figure of a son closer to that of a mother,
while less well-adjusted males would place the son figure
closer to a figure of a father.   Male undergraduates coming from intact families were subjects.   Each was given
a questionnaire to measure social adjustment and Kuethe's
(1962) Felt Figure Technique to determine familial schema.
The stimuli figures were those representing a father, a
mother, a son, and a sister.   It was found that subjects
with poor social adjustment placed the son closer to the
father, while those with good social-adjustment placed
the son closer to the mother.   The combined groups placed
the sister closer to the mother than to the father.   Additionally, poor social-adjustment subjects placed a greater
number of intervening figures between the son and mother
than between the son and father, whereas the good social-
adjustment subjects more frequently placed intervening
figures between the boy and father than the boy and
mother.

220. Hinde, R. A. (Ed.).   Nonverbal communication.   Cambridge,
England: Cambridge University Press, 1972.

Hinde presented 15 articles by various authors covering
different aspects of nonverbal communication in humans as
well as in animals.   The articles on humans discussed
nonverbal behavior in children, in the mentally ill, the
way the phenomenon is expressed in Western art, and the
influence of culture on nonverbal expression.   Some of
the contributing authors were W. H. Thorpe, M. Argyle,
N. G. Blurton-Jones, and I. Eibl-Eibesfeldt.

221. Hobson, G. N., Strongman, K. T., Bull, D., and Craig, G.
Anxiety and gaze aversion in dyadic encounters.   British
Journal of Social and Clinical Psychology, 1973, 12, 122-129.

A systematic study was made of the affects of anxiety on
eye contact.   Male and female subjects were tested in
three conditions--no anxiety, anxiety by verbal negative
reinforcement, and positive verbal reinforcement.   Results showed that gaze aversion was not a function of

anxiety. Other nonobservable bodily movements were suggested as occurring instead of gaze aversion.

222. Hochberg, J. and Galper, R. E. Attribution of intention
as a function of physiognomy. Memory and Cognition, 1974, 2,
39-42.

Hochberg and Galper wanted to determine whether or not
attributions of intention could be obtained in response
to pictures of faces. Seventy-three college students
were subjects. They were shown six photographs of female
faces chosen from a college yearbook. The faces had been
judged to display levels of either sexuality or social
desirability. The subjects were required to match an
explanation of the targets' behavior with one of the
faces. The explanations were four alternatives provided
as the endings of two scenarios--one concerning a secre-
tary and her boss, the other a social worker and her
client. The study was conducted on two samples of subjects, one year apart. The researchers found that expectations about a person's intentions were influenced by
his photograph.

223. Hocking, J. E. Detecting deceptive communication from
verbal, visual and paralinguistic cues: An exploratory experiment. Dissertation Abstracts International, 1977(May),
Vol. 37(9-B), 4756.

Hocking explored how differences in nonverbal and verbal
behavior availability influenced the ability of individuals to detect deception. Hocking videotaped samples of
lying and truth-telling behaviors for 16 targets. Eight
of the targets made true or false statements about factual events. The remaining eight made true or false
statements about their emotions. Male and female college
students saw the tapes under varying exposures of nonverbal cues. The subjects judged the veracity of the 16
targets. Different aspects of nonverbal cues were influential for each of the conditions (factual true-false
and own emotions true-false). Hocking's findings replicated the Ekman and Fuesen (1974) results when the communication involved emotions but not when it involved
factual events. Significant results were also found for
audio versus visual information given to the subjects.

224. Hollender, J. W., Duke, M. P., and Nowicki, S. Interpersonal distance: Sibling structure and parental affection
antecedents. Journal of Genetic Psychology, 1973, 123, 35-45.

The research examined the affects of maternal affection
on interpersonal closeness using third- and fourth-grade
White students from a rural lower-socioeconomic school
and college undergraduates. In Study I, the children
were given the Comfortable Interpersonal Distance (CID)
scale and the Parental Contact scale. In Study II, the
college students were given a scale highly correlated

with the Parental Contact scale as well as the CID. The
number of older brothers and sisters was obtained from
the college subjects, and the younger subjects gave information about birth order and family size. Results for
Study I showed that for males greater physical contact
with the mother allowed closer frontal approach by an
opposite sex-opposite race stimulus. Closer contact with
fathers allowed for a closer rear approach for males with
the same kind of stimulus. In Study II for males, reports of having received maternal physical affection led
to closer approaches by stimuli on the CID. Other distance results were also discussed.

225. Holman, R. M. H. Communicational properties of women's
clothing: Isolation of discriminable clothing ensembles and
identification of attributions made to one person wearing
each ensemble. Dissertation Abstracts International, 1976
(Nov.), Vol. 37(5-A), 3141.

   Holman examined the communicational properties of the
   usage of women's clothing among college students at the
   University of Texas at Austin. Slides were made of women
   students at the university. The clothing of 392 women
   was described on a 171-item scale. Six groups of inter-
   pretable clothing ensembles emerged from a cluster analysis. Pictures were taken of women dressed similarly to
   clothing in each of the six groups. College students
   gave their impressions of the women on a forced-choice
   scale. In general, the variance accounted for by clothing was small; however, there were differences on eight
   variables. Holman suggested that her study may prompt
   other research in other areas--marketing, for example.

226. Horowitz, M. J. Human spatial behavior. American
Journal of Psychotherapy, 1965, 19, 20-28.

   Horowitz discussed personal space and body-buffer zones
   in interpersonal interactions emphasizing the clinical
   importance of observations of patients' feelings about
   space, specifically with respect to their proximity to
   others. The use of such observations in treatment was
   also discussed.

227. Huneycutt, M. E. An investigation of the relationship
between teachers' attitudes and teachers' perceptions of
students' communication behaviors. Dissertation Abstracts
International, 1977(Aug), Vol. 38(2-A), 705.

   Huneycutt conducted a field study in an elementary school
   to determine whether or not certain nonverbal and verbal
   behaviors were perceived to be characteristic of students
   toward whom teachers expressed certain attitudes. Forty-
   nine teachers from two predominately Black schools were
   subjects and responded to two questionnaires. She found
   that the nonverbal behaviors direct eye contact, facial
   expression of happiness, and pseudo-relevant responses

were characterized by Attachment behavior. Behavior
irrelevant responses were associated with Rejection-type
students. Behaviors were associated with the nomination
of males across the attitude groups more than they were
associated with females. Finally, she found that none
of the behaviors was sex related.

228. Hunt, R. G. and Lin, T. K. Accuracy of judgments of
personal attributes from speech. Journal of Personality and
Social Psychology, 1967, 6, 450-453.

Hunt and Lin investigated whether or not judges could
accurately judge personality from speech; whether they
were consistently accurate across samples of speech produced by dissimilar personalities, whether there were
individual differences in judgment accuracy and whether
traits differed in their ease of apprehension, whether
speakers who performed in-character verbal parts would be
perceived more accurately than those in out-of-character
parts, whether open-minded and closed-minded judges performed differently, and whether judgment accuracy and
interpersonal similarity were related. Male and female
undergraduates were judges. They listened to speakers
reading prose. After listening to the speaker, the
judges predicted the speaker's responses to various
adjectives. Hunt and Lin found that, for example, judges
could make accurate judgments of personality from speech,
accuracy was a general ability, there was no significant
difference between open- and closed-minded judges, and
similarity between judge and speaker was not a significant effect.

229. Imada, A. S. and Hakel, M. D. Influence of nonverbal
communication and rater proximity on impressions and decisions in simulated employment interviews. Journal of Applied
Psychology, 1977, 62, 295-300.

Imada and Hakel looked at the effects of a rater's proximity and applicant's nonverbal behaviors on interview
decisions and impressions. Female college student subjects acted as interviewers, in-person observers, or TV
observers as they watched an applicant (research assistant) in an immediate or nonimmediate behavioral condition. Immediacy included eye contact, posture, smiling,
gestures, distance, and body orientation. Following the
interview, the subjects rated their liking of the applicant. The findings were that ratings of liking were
higher for the immediate condition. There were no significant rater proximity main effects or interactions
with immediacy. Imada and Hakel suggested further research into the effects of these behaviors on impressions.

230. Jancovic, M., Devoe, S., and Wiener, M. Age-related
changes in hand and arm movements as nonverbal communication:
Some conceptualizations and an empirical exploration. Child
Development, 1975, 46(4), 922-928.

The researchers investigated the possibility that the use
of communicative hand and arm movements would increase
with age. Their subjects were 60 children between the
ages of four and 18. Videotapes were taken of each subject individually as he watched a cartoon. Each subject
was told that he was to judge the cartoon in terms of
how funny it was and how funny he thought his friends
would think it was. Two judges viewed the videotapes
and scored the number of hand and arm movements for each
subject. The results showed an increase in the measured
gestures with age, that the number of pantomimic gestures
decreased with age, and the youngest children showed
little use of the hand and arm movements while viewing
the cartoon. The researchers discussed the relevance
of their data for nonverbal communication research.

231. Johnson, K. R. Black kinesics: Some nonverbal communication patterns in the Black culture. Florida FL Reporter,
1971(Spr/Fall), 9, 181-189.

Johnson discussed some of the nonverbal communication
patterns among Blacks. He focused chiefly upon those
patterns of behavior which had been called kinesics by
Birdwhistell. Johnson discussed the use of the eyes,
standing, walking, and body orientation. Some of the
postures were specifically related to the sex of the
reactant. Johnson noted the importance of knowing about
such behaviors for people who interact with Blacks so
that better understanding and relationships may occur.

232. Jones, R. A. and Cooper, J. Mediation of experimenter
effects. Journal of Personality and Social Psychology, 1971,
20, 70-74.

Jones and Cooper conducted two experiments in order to
determine whether or not subjects' projection of the feeling tone of their interaction with an assistant would influence person-perception judgments. They also examined
whether or not mutual glances between the subject and the
assistant affected the feeling tone. Male high school
students were subjects. Pairs of subjects were used with
one acting as an assistant. Two eye-contact conditions
were used--high and low. The nonassistant subjects were
instructed by the assistant subjects to rate photographs
of individuals while the assistant subjects engaged in
one of the levels of eye contact. One-half of the subjects also filled out a mood questionnaire following the
photo ratings. It was found that high eye-contact subjects felt more positively about themselves on the mood
questionnaire than low eye-contact subjects. High eye-
contact subjects rated the photos as more successful than
low eye-contact subjects, in support of the hypothesis.

233. Jones, S. E. A comparative proxemics analysis of interaction in selected subcultures of New York City. Journal of
Social Psychology, 1971, 84, 35-44.

In two studies, Jones attempted to test Hall's hypothesis
concerning the existence of subcultural differences in
proxemic behavior. Two-person groups were observed on
the streets of New York City. The subjects were from
Black, Puerto Rican, Italian, and Chinese subcultures.
Hypotheses for Study I were that there would be differences in interaction distances and axis between the subcultures, and that Blacks would stand less directly than
Puerto Ricans and Italians. These hypotheses were not
supported. In Study II, using all four groups, it was
hypothesized that distance and axis differences would
exist, that Black males would stand less directly than
males in the other subcultures, and that male-male axis
would be less direct than female-female axis regardless
of the subculture. Once again, distance and axis were
not significantly different between the groups. However,
the last hypothesis concerning sex differences was
supported.

234. Jones, S. E. and Aiello, J. R.   Proxemic behavior of
black and white first-, third-, and fifth-grade children.
Journal of Personality and Social Psychology, 1973, 25(1),
21-27.

The authors noted that a source of ambiguity in previous
research on the acquisition of proxemic behavior existed
because studies did not report whether subcultural differences were subject to change with increasing age.
Thus, unobtrusive observations of the distance and axis
behavior of same-sex, same-race pairs of first-, third-,
and fifth-grade children in a classroom setting in an
upper lower-class Black elementary school and a middle-
class White elementary school were made. For both of
the subcultures, males were found to stand less directly
than females, especially in the fifth grade. Blacks
faced each other less directly than Whites in the early
grades. Blacks were found to stand closer to each other
than Whites at the earliest grade level; however, this
difference disappeared by the fifth grade. Additionally,
axis behavior was the same across ages. It was suggested
that although subcultural differences in distance and
axis are learned early, only axis seemed to remain as a
likely communication barrier between Blacks and Whites
later in their elementary school years.

235. Jourard, S. M. and Friedman, R.   Experimenter-subject
"distance" and self-disclosure.   Journal of Personality and
Social Psychology, 1970, 15(3), 278-282.

Jourard and Friedman conducted two experiments which were
extensions of the Argyle and Dean (1965) study. Distance
between subject and experimenter was the focus of the
study, and the question raised was: Would a subject who
was approached in various ways by an experimenter retreat
or would there be conditions under which the subject
would respond to the experimenter's approach by further

decreases of distance? The distance-reducing behavior used by the experimenters were eye contact, decreases in physical distance, and self-disclosure. The authors were concerned with the effects of these degrees and modes of distancing on the subject's readiness to disclose personal information to the experimenter. In Experiment I, with a male experimenter, it was found that as distance decreased, female subjects disclosed less while males showed no significant change. In Experiment II, the experimenter interacted at further decreases of distance ranging from being present, but silent, to making physical contact with the subject and disclosing himself. A linear increase was found in the subject's disclosure as "distance" was reduced, contrary to the expectation based on Argyle and Dean's hypothesis. Self-disclosure from the experimenter, along with minimal physical contact, facilitated self-disclosure from the subjects rather than inhibiting it. Furthermore, reductions in "distance" were accompanied by increased positive experience as indicated by the subjects and by increased change in the subjects' impressions of the experimenter.

236. Kasl, S. V. and Mahl, G. F. The relationship of disturbances and hesitations in spontaneous speech to anxiety. Journal of Personality and Social Psychology, 1965, 1, 425-433.

Kasl and Mahl noted that previous research suggested that speech disturbance could be used as a measure of ongoing anxiety. Twenty-five experimental and 20 control subjects were used. All were males. The experiment was conducted in two sessions and involved being in an interview situation. In addition, the subjects took the MMPI and a Palmar Moisture test was made at each session. Recordings were made of the interviews. Three speech-disturbance measures were used: number of "ah's" divided by the number of words spoken, the sum of all disturbances except "oh" divided by the number of words spoken, and ratios for the individual speech categories. It was found that under anxiety the frequency of all speech disturbances (except "ah") increased. The experimenters also looked at the stability of certain speech characteristics within individuals.

237. Kates, R. W. and Wohlwill, J. F. Man's response to the physical environment: Introduction. Journal of Social Issues, 1966, 22, 15-21.

Kates and Wohlwill provided an introduction to a group of papers concerned with various topics of man's spatial environment and his conception of it.

238. Kendon, A. and Cook, M. The consistency of gaze patterns in social interaction. British Journal of Psychology, 1969, 60, 481-494.

The authors reviewed previous work on gaze direction in
social interactions and made suggestions for further
work. An experiment was done in which 11 subjects interacted with each of four other subjects. They found that
amount, length, and frequency of gazes and actions were
related. They also found that the longer the subjects'
utterances and the greater the percentage of the time he
spoke, the shorter and more frequent were his gazes while
speaking; however, there was also a correlation between
the amount and length of the speaker's utterances and
his own length and frequency of gazes while listening.
Significant sex differences were found for the four subjects. The 11 subjects showed differences according to
the sex of their partner. It was concluded that different aspects of gaze direction are related and are consistent aspects of the subject's social performance, although his gaze patterns are also affected by the behavior of the other person.

239. Kendon, A., Harris, R. M., and Key, M. R. (Eds.). Organization of behavior in face-to-face interaction. Paris:
The Hague; Monton Publishers, 1975.

The book presented a collection of articles by psychologists, sociologists, linguists, anthropologists, ethnolo-
gists, and mathematicians. The articles concerned the
behavior of people interacting in face-to-face situations.
The book had five parts, some of which covered theories,
methods, and cultural differences in interactional behavior. The articles used in the book were originally presented at a Research Conference held at the Department
of Psychology, University of Chicago, and were later reported to a session of the Ninth International Congress
of Anthropological and Ethnological Sciences.

240. Kerkhoff, T. R. The effects of encoder communicative
incongruence on decoder verbal and nonverbal behavior. Dissertation Abstracts International, 1977(Jan), Vol. 37(7-B),
3614.

Kerkhoff investigated the effects of interview noncongruent and congruent nonverbal and verbal behavior on the
verbal and nonverbal behavior of an interviewee in terms
of anxiety responses. Male inmates in a correctional
institution were subjects. The results showed that the
noncongruent and congruent interview behaviors were related to the subject's perception of the interview relationship. Results concerning stress and interview question content were unaffected by the subject's perception
of the interview relationship. Young presented a discussion of methodological issues and implications for
future research.

241. Kersey, J. F. Eye-contact phenomena related to choice
of partner and aggressive/passive role playing. Dissertation
Abstracts International, 1970(Jul), 31(1-A), 466.

Male and female subjects were interviewed by three males, three females, or a two-and-one combination of the sexes. Individual panel members portrayed one of three eye-contact availability conditions. On the postinterview questionnaire the subjects were to indicate a preference for one of the interviewers. Results showed that male subjects chose least frequently male interviewers who portrayed the constant availability condition and female interviewers who portrayed the never available condition. Female subjects chose least frequently interviewers of either sex who portrayed the never available condition. A second experiment tested Argyle's hypothesis that eye contact is positively related to aggressiveness. Subjects were required to role play an aggressive and vital debater or a passive and retiring one. A measure of the eye-contact availability used by the subjects in defining the roles toward male and female targets was taken, and contrary to Argyle's hypothesis only the male subject/ male target condition elicited a positive relationship between eye contact and aggressiveness. The results were interpreted as reflecting societal norms which disallow overt aggression toward females.

242. Key, M. R. Nonverbal communication: A research guide and bibliography. Metuchen, N. J.: Scarecrow Press, 1977.

Key compiled numerous works on nonverbal communication in man. The works included cross-cultural studies as well as studies done on Americans. She also included sections concerning various ideas about human communication both verbal and nonverbal. Another inclusion concerned a discussion of the various nonverbal notation systems. The bibliographies were presented in order by author.

243. Kiker, V. L. and Miller, A. R. Perceptual judgment of physiques as a factor in social image. Perceptual and Motor Skills, 1967, 24, 1013-1014.

The experimenters were concerned with the affects of body build on stereotypes. Male and female subjects arranged pictures of endomorphs, mesomorphs, and ectomorphs in the order in which they were most suited to a certain concept to least suited to the concept. Eight concepts were used. The results indicated that the same criterion was being used by most of the subjects for ranking the pictures, since five of the concepts were statistically significant for the subjects. The results also supported the idea that stereotypes based on physiques existed and were measurable. The researchers noted that they wanted to extend the research to include various other factors such as parental image and group affiliation.

244. King, M. J. Interpersonal relations in preschool children and average approach distance. Journal of Genetic Psychology, 1966, 109, 109-116.

King examined some questions concerning whether or not
approach distances could be demonstrated in preschool
children and the existence of a "peck-dominance" type of
relationship between members of a group. One question
was: Since the subordinate in a peck-dominance relationship may noxiously stimulate the dominant, does the dominant maintain a characteristic distance from the subordinate? Alternatively, since the subordinate may noxiously stimulate the dominant, would this make it more
likely for the subordinate to approach the dominant
closer? Three five-year-old kindergartners were viewed
in same-sex, similar-age triads and were observed during
free-play periods. The number of friendly and unfriendly
acts made by each subject to the other's approach distances between pairs was recorded by photographs. The
ratio of unfriendly acts to the total number of acts made
by one subject to another was strongly related to the
mean distance maintained by the second subject from the
first. Mean distances, however, were found to reduce in
most cases when a prized toy was juxtaposed with the first
subject.

245. Kinzel, A. F. Body buffer zone in violent prisoners.
American Journal of Psychiatry, 1970, 127, 99-104.

A 12-week study was undertaken to attempt to answer the
following: (1) do violent prisoners have larger body
buffer zones than nonviolent prisoners? (2) do the zones
of violent prisoners have a different shape from those
of nonviolent prisoners? and (3) do the size and shape
of the zones change in either group over repeated deter-
minations? An approach technique was used. The subject
was asked to indicate when he felt the experimenter had
come too close at which point toe-to-toe distance was
recorded. The experimenter then made approaches from
other directions around the subject. The area within the
eight closest distances tolerated by the subject was
called his body-buffer zone. Results showed that the
zones for violent prisoners were larger than those for
nonviolent ones. Rear zones were larger than front zones
for the violent group, while the reverse was true for the
nonviolent group. Zone areas decreased for both groups
over the 12 weeks of the experiment.

246. Kleck, R. E. Interaction distance and nonverbal agreeing responses. British Journal of Social and Clinical Psychology, 1970, 9, 180-182.

Kleck examined the hypothesis that at highly proximate
interaction distances statements of opinion made by one
member of a dyad would be more likely to elicit nonverbal
indicators of agreement than when similar statements of
opinion were made at less proximate interaction distances.
The measurement of agreement was positive head nodding.
Male subjects were used, and videotapes were made. More
head nodding occurred in the near condition than in the

far condition supporting the hypothesis. Smiling and
self-manipulation were also explored with the results
that the latter was affected by distance and occurred
more often in the near condition than in the far condition. It was suggested that more proximity caused
arousal, resulting in self-manipulation and positive
head nodding.

247. Kleck, R. E. and Rubenstein, C. Physical attractiveness, perceived attitude similarity, and interpersonal attraction in an opposite sex encounter. Journal of Personality
and Social Psychology, 1975, 31(1), 107-114.

Four experiments were conducted. Physical attractiveness
and attitude similarity were varied within each experiment. Forty-eight male college students were subjects.
Five female students were used as confederates. The subjects rated the confederates on physical attractiveness
and attitude similarity during the experimental situation
and two and four weeks after the experiment on seven-
point scales. The interaction between the subject and
confederate was recorded. Results for recordings of nonverbal behaviors showed that, for instance, subjects
spent more time looking at the physically attractive
confederate when talking to her than did subjects who
spoke to the less-attractive confederate. No effect
was found for attitude similarity.

248. Kleck, R. E., Buck, P. L., Joller, W. L., Condon, R. S.,
Pfeiffer, J. R., and Vukcevic, D. P. Effect of stigmatizing
conditions on the use of personal space. Psychological Reports, 1968, 23, 111-118.

Two studies were done in order to examine the affect of
the presence of a stigmatized person on the use of personal space by male college students. In Experiment I,
a figure-placement task was used. Additionally, the
French Test of Insight and two attitude measures were
given. Results showed that self-rectangles were placed
significantly farther from rectangles described with
stigmatisms than those positively defined. The result
did not hold only for the case of blindness, but it was
in the expected direction. In Experiment II, interactions involving an individual believed to have epilepsy
were examined in regard to initial interaction distance
and eye contact. The hypothesis that less proximate interactions would occur with persons described as epilep-
tic was confirmed; however, there was no significant
difference in the use of eye contact between stigmatized
and nonstigmatized individuals.

249. Kleck, R. E., Vaughan, R. C., Cartwright-Smith, J.,
Vaughan, K. B., Colby, C. I., and Lanzetta, J. T. Effects
of being observed on expressive, subjective, and physiological responses to painful stimuli. Journal of Personality
and Social Psychology, 1976, 34(6), 1211-1218.

Two experiments were conducted to determine whether or
not the presence of an observer would attenuate nonverbal
expression of pain as well as augment arousal. Male
undergraduates were used as subjects in both experiments.
The subjects experienced various levels of shocks either
alone or observed. It was found that when they believed
they were being observed, subjects were less expressive
in response to the shocks than when they believed they
were alone. In addition, autonomic measures also showed
less arousal in the observed condition than in the alone
condition. Lastly, the sex of the observer did not influence the subjects' responses.

250. Kleine, S. H. A study of raters' identification of
counselors' verbal responses to client nonverbal behavior.
Dissertation Abstracts International, 1977(Apr), Vol. 37
(10-A), 6277.

The purpose of the study was to measure the degree to
which trained raters could identify counselor verbal responses to client nonverbal behavior better than untrained raters. Four counseling sessions involving one
of two male counselors and a female client were videotaped. Male and female undergraduates who had been
designated as trained or untrained were subjects. The
subjects were further divided into an informed and an
uninformed group based upon their knowledge that one of
the counselors was blind. Judges' ratings of the counselors' verbal responses to the clients' nonverbal responses were used as a criterion base rate. Results
showed differences between trained and untrained subjects.
In addition, trained subjects' responses differed from
the judges' responses. Kleine made some suggestions
concerning training.

251. Kleinfeld, J. S. Effects of nonverbally communicated
personal warmth on the intelligence test performance of
Indian and Eskimo adolescents. Journal of Social Psychology, 1973, 91, 149-150.

Kleinfeld examined the effects of nonverbally communicated personal warmth on the intelligence test performance of Indian and Eskimo high school students. Smiling,
close body distance, and mutually seated posture were
used as the nonverbal behaviors. The students had originally taken the WAIS which was used as a baseline measure
of intelligence. They were assigned to either a cold or
warm condition and retested on the Digit-Symbol and Information subtests by a Black male. The results were that
for the Digit-Symbol test and in the cold condition,
three of the eight subjects lost points, while four remained the same. In the warm condition, six of the seven
subjects gained points, one remained the same. For the
Information test, five of the seven students gained
points in the warm condition. Finally, five of the
eight students lost points in the cold condition.

252. Kleinfeld, J. S.   Effects of nonverbal warmth on the learning of Eskimo and White students.   Journal of Social Psychology, 1974, 92, 3-9.

Kleinfeld wanted to determine whether or not an instructor's warmth as communicated by smiling and close body distance would increase the learning, question asking, and question answering of Eskimo students.   Changes in learning and verbal productivity were also compared between Eskimo and White students.   The subjects came from the ninth grade at an urban high school.   Each subject was assigned to a neutral-warm or a warm-neutral sequence condition.   During the condition the three dependent variables were manipulated: the subjects were to answer questions, the subjects were to ask questions, and the subjects were tested on some information they were to have learned.   Kleinfeld found that among White males there was significantly higher learning in the neutral-warm condition.   For the Eskimo males, warmth led to higher learning in both conditions.   For question answering, warmth had significant effects only for females.   This occurred for a warmth-by-sequence interaction.   Lastly, for question answering, warmth had a significant effect for male and female Eskimo subjects in the warm-neutral condition.

253. Kleinke, C. L.   Compliance to requests made by gazing and touching experimenters in field settings.   Journal of Experimental Social Psychology, 1977, 13, 218-223.

Two experiments were conducted to examine the effects of gazing and touching on compliance to unambiguous requests. In Experiment I, four female college students were assistants.   They approached male subjects who left certain phonebooths in an airport in which a dime had been left. The subjects were asked whether or not they had found the dime.   Gaze, touch, and distance (due to the touch condition) were manipulated.   Results showed that more dimes were returned when the experimenters touched the subjects than when they did not.   There was also a nonsignificant tendency to return the dimes in the gaze condition.   In Experiment II, eight female assistants approached male and female subjects and asked to be lent a dime.   Gaze and touch were again manipulated.   Results were that the subjects gave more dimes when they were touched than when not touched.   They gave more under the gaze condition, and males complied more than females.

254. Kleinke, C. L. and Pohlen, P. D.   Affective and emotional responses as a function of other person's gaze and cooperativeness in a two-person game.   Journal of Personality and Social Psychology, 1971, 17(3), 308-313.

The experimenters wanted to investigate the influence of certain behavioral variables on reactions toward gaze. A second purpose for their study was to test the

hypothesis that gaze would increase emotional arousal.
Fifty male college students were subjects. They participated in the Prisoner's Dilemma Game within a large
experimental room. The manipulations of gaze involved a
condition in which the confederate gazed steadily at the
subject during all trials of the game, and a condition
in which the confederate gazed at the table before him.
There were also manipulation conditions for the confederate's level of cooperation. The subjects later evaluated the confederate in terms of how much they liked him
and how much they would enjoy working with him again.
One result was that subjects in the gaze condition had
higher heart rates than subjects in the no-gaze condition. Another finding was that there was no relationship
between the manipulated variables and the distance left
between a subject and a confederate during the post-
experimental discussion. This was unexpected. Another
result was that there was no significant effect due to
the confederate's gaze upon answers to the two questions
evaluating the confederate.

255. Kleinke, C. L., Desautels, M. S., and Knapp, B. E.
Adult gaze and affective and visual responses of preschool
children. Journal of Genetic Psychology, 1977, 131, 321-322.

Kleinke et al. required three-, four-, and five-year-old
boys and girls to play a word game for five minutes during which time they were gazed at during each answer or
during each seventh answer by a female assistant. A
distance of three feet was maintained between the assistant and the child. The child's visual behavior was recorded by an observer behind a one-way mirror. It was
found that girls gazed more at the assistant than did
boys. They also gazed longer than boys. The children
gazed more at the high- than the low-gazing assistant.
A sex-by-assistant gaze result showed that girls liked
the high-gazing assistant more, while the boys liked
her less.

256. Kleinke, C. L., Staneski, R. A., and Berger, D. E.
Evaluation of an interviewer as a function of interviewer
gaze, reinforcement of subject gaze, and interviewer attractiveness. Journal of Personality and Social Psychology,
1975, 31(1), 115-122.

The study was done to determine whether or not a subject's gaze duration toward an interviewer could be effected by a reinforcement procedure. Fifty-four male
college students were subjects. Nine female students
served as interviewers. Whenever the subject gazed at
the interviewer he was reinforced by being shown a green
light. He was punished for not gazing by being shown a
red light. Control subjects received noncontingent green
and red light responses. In regard to the responses
given by subjects to the interviewers, they rated non-
gazing interviewers unfavorably. This included rating

them as unattractive, sitting farthest from them during debriefing, and giving them the shortest answers. The experimenters found that the subjects did not discriminate between attractive and unattractive confederates except for rating unattractive interviewers lower on attentiveness if they did not gaze at the subject.

257. Klukken, P. G.   Personality and interpersonal distance. Dissertation Abstracts International, 1972, 32(10-B), 6033.

The use of interpersonal distance was analyzed in terms of personality factors, topic intimacy, relationship, setting, and sex using male and female undergraduates. Results were that (1) personality was not linearly related to individual use of interpersonal distance; (2) subjects with high scores on the personality inventory did not interact at closer distances than those with low scores; (3) interaction distances in natural and laboratory settings did not differ significantly; (4) females did not use closer distances in all conditions, although in most; (5) when interacting with friends, females used closer distances for high-intimacy than low-intimacy topics; and (6) when in a natural setting, interaction of high intimacy with a stranger resulted in greater distances than interaction of low intimacy. Klukken also discussed other data and proposed hypotheses and questions.

258. Knight, D. J., Langmeyer, D., and Lundgren, D. C.   Eye contact, distance, and affiliation: The role of observer bias.   Sociometry, 1973, 36(6), 390-401.

The authors conducted two experiments in order to clarify the issue of observer bias in recording eye-contact behavior. It was hypothesized that as interaction distance became greater, the amount of eye contact recorded would become greater. The second of these two experiments was done in order to check the possibility of observer biases other than inaccuracy over distance, and the hypothesis for this experiment was that no significant difference in eye contact would be found between the three interaction distances used. Subjects in Experiment I were males. A male confederate was also used and was trained to gaze at the subject's eyes with a pleasant facial expression. An observer recorded the times the subject looked into the confederate's eyes. Results from Experiment I supported the hypothesis and replicated the findings by Argyle and Dean. In Experiment II, the confederate was told to look at the eye, ear, or shoulder of the subject for one-minute periods until given a signal to change. Additionally, the observers were told to record the amount of eye contact engaged in by the confederate with the subject. Results showed that even though the actual eye-contact behavior of the confederate was the same for each of the three interaction distances, observers reported greater eye contact with greater

distances, thus overestimating eye contact at all distances. Results for shoulder and ear gazes were also
discussed.

259. Knower, F. H.   Studies in the symbolism of voice and
action: V. The use of behavioral and tonal symbols as tests
of speaking achievement. Journal of Applied Psychology,
1945, 29, 229-235.

Knower wanted to develop a valid and reliable objective
group test of a speaker's skill in using both tonal and
behavioral symbolism. He also wanted to learn the relationships of such skills to the total effectiveness of
the speaker while speaking and to various other characteristics of the speaker. Judges rated the tonal expressions as well as the facial expressions of various persons in a class situation. One result was that skill in
using tonal symbolism varied less than skill in using
behavioral symbolism as a result of retesting. Furthermore, the mean level of performance in using tonal symbols was lower than the mean level of performance for
behavioral symbols. Results for data comparing a group
of sophomores and a group of freshmen were also reported.

260. Knowles, E. S.   Boundaries around group interaction:
The effect of group size and member status on boundary per-
meability. Journal of Personality and Social Psychology,
1973, 26(3), 327-331.

Knowles investigated whether or not the interaction between members of a small group would be as impermeable
as the boundary for an individual, and whether or not
observations from studies using individuals or pairs of
subjects could be generalized to a larger group. Two or
four confederates (males and females) of high or low
status (determined by age and dress) interrupted the flow
of traffic in a university hallway. The results showed
that the sex of passersby did not affect penetration.
When wastebarrels were placed where the confederates were
to stand (for a control condition), 75.6% of the passersby penetrated the space between the objects. However,
when the confederates were in place, only 25.1% of the
passersby walked between them. Another finding was that
the size of the interacting group decreased the percentage of penetration. Additionally, fewer people walked
through the high-status group than through the low-status
group.

261. Konečni, V. J., Libuser, L., Morton, H., and Ebbesen,
E. B.   Effects of a violation of personal space on escape and
helping responses. Journal of Experimental Social Psychology,
1975, 11, 288-299.

The investigators conducted four experiments to examine
the effects of a violation of personal space on the subsequent behavior of the subject. Male and female

pedestrians were manipulated in various conditions by
male or female confederates at an intersection while waiting to cross the street. Each manipulation was designed
to violate the subject's personal pace for different
lengths of time and under different conditions. Some
general findings were that violation of personal space
caused the subject to flee. Also, the subject's helping
behavior diminished when his personal space was violated
for an extended period of time and presumably because he
had imputed certain personality characteristics to the
violator. The experimenters suggested that an interesting extension of their study would involve the investigation of the possibility that a person whose space had
been violated would not only become less likely to help
the violator but other individuals as well.

262. Korner, I. N. and Misra, R. K. Perception of human relationship as a function of inter-individual distance. Journal of Psychological Researches, 1967, 11, 129-132.

Teen-age boys (14-16 years old) were subjects. Their responses as to the relationship of two figures placed at
various degrees and kinds of physical distances on a
wooden board showed that relationship was a function of
the dimensions they vary along--horizontal dimension indicated a stronger relationship and the vertical dimension
indicated a family relationship.

263. Kramer, E. Elimination of verbal cues in judgments of
emotion from voice. Journal of Abnormal and Social Psychology, 1964, 68(4), 390-396.

Kramer investigated three methods of eliminating verbal
cues from expressions of emotion: (a) an ambiguous set
of words expressing various emotions, (b) filtering out
those frequencies which allow word recognition, and (c)
speech in a language which was unknown to the listener.
Five emotions were used in the study. Six male students
from the university speech department and the experimenter
initially recorded passages incorporating each emotion.
The passages were then filtered, translated into Japanese,
and, finally, some of the Japanese recordings were alternated with English recordings. The results showed that
the emotions presented in English were usually judged as
the actor had intended it to be, errors with the filtered
speech tended to be similar to those from normal speech
(with certain exceptions), and foreign speech seemed to
still permit accurate judgment of emotions.

264. Kramer, E. Judgment of personal characteristics and
emotions from nonverbal properties of speech. Psychological
Bulletin, 1963, 60, 408-420.

Kramer reviewed articles done over a 30-year period concerning studies of the judgment of personal characteristics from the voice. He pointed out that many studies

had used inadequate measurement techniques and thus had
not been able to eliminate verbal content wholly. He
also noted certain areas within the research which had
been neglected.

265. Kraut, R. E. Verbal and nonverbal cues in the perception of lying. Journal of Personality and Social Psychology,
1978, 36(4), 380-391.

Kraut conducted two studies in which observers distinguished truths from lies. Study I was done to determine
some of the cues influencing an observer's judgment about
another person's statement in terms of whether it was
true or not. It also explored whether or not observers
agreed with each other and were accurate when evaluating
such statements. Observers viewed videotapes of college
students who lied or told the truth during simulated job
interviews. Some judges rated lying; others rated verbal,
nonverbal, and paralinguistic characteristics of each
answer. The results showed that judges tended to use
less smiling, postural shifting, and more grooming as
signs that the subject was lying. They also used longer
hesitations between answers as a measure of lying. In
the second experiment, the content of an answer and a
nonverbal cue were manipulated. Nonverbal cues also effected the judgments about lying and there was an interaction effect between the cue (long pause between answers)
and the subject's attitude about an issue.

266. Krebs, G. M. Utilization of incongruent communication.
Dissertation Abstracts International, 1976(Apr), Vol. 36
(10-B), 5263.

Krebs hypothesized that (1) simultaneous verbal and nonverbal cues would be combined or integrated, (2) that an
intuitive mode of perception would be related to greater
responsiveness to the nonverbal component of a congruent-
incongruent communication, and (3) sensitization would
act to increase the communicational significance of nonverbal cues. Hypothesis 1 was the only confirmed prediction. Krebs found that the anxiety level of a client was
rated higher when both his nonverbal and verbal anxiety
cues were high. In turn, his anxiety was rated lowest
when both cues were low. These two extremes represented
the congruent conditions of communication. Under incongruent conditions (one form of communication high, the
other low), rated anxiety fell between the high- and low-
rating extremes.

267. Krout, M. H. An experimentation attempt to determine
the significance of unconscious manual symbolic movements.
Journal of General Psychology, 1954, 51, 121-152.

Krout's study was done in order to examine certain manual
gestures. His research was exploratory since he was not
certain of the nature of the gestures he might observe.

He manipulated certain attitudes and looked at the manual
gestures which accompanied these. There were 1,601 experiments conducted on 100 male and female subjects. Sex
differences were found in terms of such things as number
of gestures observed, type of gesture, and reaction time
in displaying a gesture. In addition to the nonverbal
behaviors, Krout also asked his subjects to select those
terms from a predefined list of attitudes which they had
experienced while the nonverbal portion of the experiment
had been taking place. Krout was able to equate 10 manual
gestures with verbalized attitudes. He discussed further
research which could develop from his findings.

268. Kuethe, J. L. Pervasive influence of social schemata.
Journal of Abnormal and Social Psychology, 1964, 68, 248-254.

Subjects were required to place felt human figures on a
board under free-response instructions and then to reconstruct displays of the figures in a judgment task
where figures were presented with a fixed separation
and replaced by subjects. Then, subjects attempted to
replace human statutes while blindfolded. Lastly, they
were given a word-association test. Subjects who kept
man and woman figures together in free placement made
the largest replacement errors of opposite-sex pairs in
the visual and blindfolded conditions. Additionally,
these subjects were more likely to give "man" and "woman"
as reciprocal verbal associations on the word-association
test. (Summary of author abstract.)

269. Keuthe, J. L. Social schemas and reconstruction of
social object displays from memory. Journal of Abnormal and
Social Psychology, 1962, 65, 71-74.

Kuethe wanted to determine whether or not social schemas
other than the man-woman schema interfered with judgments
of figures having specific content; and using a different
technique, he wanted to discover the manner in which a
schema introduced error into the judgment process. In
Experiment I, subjects reconstructed pairs of stimulus
figures from memory. Results showed that male undergraduates placed the two male figures which were facing outward the farthest apart; rectangles were placed the next
farthest, followed by the female pair, the male-female
pair, and the male pair facing inward. In Experiment II,
male subjects were asked to place a man, a woman, and a
cat in any manner they wanted. Results showed that the
ordering man, woman, cat was preferred most often. In
Experiment III, male subjects were required to replace
from memory figures of a cat and a woman and then of a
dog and a man. The woman-cat pair was replaced at a
closer distance than the man-dog pair. In a final experiment, subjects were asked to replace a man and woman
pair with two rectangles and then to replace two rectangles with a man and woman pair. The man and woman
figures were placed closer together then the rectangles.

270. Keuthe, J. L. Social schemas. Journal of Abnormal and Social Psychology, 1962, 64, 31-38.

Kuethe asserted that when a person indicates that two things belong together, he has employed some schema or plan. If these objects are people or people symbols, the schema employed may be considered, by definition, a social schema. The purpose of Kuethe's first investigation was to determine whether or not objects are thought of as belonging together and the degrees of belongingness. Subjects were male undergraduates who were to place two or more cutouts of men, women, a child, a dog, and three rectangles on a felt board in any manner they wished. In general, the woman and child were placed closer together than the man and child. Height ordering was used for the three rectangles. This tendency was also shown for the man, woman, and child. Additionally, subjects generally grouped the man and woman figures rather than the two women figures. In a second experiment, the experimenter looked at the subject's replacement responses after he had removed a display which had been looked at for five seconds. Errors of reconstruction were found. Thus, Kuethe concluded that the schema that men and women belong together induced error.

271. Keuthe, J. L. and Stricker, G. Man and woman: Social schemata of males and females. Psychological Reports, 1963, 13, 655-661.

Fifty male and 50 female undergraduates placed felt human figures on a felt field. Subjects were to arrange the figures in any manner. Both male and female subjects used the same generic social schemata: human figures were kept together, males with females, and rarely paired by same sex. When one man and two women sets were used, the dominant schema was to place the male figure between the two females; and when there was one woman and two men, the woman was placed in the middle.

272. Keuthe, J. L. and Weingartner, N. Male-female schemata of homosexual and nonhomosexual penitentiary inmates. Journal of Personality, 1964, 32, 23-31.

The experimenters explored the social schemata used by individuals who were overt homosexuals and those who were nonhomosexuals. It was predicted that (1) in the free-placement condition, using a man and a woman figure as well as other objects, homosexuals would separate the man and woman more often than nonhomosexuals; (2) with sets of figures containing two men and two women, homosexuals would form man-man pairs more often than nonhomosexuals; and (3) in the reconstruction from memory condition, homosexuals would replace two male figures closer together than male-female figures, and nonhomosexuals would err in the opposite direction. The subjects were inmates of the Maryland Penitentiary. The results supported the hypotheses.

273. Kushner, R. I. and Forsyth, G. A.   Judgment of emotion
in human face stimuli: An individual differences analysis.
Journal of General Psychology, 1977, 96, 301-312.

   Kushner and Forsyth used an individual differences analysis approach to identify groups of subjects and to char-
   acterize their use of different parts of the face in
   judging affects.   Male and female college students were
   subjects.   The pictures of the face of a male student
   were each divided into four segments which were inter-
   changed to examine the interactive and additive use of
   various regions of the face for making judgments.   The
   student had posed with an angry face, a pleasant face,
   and a neutral pose.   Dissimilarity in pleasure and dissimilarity in anger were judged by the subjects for the
   various face-pair stimuli.   Five subgroups were determined from the subjects' ratings.   The subgroups differed
   in terms of the region of the face they used to make
   anger and pleasure judgments.

274. LaBarre, W.   The cultural basis of emotions and gestures.
Journal of Personality, 1947, 16, 49-68.

   LaBarre discussed the cultural bases of various gestures
   and emotions and pointed out that even though the physiological behavior displayed in different individuals may
   be similar, its emotional and cultural functions may be
   different.   He also noted that forgetting the possibility
   of differences may lead to misunderstanding.   Another
   point was that gestures may change culturally and his-
   torically.

275. LaFrance, M. and Mayo, C.   Racial differences in gaze
behavior during conversations: Two systematic observational
studies.   Journal of Personality and Social Psychology, 1976,
33, 547-552.

   LaFrance and Mayo conducted a laboratory and naturalistic
   study to investigate differences in eye-contact behavior
   during conversations between Black-Black and Black-White
   pairs.   In Study I, films of dyadic interactions were
   rated.   Subcultural differences in eye-contact behavior
   were found.   Differences in looking, depending upon
   whether or not the individual was listening or talking,
   were also observed.   In Study II, same-race dyads were
   observed in college cafeterias, hospitals, airport waiting rooms, and fast-food stores.   It was found that Black
   interactants engaged in less other-directed eye contact
   during listening than did White interactants.   A main
   effect for sex was not significant.   Other interaction
   results were presented.

276. Laird, J. D.   Self-attribution of emotion: The effects
of expressive behavior on the quality of emotional experience.   Journal of Personality and Social Psychology, 1974,
29, 475-486.

Laird conducted two studies in which undergraduate males
and females were to indicate their subjective feelings of
emotions after being required to smile or frown during
various conditions. In the first experiment, apparatus
purported to measure muscle activity of the face was attached to the subject. After his face was positioned
into a smile or frown, he watched pictures of Ku Klux
Klan members and of children playing. Following this,
he filled out a mood adjective checklist. The results
were that the subjects described themselves as happier
when the smile was positioned and angrier when their
faces were positioned in a frown. In the second experiment, the subjects were to rate humorous stimuli while
their faces were in the smile and frown positions and
while they were attached to the bogus apparatus. Results similar to the first experiment were found.

277. Lambert, S.   Reactions to a stranger as a function of
style of dress.   Perceptual and Motor Skills, 1972, 35, 711-
712.

The study was done to measure the reactions of individuals to different conditions of dress in a real-life
situation. The subjects were 200 individuals who used
a suburban subway station. They were adult Whites who
were traveling alone. A female confederate who was
either neatly or sloppily dressed approached each subject and pretended to be conducting a market research
survey. The results were that there were no main effects
for condition of dress, age of subject, and sex of subject in terms of their refusal to answer the questions.
However, age interacted with the condition of dress such
that older subjects preferred or responded to the confederate when she was neatly dressed than when she was
dirty. In addition, for age by sex by condition of
dress, older females generally refused to be interviewed
when the confederate was dirty.

278. Lanzetta, J. T. and Kleck, R. E.   Encoding and decoding
of nonverbal affect in humans.   Journal of Personality and
Social Psychology, 1970, 16(1),   12-19.

Lanzetta and Kleck wanted to determine whether or not
individuals who were good at displaying nonverbal cues
would be good judges of the nonverbal behavior of themselves and of others. Twelve male college students were
subjects in the study. Their nonverbal responses to
sequences of red and green lights, in which the red
light signaled the advent of a shock, were videotaped.
The subjects and other individuals viewed the tapes.
The investigators' results were that there was no evidence to support the idea that people whose nonverbal
cues were easily decoded by others were good judges of
nonverbal cues themselves. The experiment had been an
attempt to further document the results of a study by
Levy (1964). The present investigators offered possible

explanations for the divergent findings between their study and Levy's.

279. Latta, R. M. There's method to our madness: Interpersonal attraction as a multidimensional construct. Journal of Research in Personality, 1976, 10, 76-82.

Latta investigated six measures of attraction in order to determine whether or not the results observed in any given experiment depended upon the kind of measure used. He also examined whether or not the various measures of attraction were measuring the same thing. Sixty-four female college students were subjects. Nonverbal measures of attraction were taken in regard to the subjects' choice of seat at one of various tables in relation to a seated female confederate. Head orientation, eye contact, shoulder orientation, and distance from the confederate were also recorded. In addition, each subject rated the confederate on an impression formation scale. Of these measures, three verbal and three nonverbal were used. The three verbal measures included three characteristics from the impression formation scale. The three nonverbal measures were seating position, distance, and head orientation. Latta found that the verbal and nonverbal measures were not significantly related. Factor analysis showed no general attraction factor which was related to all six measures. Latta suggested that a theoretical framework is needed to try to specify how and when the two dimensions may be related.

280. Lauffer, M. B. Gestural behavior during a stressful interview. Dissertation Abstracts International, 1975(Oct), Vol. 36(4-B), 1905.

Sixty-four subjects were videotaped while they responded to Rorschach and TAT cards during a stressful interview. Lauffer was interested in recording two types of nonverbal responses: emphasis in which gestures did not touch the body, and Active Comfort in which gestures did touch the body. She found individual differences in patterns of gestures such that certain types of behaviors were consistent across the two test conditions. She also looked at the relationship between emotional style and gestures. Decoders watched the videotapes, and they attributed significantly different moods to individuals who showed high rates of one or the other gesture.

281. LeCompte, W. F. and Rosenfeld, H. M. Effects of minimal eye contact in the instruction period on impressions of the experimenter. Journal of Experimental Social Psychology, 1971, 7, 211-220.

The investigators studied the importance of gaze direction on various factors such as impressions of the experimenter, accuracy of memory of factual material, and awareness of the experimenter's nonverbal behavior.

Twenty-eight female and 28 male college students were
subjects. Two male experimenters were used. The experimenters were filmed in two conditions of presenting test
instructions: one in which they did not look up from the
instructions, and the other in which they glanced up
twice and fixed their eyes into the camera. The investigators found that impressions of tension and formality
were inversely related to the experimenter's glancing
behavior. No significant results were found for questions concerning the subject's awareness of the experimenter's nonverbal behavior. No significant differences
were found concerning remembering the information and
the experimenter's gaze condition. Lastly, no significant sex of subject effect was determined.

282. Lee, D. Y., Zingle, H. W., and Patterson, J. G. Development and validation of a Microcounseling Skill Discrimination Scale. Journal of Counseling Psychology, 1976, 23(5),
468-472.

The researchers developed a Microcounseling Skill Discrimination Scale to measure an individual's ability to
discriminate between effective and ineffective nonverbal
and verbal helping messages. Trained and untrained groups
(faculty members in counseling, graduate students in counseling, undergraduates, and high school students) were
successful at discriminating between ineffective and effective helping measures, regardless of whether they had
seen the behaviors on tape or had read them from a script.
However, the trained subjects rated the ineffective behavior more negatively than the effective behavior, while
the untrained subjects did the reverse. Other results
were discussed, among which was the report that the Microcounseling Skill Discrimination Scale was useful in measuring a judge's ability to discriminate between ineffective and effective verbal as well as nonverbal messages
and in determining the contribution of nonverbal versus
verbal cues in this judgment.

283. Leginski, W. and Izzett, R. R. The selection and evaluation of interpersonal distances as a function of linguistic
styles. Journal of Social Psychology, 1976, 99, 125-137.

The researchers conducted two experiments to determine
the effects of a speaker's linguistic style on interpersonal distance. In Experiment I, college students were
subjects. They were required to imagine they were interacting with a person represented by a life-size male or
female silhouette. Four linguistic styles which had been
recorded by male and female drama students were stimuli.
They represented an intimate, personal, consultative, and
public style. After listening to eight tapes for the
four styles by male and female speakers, each subject was
to assume a distance in relation to the silhouette. A
sex of speaker effect was found such that subjects stood
closer to the female silhouette than the male. In

addition, a linguistic style effect was found with the
closest distance occurring for the intimate style and the
farthest for the public style. In Experiment II, college
students were to again imagine they were interacting with
the silhouette and to mark the distance they would be
standing from the figure on a scale. No sex of speaker,
sex of subject, or interactions between these factors
were found. However, as in Experiment I, a strong linguistic style effect was found.

284. Leipold, W. E. Psychological distance in a dyadic interview. In R. Sommer (Ed.), Personal space: The behavioral
basis for design. Englewood Cliffs, N. J.: Prentice-Hall,
1969.

Leipold studied the distance at which introverted and
extroverted college students placed themselves in relation to an interviewer in a stress or nonstress situation.
When the subject entered the room he was given one of
three types of instructions: stress, praise, or neutral.
Results showed that students given praise sat closest to
the experimenter's chair, followed by those in the neutral
condition. Those in the stress condition sat farthest.
Additionally, introverted and anxious subjects sat farther
away from the experimenter than did extroverted subjects
with lower anxiety.

285. Lerner, R. M. Some female stereotypes of male body
build-behavior relations. Perceptual and Motor Skills, 1969,
28, 363-366.

Lerner investigated the relation between body build and
behavior. Ninety female college students were required
to indicate which photograph of a male (endomorph, mesomorph, and ectomorph) best fit each of 30 behavioral
descriptions. He found that the subjects had a common
stereotype of male body build-behavior relations. For
example, the mesomorph was described as assuming leadership, having many friends, and not smoking. The endomorph was described as being a poor athlete, drinking
more than the other types, and eating the most often.
Finally, the ectomorph was described as eating the least,
smoking three packs of cigarettes a day, and being most
likely to have a nervous breakdown.

286. Lerner, R. M. The development of personal space schemata toward body build. Journal of Psychology, 1973, 84,
229-235.

Lerner investigated the development of personal space
schemata toward endomorphs, mesomorphs, and ectomorphs
using male and female children in kindergarten to third
grade. Each subject was tested individually. Subjects
were required to move a marker, attached to a board, in
order to indicate the preferred distance from stimulus
figures. To check the affectiveness of the projective

measure, the subjects were then required to give preferred distances from objects having a high probability
of evoking different affective responses--an ice cream
cone and a syringe. As noted by the experimenter, consistent with a negative stereotype toward chubbiness,
the greatest distance was used toward the endomorph.
However, no differential spatial usage was found between
the similarly negatively stereotyped ectomorph and the
positively evaluated mesomorph. The experimenter suggested that the precise correspondence between projective
and behavioral measures of personal space still needs
direct empirical determination.

287. Lerner, R. M. and Korn, S. J. The development of body-
build stereotypes in males. Child Development, 1972, 43,
908-921.

Lerner and Korn studied three different age groups of
young males to determine the development of a preference
for a certain physique. During the first session, the
subjects were asked to rate on an adjective checklist
the terms they felt described an endomorph, mesomorph,
and an ectomorph. Following this, they were to give
evaluative (good-bad) responses to the adjectives.
Finally, they were required to judge whether or not
they felt the items were like or unlike themselves.
During the second session, the subjects were asked to
indicate which of the physiques they would prefer to
look like. The subjects were either chubby or of average build. The results were that all ages of subjects
had a more favorable view of the mesomorph than of the
two other types with the endomorph receiving the least
favorable evaluation.

288. Levine, M. H. The effects of age, sex, and task on
visual behavior during dyadic interaction. Dissertation
Abstracts International, 1972(Nov), Vol. 33(5-B), 2325-2326.

Levine examined the development of gazing between same-
sex pairs of subjects ranging in years from four to college age. Subjects participated in a conversation task
and a construction task. It was hypothesized that gazing
would increase with age during conversations and that
females would gaze more than males. The dependent variables were total time gazing, total time in mutual gazing,
percentage of subject's speaking time spent in gazing,
and percentage of partner's speaking and listening time
spent in gazing. This behavior was recorded, and significant age differences were found with increased gazing
occurring except at ages 10, 11, and 12. Predicted sex
differences occurred during conversation and for total
mutual gazing and gazing while speaking. No correlational trends were found between gazing, influence attempts, height, and liking for age, sex, or task. Partner's gazing tended to be positively correlated. Differences in gazing with age were concluded to be due to the

interaction of various factors. More gazing occurred
during conversations than constructions.

289. Levy, E. The effect of focused videotape feedback of
group process on facilitative skills and responsibility to
verbal or nonverbal cues of counselors in practicum training.
Dissertation Abstracts International, 1975(Feb), Vol. 35
(8-A), 5027-5028.

Levy wanted to determine whether or not focused videotapes of group processes could be used as a training procedure since the importance of nonverbal communications
in counseling was recognized but little studied. Several
hypotheses were developed. Six graduate students were
involved in the study for six weeks. They were either
shown videotapes of their interactions with clients or
heard audiotapes of this interaction. Levy found that
there was a significant difference between the post-
treatment ratings of counselors using video and audio
feedback. For example, those who had experienced video
feedback were more responsive to facial cues and more
often acknowledged nonverbal behaviors.

290. Lewis, P. Smiling elicited from an interviewer as a
function of subjects' history of interpersonal distances.
Paper presented at the 43rd Annual Meeting of the Eastern
Psychological Association, Boston, April 1972.

Lewis predicted that low-distance individuals, as determined by Mololla's History of Interpersonal Distance
(1968) questionnaire, would be more likely than high-
distance individuals to elicit active involvement from
others and, specifically, that those subjects who had a
history of close relationships would elicit more nodding
and smiling from an interviewer than subjects who had a
history of distant relationships. Female college students were subjects. The subjects were randomly assigned
to one of two male interviewers who were trained to gaze
continuously in the direction of the eyes during a seven-
minute interaction. One observer recorded the nodding
and smiling responses of the interviewer who believed
that the observers were recording the eye movements of
the subject for reliability purposes. It was found that,
contrary to the hypothesis, subjects in the different
groups did not elicit differential amounts of nodding
from the interviewers. Concerning smiling, while results
were in the predicted direction, there was not a significant difference between groups. There was, however, a
significant main effect for interviewers in terms of
smiling with Interviewer 1 smiling more than Interviewer
2. Lastly, as predicted, low-distance subjects elicited
more smiles, but only from Interviewer 2.

291. Lewit, D. W. and Joy, V. D. Kinetic versus social schemas in figure grouping. Journal of Personality and Social
Psychology, 1967, 7, 63-72.

The experimenters suggested that biased responses in the recalled spacing of human-like figures in displays may have been due to unit-defining cultural stereotypes, as hypothesized by Kuethe, or to physical requirements for communication between individuals represented by these figures. In a number of experiments the following conditions were used: lateral orientation of figures, implied speed of figures by posture, pairs of animals, tachistoscopic exposure, and indirect manipulation of figures. It was hypothesized that external situation cues would dominate internal autistic ones. Male and female college students were subjects. Some of the results were as follows: contrary to Kuethe's hypothesis for normal subjects, the male pairs of figures facing forward were grouped more closely than male-female pairs, there was a tendency for the subjects to group the figures closely with the briefer exposure time, and for kinetic schemas it was found that orientation was a significant factor with together-facing figures yielding more displacement toward closure than away-facing figures.

292. Libby, W. L.   Eye contact and direction of looking as stable individual differences.   Journal of Experimental Research in Personality, 1970, 4, 303-312.

Four ocular responses by an interviewee to specific questions were identified: (1) maintaining eye contact, (2) breaking eye contact before completion of a question, (3) looking up or down at or after the end of a question, and (4) looking right or left.   Male and female subjects tended to look up rather than down, left rather than right.   Women and subjects with more social experience tended to maintain eye contact.   The experimenter suggested the implications of directional responses for personality assessment in face-to-face interactions.

293. Libby, W. L. and Yaklevich, D.   Personality determinants of eye contact and direction of gaze aversion.   Journal of Personality and Social Psychology, 1973, 27, 97-206.

The authors studied the affects of three personality needs, nurturance, intraception, and abasement of 35 male and 35 female undergraduates on their ocular responses during a structured interview by a female interviewer. The subjects' responses to each of 48 questions were scored as (a) maintenance of eye contact throughout verbal responses, (b) breaking of eye contact before the end of the question, (c) lateral gaze aversion, and (d) vertical gaze aversion.   Subjects high in need abasement looked away markedly more often to the left than subjects low on this need.   Also, subjects high on nurturance maintained eye contact more than low-nurturance subjects.   It was suggested that the face "leaks" information regarding the personality.

294. Liebman, M. The effects of sex and race norms on personal space. Environment and Behavior, 1970, 2, 208-246.

Liebman investigated the relationship between the race
of another individual and two forms of spatial behavior--
distance and intrusions. The subjects were females employed in secretarial or editorial capacities. Four confederates were used: a Black and a White female, and a
Black and a White male. In one condition the subject was
to choose a seat on a bench which was already occupied at
one end by a confederate. In an intrusion-choice condition, the subject could choose between two benches occupied by a confederate varying in race or sex. In the
intrusion-nonintrusion condition, subjects were given a
choice between an empty bench and one occupied by a White
female confederate. Only White subjects participated
here. Results showed that the subjects sat at similar
distances from all four confederates. However, larger
distances tended to occur in relation to male confederates and smaller distances to female confederates. Intrusion of personal space was avoided when possible.
The hypothesis predicting that females would be more
likely to choose to intrude upon another female rather
than a male was supported. However, an hypothesis concerning intrusion preferences and race was not confirmed.

295. Lindenfeld, J. Syntactic structure and kinesic phenomena in communicative events. Semiotica, 1974, 12, 61-73.

Lindenfeld attempted to examine relationships between two
components--the addresser and the code. She hypothesized
that there are definite relationships between the syntactic structure of speech and certain body movements accompanying speech. A second hypothesis concerned the co-
variation of syntactic complexity and frequency of movement during various affective states. Lindenfeld used
data from two sources. One case was obtained from a
study by two other researchers. Her remaining data were
collected from manic-depressive patients and normal control subjects. In normal subjects she found that as syn-
tactive complexity decreased, movements increased, and
vice versa. For the case borrowed from a previous study,
she found that certain body movements were negatively
related to syntactic structure during the affective states
under consideration. Finally, the relationship between
syntactic complexity and movement frequency was unaffected
by the addresser's affective state in both kinds of subject data.

296. Lippa, R. A. The effect of expressive control on expressive consistency and on the relation between expressive behavior and personality. Dissertation Abstracts International,
1977(Apr), Vol. 37(10-B), 5440.

Lippa conducted his study to determine the effects of expressive control on expressive behavior and personality

judgment. Sixty-eight subjects who had been determined
to be high or low on extraversion, neuroticism, and self-
monitoring role played teaching triangles on two succes-
sive trials and were videotaped. One group of judges
rated the subjects on the personality variables and
another rated them four different types of expressive
behaviors. The findings indicated that expressive control affected expressive behavior and person perception.
Subjects classified as low self-monitors showed smaller
expressive behaviors than high self-monitors. Extraversion and neuroticism showed no effects on the measures.
Various other results were also presented.

297. Little, K. B. Cultural variations in social schemata.
Journal of Personality and Social Psychology, 1968, 10, 1-7.

Little asked five national groups (Americans, Sweds,
Greeks, Southern Italians, and Scots) to place dolls in
order to determine different social schemata. His hypothesis suggesting that the Mediterranean subjects would use
closer interaction distances as compared to the Northern
European subjects was confirmed. However, the hypothesis
that interactions involving female surrogates would always be seen as occurring at closer distances than those
involving males was not supported. Situational variables
had an affect on these perceptions.

298. Little, K. B. Personal space. Journal of Experimental
Social Psychology, 1965, 1, 237-247.

Little assessed the affect of the degree of acquaintance
between members of a dyad on interaction distances in
different settings and the degree of congruence between
the measurement of personal space by a quasi-projective
technique and by live interactions. Sixty female and 32
male students were subjects. In both studies the degree
of acquaintance strongly influenced perceived interaction
distances. When the pair was labeled friends, they were
seen as interacting closer than if they were called acquaintances or strangers. The setting in which a live
interaction took place influenced behavior substantially
for females, but less so for males--open air settings
elicited the closest distances, while office waiting
rooms elicited the greatest distances.

299. Little, K. B., Ulehla, Z. J., and Henderson, C. Value
congruence and interaction distances. Journal of Social
Psychology, 1968, 75, 249-253.

Male undergraduates judged interaction distances between
individuals sharing the same presidential preference and
those holding opposite preferences using placement of
silhouette figures. Value congruence produced closer
assigned distances for the Goldwater supporter pairs,
but not for Johnson supporter pairs. It was suggested
that the Goldwater supporters were seen as forming a

homogenous ingroup, while Johnson supporters were held together primarily by opposition to Goldwater.

300. Lothstein, L. M. Human territoriality in group psychotherapy. International Journal of Group Psychotherapy, 1978, 28, 55-71.

Lothstein discussed the need for studying the effects of human territoriality in group therapy. Such things as comfortable conversation distances, seating arrangements, and placement of furniture should, he asserted, be considered important aspects of the therapy environment. He also discussed the use of a recorder and how his or her presence should be as unobtrusive as possible so as not to intrude upon the territorial boundaries of the therapy group.

301. Lott, D. F. and Sommer, R. Seating arrangements and status. Journal of Personality and Social Psychology, 1967, 7, 90-95.

The authors questioned how a subject would locate himself in regard to a person of higher, lower, or equal status. In the first two studies, using paper-and-pencil diagrams of rectangular tables, there was a clear association of the head position with the higher status figure. In the questionnaire study, using square tables where all positions were equal, people sat farther from both high- and low-status individuals than from peers. In the fourth study, the subject was asked to go into a room and sit at a table containing a surrogate of a high-, low-, or equal-status person. The results showed that subjects sat farther from higher and lower status individuals than from peers.

302. Luft, J. On non-verbal interaction. Journal of Psychology, 1966, 63, 261-268.

The study was done by Luft to find ways of measuring and understanding what takes place affectively between two people in a nonverbal task-free situation. Female college students were instructed (in pairs) to sit across from each other in a room leaving seven to nine feet between them. They were not permitted to talk to each other, and at the end of five 15-minute sessions, they were required to fill out a 20-point like-dislike scale concerning how each felt about the other. Interviews given later determined that the subjects felt discomfort and anxiety. Another group of subjects interacted nonverbally with a standard stimulus subject. Results showed that attitudes toward the self was positively related to attitudes toward strangers, and that affect ratings expected from others followed the rating given to others.

303. MacCannell, D. A note on hat tipping. Semiotica, 1973, 7, 300-312.

MacCannell made observations of the ritual of hat tipping in urban areas in the Northeastern United States.
He found that hat tipping occurred not so much because
of the social class of the individual tipping his hat,
but because of the individual's perception of the relationship between his social class and the positions
of the individuals who will see him make the gesture.
MacCannell also discussed some of the other usages of
hat tipping such as avoidance and insult.

304. Mackey, W. C. Parameters of the smile as a social
signal. Journal of Genetic Psychology, 1976, 129, 125-130.

Mackey tested three hypotheses in two separate studies:
(1) sex would influence rates of smiling, (2) smiles
elicit smile responses, and (3) a social milieu would
increase smile responses. Male and female college students were subjects for Study I. When tested in pairs,
only members of the same sex were put together. Observers behind a two-way mirror recorded subject smiles
while they listened to a tape recording. Results for
Study I showed that females who were alone smiled significantly more than males alone. When pairs of females
were tested, they increased their rate of smiling. Smiling was unaffected for male pairs. Study II used adults
from rural and urban areas. Observers were to greet six
people of their choice, and to smile at three and not
smile at the remaining three. Mackey found that greet-
ings accompanied by a smile elicited a return smile. An
interesting sex-of-subject by sex-of-observer interaction occurred such that male-female pairs smiled more
than male-male pairs.

305. Malpass, R. S. and Kravitz, J. Recognition for faces
of own and other race. Journal of Personality and Social
Psychology, 1969, 13, 330-334.

The researchers were interested in the ability of subjects to recognize faces of members of their own and
another race. Black and White students from two universities were subjects. They were shown slides of 20 Black
and White college-age males. After seeing these, 80 other
pictures of Black and White males were mixed with the 20,
and the subjects were to indicate on an answer sheet
whether or not they recognized the original 20. The
interval between the initial presentation of 20 and the
recognition phase was one minute. The results were that
White male faces were more discriminate than Black male
faces. In addition, the subjects were found to recognize
faces of members of their own race than the other race.
The researchers also briefly discussed some findings from
questionnaire data collected in their study.

306. Marcelle, Y. M.   Eye contact as a function of race, sex, and distance. <u>Dissertation Abstracts International</u>, 1977 (Jan), Vol. 37(7-A), 4238.

   Marcelle studied differences in frequency, duration, and average duration of eye contact between various cultural groups. Eight Black and eight White male and female subjects were used. Each subject engaged in a conversation with a Black or White male or female assistant at various distances. The race of the assistant had a significant effect. Sex of subject and race of subject were significant effects. Females engaged in more eye contact than males, and Whites engaged in more eye contact than Blacks. Distance did not have a significant effect.

307. Marks, H. E.   The relationship of eye contact to congruence and empathy. <u>Dissertation Abstracts International</u>, 1971(Aug), Vol. 32(2-B), 1219.

   Marks predicted that those who were more able to engage in eye contact with another would be more congruent and more empathic with others. Groups of eye-contact maintainers and avoiders were formed. It was found that maintainers were significantly more congruent and empathic than avoiders. Furthermore, congruence and empathy were felt to be stronger when both persons looked than when only one looked--persons referred to one subject and one experimenter. This was felt to result from an optimal arousal level facilitating more accurate utilization of cues from the other. The experimenter also explored the implications of eye contact for therapy.

308. Martin, D. S.   The effects of using different response criteria in assessing conservation in children. <u>Dissertation Abstracts International</u>, 1976(May), Vol. 36(11-B), 5765.

   The study was conducted in order to compare the differential effects of verbal judgments, nonverbal judgments, and explanations in identifying children who were conservers and nonconservers. Elementary school children were given conservation tasks which required the three types of responses. The results showed that the use of nonverbal judgment produced younger and more children who were identified as conservers than did the other two types of responses. Another result was that differences between performances on the three response types decreased as the children's ages increased.

309. Martin, T. P.   The effects of psychological modeling, descriptive and exhortative instructions and written programmed instructions on the learning of verbal and nonverbal attending behavior among counselor trainees. <u>Dissertation Abstracts International</u>, 1977(Oct), Vol. 38(4-A), 1894-1895.

Thirty-two counselor trainees were exposed to one of four
training treatments to determine the effectiveness of
each. The four conditions were: videotape models with
instructions, videotape models without instructions,
written programmed instructions, and no treatment. Independent raters counted eye-contact breaks, inattentive
gestures and movements, verbal topic jumps, and verbal
following statements. Martin found that the three treatment conditions increased attending behavior in terms of
eye contact and verbal topics. Those subjects in the
videotape models with instructions showed greater amounts
of attending behavior than subjects in the no-instruction
group. Lastly, subjects in the videotape-instruction
group as opposed to the videotape-no instruction group
reduced the emission of eye-contact breaks. Various
other results were reported.

310. McBride, G., King, M. G., and James, J. W. Social
proximity effects on galvanic skin responses in adult humans.
Journal of Psychology, 1965, 61, 153-157.

The experimenters studied the motivation for spacing behavior in terms of arousal using GSRs as indications of
the level of arousal associated with the proximity of
another. Males and females between the ages of 19 and
23 were subjects. Four experimenters, two males and two
females, were used. The GSRs for five subjects of each
sex to each experimenter were recorded. Experimental
conditions consisted of the following: The experimenter
positioned him or herself at various seated distances,
with eyes fixated on the eyes of the subject; and the experimenter approached the subject from the back, side,
or front, and a square white card was drawn at eye level
for the subject, from 12 feet in front, over the subject's head (just brushing the hair), to 12 feet behind
and back to the starting position to determine responses
to a moving, inanimate object. Results showed that the
GSRs to experimenters at one, three, and nine feet (with
the eyes of both individuals fixated) were not different
on the average between one foot and three feet, although
the response was significantly less at nine feet. Responses to male experimenters were greater than to female experimenters at one foot with eyes fixated. GSRs
were greatest when the subject was approached from the
front, and side approach yielded a greater effect than
rear approach. Lastly, responses to experiments of the
same sex were less than to experimenters of the other sex.

311. McDowell, K. V. Accommodations of verbal and nonverbal
behaviors as a function of the manipulation of interaction
distance and eye contact. Proceedings of the 81st Annual
Convention of the American Psychological Association, 1973,
8, 207-208.

McDowell tested the hypothesis that the "eye-contact
equilibrium" notion presented by Argyle and Dean (1965)

would only hold in those situations in which there was
no verbal communication or in which the recipient of more
eye contact could control the level of intimacy by talking more. Two hundred and forty undergraduates were subjects. A subject interacted with a confederate for five
minutes and varied interaction distances and eye contact
conditions. During that time they were to talk about
anything they wished. They were recorded on camera in
a standing position. The data did not show significant
main effects or interactions due to distance manipulation
in conjunction with looking and speech. The data did
support the hypothesis that increased eye contact pro-
duces more talking, and suggested that increased eye
contact was interpreted as an attempt for more intimacy.

312. McDowell, K. V. Violations of personal space. Dissertation Abstracts International, 1970(Jul), Vol. 31(1-A), 467.

McDowell conducted a study of violations of personal
space by an interacting stranger as a means of determining attribution of the violator's personality characteristics as well as whether or not the violated person
would move away from the violator. Interaction distance,
sex of subject, and sex of confederate were varied. College students were subjects. The results showed that
violations of personal space by a stranger elicited a
significant movement away from the violator, but no dis-
tinctly different evaluations of his or her personality.
It was suggested that the subjects may have been reluc-
tant to attribute violations of their personal space to
the confederate's personality.

313. McGovern, T. V. The making of a job interviewer: The
effect of nonverbal behavior on an interviewer's evaluations
during a selection interview. Dissertation Abstracts International, 1977(May), Vol. 37(9-B), 4740-4741.

McGovern showed videotapes of interviews to personnel
representatives from business and industry. The content
of the films was identical; however, sex of the interviewee and level of nonverbal behavior were manipulated.
The representatives evaluated the interviewees every four
minutes during the interviews. Dimensions which had previously been identified as critical in influencing on
interviewer's decisions were the criteria for the representatives. McGovern found that nonverbal behaviors significantly influenced decisions with "high nonverbal"
interviewees receiving comments of the possibility of
their being brought back for a second interview. McGovern
discussed his results in terms of their implications for
preparing for job interviews.

314. McGinley, H., LeFevre, R., and McGinley, P. The influence of a communicator's body position on opinion change in
others. Journal of Personality and Social Psychology, 1975,
31, 686-690.

The researchers wanted to determine whether or not a
communicator's use of open-body positions would effect
greater attitude change in a listener than his use of
closed-body positions. Female college students were
subjects. The subjects were shown bogus questionnaires
either agreeing or disagreeing with the questionnaire
responses they had given. They then viewed slides of
the female whose responses they purportedly had read.
She was shown discussing her responses. Subjects gave
their impressions of the speaker on another questionnaire. Results showed that at retesting, subjects who
had seen the addresser display open-body postures
changed toward her viewpoint as compared to subjects
who had seen the addresser display closed-body postures.

315. McGinley, H., Nicholas, K., and McGinley, P. Effects
of body position and attitude similarity on interpersonal
attraction and opinion change. Psychological Reports, 1978,
42, 127-138.

McGinley et al. hypothesized that a communicator who
displayed open-body positions and who had attitudes similar to an addressee would elicit more positive evaluations. One hundred and sixty-five female college students were subjects. They watched slides of a female
model who they believed had similar or dissimilar attitudes to their own. The face of the communicator was
inked out so as not to be confounded with the affects
of body position. The subjects also filled out the
semantic differential. The results were that subjects
rated the communicator as more active when she expressed
open-body movements. These results were accentuated
when the communicator and subject had similar attitudes.
Communicators with similar attitudes were rated more
positively than those with dissimilar attitudes. However, there was no overall support for the hypothesis
that communicators using more open-body positions would
be evaluated more positively.

316. McKelvie, S. J. The role of eyes and mouth in the
memory of a face. American Journal of Psychology, 1976, 89,
311-323.

The purpose of McKelvie's study was to investigate the
importance of the eyes and the mouth on recognition of
faces. Two types of facial transformation were used--
masking the eyes or the mouth. One hundred and fifteen
adults were used as subjects. They were divided into
six groups of 14 and one group of 31 subjects. This
latter group was a control. One hundred and eight pictures of adult males were used as stimuli. Each subject
was shown 27 pictures which he was later to pick out
from among the total sample of stimuli. The results
showed that the subjects made more errors when the eyes
were masked than when the mouth was masked. A looking
time analysis was made, and it was found that subjects

made their responses more quickly when there were no
transformations made to the face. Some other findings
concerning confidence ratings and individual differences
were also discussed.

317. McMullan, G. R. The relative contribution of selected
nonverbal behaviors to the communication of empathy in a
counseling interview. Dissertation Abstracts International,
1975(Mar), Vol. 35(9-B), 4657.

The study was done in order to determine the contribution of nonverbal behavior to judged levels of empathy
during a role-played counseling interview. Thirty graduate students in a counseling program rated various combinations of eye contact, trunk lean, body orientation,
hand gesture, and positive head nod, along with a standardized interaction distance and a medium level of verbal empathy on an empathy scale. McMullan suggested
that his results supported the idea that empathy may be
communicated in more than one channel. He also noted
that all of the nonverbal behaviors he had used had
effects on lowering or raising the judged levels of
empathy in the counseling interview. He also discussed
his findings in relation to the role of nonverbal behaviors in the communication of empathic understanding in
therapy and counseling.

318. Mehrabian, A. A systematic space for nonverbal behavior. Journal of Consulting and Clinical Psychology, 1970,
35(2), 248-257.

Three dimensions were reported to have emerged from studies of nonverbal and verbal behavior: evaluation, potency
or status, and responsiveness. Increases in positive
evaluation are denoted by immediate positions (closer
distance, forward lean, more eye contact, and more direct
orientation); and increases in potency or status are denoted by greater degrees of postural relaxation. Increases in responsiveness are denoted by greater facial
activity and speech intonation.

319. Mehrabian, A. Nonverbal betrayal of feeling. Journal
of Experimental Research in Personality, 1971, 5, 64-73.

Mehrabian conducted three experiments in which he investigated the behaviors of deceitful communicators. He
wanted to determine the general situations in which an
individual was unwilling or unable to communicate his
feelings verbally. College students were subjects in
all of the experiments. Generally, he found that negative
affects, indicating nonverbal cues, were displayed more
frequently during deceitful than truthful communications.
Some of the behaviors of deceitful communicators were
less frequent moving, less direct orientation relative
to the addressees, slower talking, less talking, more
smiling, and more speech errors.

320. Mehrabian, A. Orientation behaviors and nonverbal attitude communication. Journal of Communication, 1967, 17,
324-331.

Mehrabian investigated the communication of affect intensity toward others via head and body orientations. He
hypothesized that more immediate communicator orientation
toward an addressee would imply a positive attitude. Female undergraduates met a female experimenter in pairs
in an experimental room. An observer looked through a
one-way mirror and recorded the duration of the experimenter's head and body orientation toward each subject.
Results showed that when a subject made inferences about
the degree of positive experimenter attitude toward herself, these judgments were influenced by a combination
of head and body orientations. On the other hand, when
the subject made inferences about the degree of positive
experimenter attitude toward another subject, judgments
were only influenced to a significant degree by head
orientation.

321. Mehrabian, A. Relationship of attitude to seated posture, orientation and distance. Journal of Personality and
Social Psychology, 1968, 10, 26-30.

In four experiments the author investigated inferred
attitudes from the posture, orientation, and distance of
a communicator. In the first three experiments a decoding methodology was used. Subjects were to infer the
individual's attitude from photographs of him as he sat
in different positions. In the fourth experiment subjects were required to role play by assuming they were
in specific situations. Findings from the first three
experiments showed that greater relaxation, a forward
lean of the trunk, and a smaller distance to the addressee communicated a positive attitude to the addressee. According to the findings of the fourth experiment on
male communicators, more eye contact, smaller distance,
and a relative absence of an arms-akimbo position were
part of an attempt to communicate a positive attitude.
However, in general, directness of orientation and openness of posture were not related to positive attitudes.

322. Mehrabian, A. Significance of posture and position in
the communication of attitude and status relationships.
Psychological Bulletin, 1969, 71, 359-372.

Mehrabian presented a review of the findings relating the
posture of a communicator to his attitude toward his addressee. The results were found to suggest the following
patterns: distance between a communicator and addressee
is a decreasing linear function of the degree of liking
toward the addressee. Eye contact is smaller for disliked and liked addressees and approaches a maximum value
for addressees toward whom the attitude is neutral. For
female communicators, the least direct orientation occurs

with disliked addressees, the highest with neutral addressees, and a relatively high degree with liked addressees. Male communicators give intensely liked
addressees a less direct body orientation. Other findings are also presented for the use of arms and legs.

323. Mehrabian, A. and Diamond, S. G.   Seating arrangement
and conversation. Sociometry, 1971, 34, 281-289.

The study examined seating preferences as a function of
sex, affiliative tendency, and sensitivity to rejection
and the affect of seating choice on conversation. Subjects were male and female undergraduates supposedly
taking part in a music-listening experiment. Groups of
four subjects were observed through one-way mirrors as
they chose from among eight seats placed in one of the
following four arrangements: circular, rectangular, two
squares, or paired. It was found that the average amount
of conversation in the groups did not differ with chair
arrangement. In terms of seating choice, the results
were that males sat at an average distance of 5.60 feet
from others, while females sat significantly closer at
5.11 feet. Additionally, high-affiliative scorers sat
at a mean distance of 5.12 feet, while low scorers sat
at 5.61 feet. Orientation was not found to be correlated
with sex or the other two variables. And, lastly, sex
was a significant determiner of conversation so that females talked more than males.

324. Meisels, M. and Canter, F. M.   Personal space and personality characteristics: A non-confirmation. Psychological Reports, 1970, 27, 287-290.

In Study I, female college students were given a test to
determine introversion-extraversion. Each subject was
then required to rate 12 topics in terms of whether she
would find them difficult to discuss with a stranger.
Half of the subjects were assigned to topics they had
rated most difficult to discuss and half were assigned
that rated least difficult. Subjects were then asked to
enter a room with four chairs, one of which was already
occupied by a confederate. The chair chosen by the subject provided the measure of personal space. There was
no significant difference between the groups for seating
choice. In Study II, female subjects were tested for
actual and subjectively felt deviancy and were then required to enter a room with 10 chairs at various distances
from one occupied by a confederate. Choice of seat was
again the measure of personal space. Additionally, topic
choices were again a variable. Results for Study II were
also nonsupportive of the hypothesis.

325. Meisels, M. and Dosey, M. A.   Personal space, anger-
arousal, and psychological defense. Journal of Personality,
1971, 39, 333-344.

The major purpose of the study was to examine the idea
that psychological defense mechanisms may, under certain
conditions, be manifested through enlarged personal space
zones. Additional purposes concerned the generality of
the phenomenon, whether defenses against aggressive im-
pulses contribute to greater interpersonal distances when
anger is not aroused, and the comparison of personal
space usage under conditions of anger and control. College undergraduates were subjects and were given the TAT,
a word-association test, differential anger and nonanger
instructions, and an approach test of personal space.
Instructions which told the subject to stop when he
reached a natural or comfortable position with respect
to the experimenter led to close proximity, while instructions which asked the subject to stop when he
reached the experimenter led to the use of greater distances. Some of the other findings were that for the
anger condition a "fight" reaction occurred so that hostile subjects retaliated by invading the confederate's
territory. And more defensive females (as determined by
the word-association test) used greater spatial distances.

326. Meisels, M., Dosey, M. A., and Guardo, C. J. Development of personal space schemata. Child Development, 1969,
40, 1167-1178.

The experimenters investigated the development of personal space schemata in 431 third to 10th graders. Subjects were given paper-and-pencil measures of spatial
usage in 20 situations involving positive, neutral, and
negative affects. Major findings were that (a) the in-
verse relationship between amount of distance and degree
of liking and acquaintance was established by the third
grade; (b) E. T. Hall's conceptualized personal space
zones applied to childhood spatial schemata; (c) children
generally used less space as they grew older; and (d) in
positive and negative affect situations, both sexes placed
themselves closer to same-sexed peers in earlier grades
and to opposite-sexed peers in later grades. Results
were in accord with knowledge about social development
and the formation of sex-role identification.

327. Michael, G. and Willis, F. N., Jr. The development of
gestures as a function of social class, educational level,
and sex. Psychological Record, 1968, 18, 515-519.

Michael and Willis examined the development of certain
gestures in children as a function of sex, socioeconomic
level, and education. Eight groups of racially mixed
subjects were used. Each child was interviewed individually during which time he was observed by two independent judges. They were to determine whether or not each
child could transmit and interpret each of 12 gestures.
The results were that for transmitted gestures, middle-
class children were significantly more accurate than
children with no schooling. Boys were more accurate at

interpreting than were girls. A class-by-education finding occurred for accuracy. Finally, the children were
more accurate at interpreting than transmitting gestures.

328. Michael, G. and Willis, F. N., Jr. The development of
gestures in three subcultural groups. Journal of Social Psychology, 1969, 79, 35-41.

329. Miller, A. R. and Stewart, R. A. Perception of female
physiques. Perceptual and Motor Skills, 1968, 27, 721-722.

Fourteen boys aged 13 to 19 and of Mexican-American background were subjects for this study. They worked individually and were required to arrange reproductions of
somatotypes taken from Sheldon's (1963) Varieties of
Human Physiques in order from the physique which they
felt most suited a certain concept, to the physique which
they felt least suited the concept. Seven concepts were
used. A statistical test indicated that there was agreement among the subjects for six of the seven concepts
and rankings of the somatotypes. However, because the
subject sample was so small and homogeneous, the experimenters suggested that further studies needed to be
done to verify their present findings.

330. Miller, R. E., Giannina, A. J., and Levine, J. M. Nonverbal communication in man with a cooperative conditioning
task. Journal of Social Psychology, 1977, 103, 101-113.

Miller et al. provided a description of a cooperative
conditioning method for investigating nonverbal sending
and receiving ability in humans. Male and female junior
medical students were subjects. The face of each subject
was videotaped as he or she tried to solve a task involving a slot machine. Half of the subjects served as stimuli, the other half as responders who were to use only
the expressive cues from the stimuli to solve the slot
machine task. Measures of skin potential were also made.
The results showed that the method was effective for
assessing nonverbal sending and receiving abilities.
They also showed that it was effective for discriminating between individuals, especially responders. The
findings in regard to physiological responses showed
that these were related to the ability to decode the
expressions of others as well as to be expressive.

331. Milord, J. T. Aesthetic aspects of faces: A (somewhat)
phenomenological analysis using multidimensional scaling
methods. Journal of Personality and Social Psychology, 1978,
36, 205-216.

The purpose of the study was to determine whether there
were certain orthogonal features of the face which dis-
tinguishes it from other faces; whether aesthetic appreciation of the face was related to any of the differences;
the extent to which interpersonal attraction was a

function of aesthetic appreciation; and the role features,
aesthetic appreciation, and interpersonal attraction
played in symbolic approach behavior. Four experiments
were conducted. Two sets of stimuli were used: a heter-
ogeneous sample containing faces of White, non-White,
male, female, young, old, expression and expressionless
individuals; and a homogeneous sample of male, White,
young, expressionless faces. It was found that beauty
and race generally affected perceptions. Also, features
and expression were influential.

332. Modigliani, A. Embarrassment, facework, and eye contact: Testing a theory of embarrassment. Journal of Personality and Social Psychology, 1971, 17, 15-24.

Embarrassment was defined as a feeling of inadequacy pre-
cipitated by the belief that one's presented self appeared
deficient to others. The experimenter tested four hypotheses in conditions of success, failure, and public/private
on their portion of a group task. Male undergraduates
were subjects. Results showed that both public-failure
and mitigated (a warning of the difficulty or easiness
of anagrams subjects were to work on) public-failure subjects decreased their level of eye contact with the confederates during embarrassing postfailure interactions.
In contrast, public-success and mitigated public-success
subjects slightly increased their level of eye contact
during their postsuccess interaction. However, the experimenter noted that other data questioned the validity
of interpreting the decreases in eye contact as manifes-
tations of embarrassment since changes in the former
variable were weakly associated with other measures meant
to reflect the degree of embarrassment. It was suggested
that the observed reduction in eye contact may have reflected a dislike for the confederates who were assessing
this behavior rather than a reflection of the affect.
Data showed that subjects criticized by confederates
reduced eye contact, while those praised by confederates
tended to maintain or increase eye contact.

333. Moore, J. E. Some psychological aspects of yawning.
Journal of General Psychology, 1942, 27, 289-294.

Moore wanted to determine whether or not the yawning
response could be invoked by auditory and visual stimuli.
In the visual stimulation part of the research, male and
female college students were trained to produce a realis-
tic-looking yawn. They displayed yawns in various public
places while an observer recorded imitation responses.
Findings were difficult to interpret because of various
extraneous factors. In the auditory stimulation part of
the study, a recording of yawns made by an experimenter
was played to subjects. Graduate nurses and eighth-grade
students in a school for the blind were subjects. Some
subjects imitated the yawns. In a third part of the
study, a film of a female yawning was shown to college

students. One-third of the students imitated the yawns,
others indicated in response to specific questions that
they felt like yawning even though they did not actually
yawn.

334. Munn, N. L. The effect of knowledge of the situation
upon judgment of emotion from facial expressions. Journal
of Abnormal and Social Psychology, 1940, 35, 324-338.

Munn wanted to determine the influence of knowledge of
a situation on the judgment of facial expressions of emotion. He gathered a group of 16 unposed emotional expressions from Life and Look magazines. Two groups of
subjects were used in the study. Group I was asked to
describe the emotion shown on the stimulus face when the
face alone was shown and when the background was included.
Group II was given a list of the most frequently used
terms by Group I and was asked to indicate which terms
represented the emotions expressed on the stimuli when
the face alone was shown and when the background was
included. The results showed that spontaneous expressions were accurately interpreted and that the face
alone was able to prompt similar responses from both
groups in many instances.

335. Murray, R. P. and McGinley, H. Looking as a measure of
attraction. Journal of Applied Social Psychology, 1972, 2,
267-274.

Murray and McGinley noted that Byrne's reinforcement
theory of attraction was based almost exclusively on
studies using the Interpersonal Judgment Scale (IJS).
They conducted a study using an unobtrusive-looking
measuring as well as the IJS. Female college students
were subjects. It was hypothesized that subjects would
spend more time looking at a stranger who had similar
attitudes to his own than at a stranger whose attitudes
differed from his own. Two methods of presenting the
attitudes were used--one videotape and one questionnaire.
Subjects' looking time at photographs of the strangers
was measured. The researchers found that degree of attitude similarity was related to looking time but not to
the IJS measure which was also completed.

336. Mutschler, E. The influence of evaluative agreement and
content relevance on social workers' expression of affect:
An experimental analysis. Dissertation Abstracts International, 1976(Jun), Vol. 36(12-A), 8300.

Mutschler hypothesized that her subjects (social workers)
would express more positive affect and less negative
affect when in agreement with a client's evaluation of
topics during the interview, and that subjects would express more positive and less negative affects under those
circumstances in which the client's communications confirmed the subject's content expectations than when they

did not meet these expectations. The affective behavior
of 64 graduate students in social work was rated on self-
report measures and by independent judges in an adjective
checklist. The results were that the prediction concerning the influence of evaluative agreement was not supported. The other hypothesis was supported.

337. Myers, G. E. and Myers, M. T. Nonverbal communication:
The sounds of silence. In The dynamics of human communication. New York: McGraw-Hill Book Co., 1976.

The article dealt with four aspects of nonverbal communication: (1) silences, (2) how people send and receive
nonverbal messages, (3) certain cultural patterns of nonverbal behavior, and (4) certain characteristics of nonverbal behavior. These four divisions were in turn
further divided, and various factors about these areas
of nonverbal behavior were briefly discussed. Some of
the subtopics which were presented were gestures, facial
expressions, time, and space.

338. Natale, M. Induction of mood states and their effect
on gaze behaviors. Journal of Consulting and Clinical Psychology, 1977, 45, 960.

Natale conducted his study in order to determine whether
or not there was a relationship between emotional states
and visual behavior among nonpsychotic individuals. Female college students read Velten's (1968) self-referent
mood statements corresponding to elated, depressed, and
neutral moods. Later, they met individually with a female assistant and were required to sit facing each other
while they discussed the world situation. Natale found
that the elated subjects engaged in more looking and
longer looks than the other subjects. However, they
looked less frequently. Depressed subjects engaged in
less total looking and less frequent looks. Natale
noted the viability of the mood-induction procedure for
measuring clinical changes in conduct due to temporary
mood states.

339. Naus, P. J. and Eckenrode, J. J. Age differences and
degree of acquaintance as determinants of interpersonal distance. Journal of Social Psychology, 1974, 93, 133-134.

The study was concerned with age differences between
interaction partners and their degree of acquaintance
as these effected the physical distance judged to be
appropriate for a dyadic social interaction. It was
predicted that young people would consider the interaction distance between an old and young person to be
larger than that between two young people. A second
hypothesis was that the distance deemed appropriate for
friends would be shorter than that for strangers. College undergraduates were asked to reconstruct eight types
of conversational interactions by placing silhouettes

representing interaction partners on a background representing an office waiting room. The first hypothesis was
supported. Main effects for degree of acquaintance and
sex were not significant. However, an interaction of age
by acquaintance by sex was significant. The experimenters
suggested that further research be done to determine
whether the effect of age differences upon interaction
distance is due to attitudinal factors or to perceived
differences in status between the old-young and young-
young interactions.

340. Newman, R. C. and Pollack, D. Proxemics in deviant adolescents. Journal of Consulting and Clinical Psychology,
1973, 40, 6-8.

The distance requirements of deviant and normal adolescents were measured using an experimenter approach subject method. Thirty deviant male ninth graders and 30
underachievers in ninth, 10th, and 11th grades were subjects. The experimenter approached each subject (who
was to remain stationary) from the front, back, and both
sides. The subject was to tell the experimenter when to
stop. It was found that the deviant boys required a
greater proxemic area than the normals. A significant
difference was also found for direction of approach.
Proxemic distance increased from front to rear with no
difference between the groups of subjects. The investigators pointed out that knowledge of the subject's group
membership by the experimenter was unavoidable and should
be controlled in future research. Another suggestion is
that developmental aspects of proxemics be studied.

341. Nichols, K. A. and Champness, B. G. Eye gaze and the
GSR. Journal of Experimental Social Psychology, 1971, 7,
623-626.

Nichols and Champness predicted that the amplitude and
frequency of GSRs shown by a subject gazing at another
person's eyes would be greater during eye contact than
during periods of unreciprocated gaze. Twenty male and
20 female students served as subjects. A male and a female student served as confederates. The subject and confederate sat three feet apart facing each other in a small
room. An approach was adopted by the investigators so
that the subject could be used as his own control. After
placement of the electrodes for the GSR, the subject was
to gaze steadily at the confederate's eyes while the confederate alternated his gaze from the subject's eyes to a
marker on the wall behind the subject's head. Each subject experienced six periods of eye contact and six of
unreciprocated gaze. The frequency and amplitude of GSRs
were recording during these periods. Results showed that
the frequency and amplitude of GSRs were greater during
eye contact than the unreciprocating condition. Additionally, no main effect for subject or confederate sex
was found.

342. Nieters, J. L.   The differential role of facial and body
cues in the recognition of disguised emotional responses.
Dissertation Abstracts International, 1976(Oct), Vol. 37(4-B),
1944-1945.

The facial and body behavior of male and female subjects
was videotaped as they described two sets of pleasant and
two sets of unpleasant slides either truthfully or un-
truthfully. In the second phase of the study, male and
female subjects viewed segments of the videotapes (either
facial or body expressions) and judged the nature of the
stimulus each filmed subject was watching and also whether
the subject was being candid or deceitful. Nieters found
that judges who rated facial expressions were more accurate at recognizing actual negative responses despite the
filmed subjects' attempts to hide them. No other hypotheses were significant.

343. Norton, L. S.   Elementary school age children's perceptions of teachers' nonverbal behavior. Dissertation Abstracts
International, 1975(Apr), Vol. 35(10-A), 6371.

Norton wanted to explore children's own perceptions of
nonverbal behavior as well as sex, cultural, and age differences in its perception. She also wanted to test the
Perceptions of Nonverbal Behavior (PNB) index which she
had developed. Black, White, and native American male
and female six-, eight-, and 10-year-olds were subjects.
She found sex differences in the perceptions of teachers'
nonverbal behaviors. She also found age and cultural
differences in perceptions. Other findings were that
the choices made by males indicated that they had more
tolerance for distant or negative behavior than did girls.
Some age by sex, sex by culture, and age by culture interactions were reported.

344. Odom, R. C. and Lemond, C. M.   Developmental differences
in the perception and production of facial expressions. Child
Development, 1972, 43, 359-369.

The researchers wanted to know whether or not there was a
developmental lag between perceiving facial expressions
and producing them. Thirty-two kindergarten and 32 fifth-
grade children (males and females within each grade) were
subjects. Each subject was tested individually by a female experimenter. Each was required to match expressions
shown in a series of pictures for a discrimination task.
For a production task, each subject was asked to produce
the expression shown to him or asked of him by the experimenter. The results were that both age groups of subjects were better at discriminating the expressions than
they were at producing them. Older children were better
at discriminating than were younger children, and the
difference between discrimination and production increased with age.

345. Osgood, C. E. Dimensionality of the semantic space for communication via facial expressions. Scandinavian Journal of Psychology, 1966, 7, 1-30.

Osgood required students to either pose various expressions or judge them on the faces of other students. His data had been collected originally in 1944; however, it was analyzed later to determine the number and nature of dimensions required to account for variance in the judgment of facial expressions. He found that, according to factor analysis, there were three main dimensions-- Pleasantness, Activation, and Control. A cluster analysis showed that there were from seven to 10 regions within the space.

346. Patterson, M. L. Compensation in nonverbal immediacy behavior: A review. Sociometry, 1973, 36, 237-252.

Patterson examined the relationships between nonverbal immediacy behaviors within the context of Argyle and Dean's (1965) compensation hypothesis. Correlational and experimental evidence was presented which supported the compensation notion. A summary was made of research on compensation with a table noting the direction of support for this phenomenon in pairs of immediacy behaviors--distance and eye contact, orientation and eye contact, distance and orientation, distance and lean, and a miscellaneous entry. Problems involved in evaluating relevant research and implications for further investigations were discussed.

347. Patterson, M. L. Interpersonal distance, affect, and equilibrium theory. Journal of Social Psychology, 1977, 101, 205-214.

Patterson tested Argyle and Dean's (1965) equilibrium theory in two studies. Study I was done in the laboratory with male and female subjects and a female assistant. Study II was done on a university campus, a shopping center, and at a church with adult dyads. In Study I, seating distance was manipulated by having subjects pull up a chair and seat themselves at a distance which was comfortable for them. The results showed that increased proximity led to less eye contact and orientation. In Study II, pairs of individuals were observed while standing. There was no difference in distance due to sex of the pairs. Another result was that less direct orientations occurred with closer interaction distances.

348. Patterson, M. L. Social space and social interaction. Dissertation Abstracts International, 1969, 29(11-B), 4368- 4369.

The author studied the effects of both the manipulation of interpersonal distance by a male or female confederate

and the disposition of that confederate upon the subject's subsequent approach to a target person. No support was found for hypotheses concerning manipulated distances or dispositions; however, the hypothesis predicting a contrast effect between the rated favorability of
the two target persons after the subject had met with a
confederate was confirmed.

349. Patterson, M. L. Spatial factors in social interaction.
Human Relations, 1968, 21, 351-361.

Patterson presented an article discussing many of the
studies of spacial use in social interactions among
humans. His discussion included such areas as small
group interactions and structure, personality correlates
of spatial usage, and invasions of personal space. He
also discussed the use of projective methods in personal
space research.

350. Patterson, M. L. and Sechrest, L. B. Interpersonal
distance and impression formation. Journal of Personality,
1970, 38, 161-166.

The experimenters examined impression formation as a
function of interpersonal distance in an interview with
college students. It was predicted that a confederate
would be rated less socially active as the distance between him and the subject increased. The hypothesis was
supported by a significant negative linear trend in the
composite ratings of friendliness, aggressiveness, extraversion, and dominance. A variation in this trend, indicating that confederates seated closest to the subject
were seen as less socially active, was explained in terms
of compensatory behaviors minimizing the effect of close
physical proximity.

351. Patterson, M. L., Mullens, S., and Romano, J. Compensatory reactions to spatial invasion. Sociometry, 1971, 34(1),
114-121.

The aim of the study was to examine specific compensatory
behaviors in response to an intruder. The study took
place in a university library so that males and females
seated alone at a study table were used as the targets
for intrusion by one of two female experimenters. It was
hypothesized that increasing immediacy of the intruder
would decrease the latency of flight responses. During
each 10-minute session the intruder attempted to maintain
a 30% rate of glancing toward the subject or his work.
Results showed that only 18 of the 80 subjects left before the 10-minute period was over. However, compensatory reactions occurred such as increased leaning or
sliding away from the intruder and turning away or using
a hand or elbow in a position to screen her. These compensatory behaviors changed with the immediacy of the
intruder.

352. Patterson, M. L., Mullens, S., and Romano, J.   Stability
of nonverbal immediacy behaviors. Journal of Experimental
Social Psychology, 1973, 9, 97-109.

The main purpose of the study was to obtain further information on the stability of immediacy behavior, specifically approach distance and orientation, eye contact,
and body lean. Additionally, compensatory relationships
between the immediacy behavior, the effect of sex of subject and sex of the interviewer on immediacy behavior,
and the relationship between personality variables and
immediacy behavior were examined. Male and female undergraduates were subjects. Two female and two male experimenters were interviewers. Each subject entered a room
with an interviewer. The subject was invited to pull up
a chair, and when he was seated the interview began.
Later, he filled out a brief personality questionnaire
in another room. Then he was taken back to the experimental room for a second interview. After this he rated
himself on social anxiety, extraversion, and dominance.
In a second study a similar format was used, but with a
one-week interval between the two interviews. Results
showed that approach distance, eye contact, approach
orientation, and body lean behavior were highly consistent over time. Another finding was that eye contact
was greater in same-sex than opposite-sex pairs, and in
the second study it was found that females showed greater
eye contact than did males. Lastly, in general, the
results supported the compensatory hypothesis.

353. Pedersen, D. M. Development of a personal space measure.
Psychological Reports, 1973, 32, 527-535.

The author described the Pedersen Personal Space Measure
which used standardized instructions and measured simulated personal space. Reliability and validity data,
as determined for 170 male undergraduates, were discussed.

354. Pedersen, D. M. Developmental trends in personal space.
Journal of Psychology, 1973, 83, 3-9.

Pedersen administered the Pedersen Personal Space Measure
children's form to males and females in grades one to six
to obtain simulated personal space scores toward stimulus
figures of a man, woman, boy, and girl. Male subjects
had a larger space than females at all grades and for all
figures. This larger space was established by the third
grade and remained until the sixth grade when the personal
space for females tended to increase to that of males.
The personal space of males and females tended to be the
same toward the man, woman, and a same-sex child figure;
but smaller toward opposite-sex peers.

355. Pedersen, D. M. Personality and demographic correlates
of simulated personal space. Journal of Psychology, 1973,
85, 101-108.

Various personality, demographic, and simulated personal space measures were given to male college students. The two former measures were given two weeks prior to the personal space measure. Correlations of the personality and demographic variables with the personal space measure showed that subjects with a smaller personal space tended to be less aggressive, more tolerant of ambiguity, more self-acceptant, and had a higher ideal self. They also tended to be of Southern European extraction which was noted to be consistent with other research findings. Subjects with a smaller back personal space tended to have higher self-acceptance, emotional stability, and a lower consumption for alcohol.

356. Pedersen, D. M.   Relations among self, other and consensual personal space. Perceptual and Motor Skills, 1973, 36, 732-734.

Pedersen administered measures of self, other, and consensual personal space in relation to a target person to 170 male undergraduates. No significant mean differences or high intercorrelations were found among the personal space measures. It was concluded that the personal space of a person is affected by the personal space of another person, and that both the space of the self and of the other determine the space between them that is consensually obtained.

357. Pedersen, D. M.   Relations among sensation seeking and simulated and behavioral personal space. Journal of Psychology, 1973, 83, 79-88.

The author gave the Pedersen Personal Space Measure to male and female undergraduates. They were required to position male and female profiles relative to a self-profile at each of nine angles. The Pedersen Behavioral Personal Space Measure was administered in which subjects were approached by a male and female at each of the nine angles. Additionally, the Sensation Seeking Scale was administered. According to results, females with high scores on the disinhibition scale of the Sensation Seeking Scale, categorized as swingers, had greater simulated personal spaces but tended to have closer behavioral space toward males, except at the sides. Males with high scores on the boredom susceptibility scale of the Sensation Seeking Measure and who, therefore, liked new and interesting experiences had greater simulated side and diagonal personal spaces. For the behavioral measure, males and females responded similarly to males and females approaching from various angles. Simulated and behavioral spaces were similar for male subjects, but almost unrelated for female subjects.

358. Pedersen, D. M. and Heaston, A. B.   The effects of sex of subject, sex of approaching person, and angle of approach upon personal space. Journal of Psychology, 1972, 82, 276-286.

The authors gave two personal space measures to male and female subjects--an approach measure with a male and female confederate, and a placement task using nine angles with male and female profiles. On the placement measure, both sexes of subjects placed females closer than males, and there was no difference between sexes for placement of male figures. For the approach measure, females permitted closer approach at sides than at front, while males permitted a closer frontal approach.

359. Pedersen, D. M. and Shears, L. M. A review of personal space research in the framework of general system theory. Psychological Bulletin, 1973, 80, 367-388.

The review by Pedersen and Shears related personal space to social interactions. General system theory was used as a framework because of its role in communicating information. For that topic, the information communicated is feelings and attitudes, and they are conveyed by the person's use of his body and the space occupied by it and his possessions. Nonverbal communication, a subpart of all forms of interpersonal interactions, was also discussed. (Summary of author's abstract.)

360. Peery, J. C. and Stern, D. N. Gaze duration frequency distributions during mother-infant interaction. Journal of Genetic Psychology, 1976, 129, 45-55.

The researchers recorded the gaze behavior of 10 twin babies and their mothers during the fourth month of the infants' lives. The behavior was observed within the home and was noted weekly. Gaze behavior was measured during play, bottle feeding, and spoon feeding. The results were discussed in terms of power functions. The researchers also presented a consistency-activation personality theory as a possible interpretation of their results.

361. Peery, J. C. and Stern, D. N. Mother-infant gazing during play, bottle feeding, and spoon feeding. Journal of Psychology, 1975, 91, 207-213.

Peery and Stern analyzed the gazing behavior of three-month-old twin infants and their mothers during spoon and bottle feeding and play. The subjects were videotaped in their homes. They found that mothers spent more of their time looking at their infants than their infants spent looking at them. This behavior occurred for all of the conditions (spoon feeding, bottle feeding, and play). Peery and Stern interpreted their data from a consistency-activation personality theory approach. This theory suggests that mothers and infants try to maintain a comfortable level of arousal.

362. Pellegrini, R. J. and Empey, J. Interpersonal spatial orientation in dyads. Journal of Psychology, 1970, 76, 67-70.

Noting that research on personal distance neglected the
measurement of the extent to which interactions assumed
a face-to-face versus a side-to-side orientation, the
experimenters examined the relationship between interpersonal proxemics and angle of regard in an effort to
clarify possible expressive functions of the two characteristics. The subjects were male and female students
who met with a same-sex confederate. The interaction
involved a three-minute seated conversation. The confederate was already in the experimental room in a designated chair and the subject had to pull up a chair in
order to engage in the conversation. It was found that
female subjects sat closer to the female confederate than
did male subjects to the male confederate. The experimenters' subjects tended to turn away from direct, face-
to-face orientations with the confederate as proximity
increased. An explanation was provided according to
Argyle and Dean's (1965) affiliative conflict theory.

363. Perky, S. D. Effects of positive and negative audience
response on actors' nonverbal performance behavior and on
their attitudes. Dissertation Abstracts International, 1977
(Feb), Vol. 37(8-A), 4715.

Perky wanted to identify variables and to observe the
attitudes and behaviors of actors in positive, negative,
and unclaqued audience response conditions. Five actors
were videotaped and audiotaped during 12 performances.
Their physical behaviors were analyzed from photos made
from the videotapes. The actors rated their performances,
the overall performance, the performances of other actors,
and the audience. The director and expert evaluators
also rated the performances. No significant differences
in nonverbal behaviors were found. It was noted that the
actors' awareness of the experimental observation biased
the data. Nonverbal behaviors which occurred most frequently were body orientation to the audience, lean, gestures, and eye focus. From the audio-videotapes, it was
found that the most frequently occurring dysfluences
were vocal pauses.

364. Pinnas, R. M. The effect of microcounseling on attentiveness and sensitivity to nonverbal cues. Dissertation
Abstracts International, 1976(Jun), Vol. 36(12-A), 7872-7873.

The study was done to investigate the effectiveness of
microcounseling upon the enhancement of counselor sensitivity and attentiveness to nonverbal cues. Two other
purposes of the study were to determine whether microcounseling and practicum training interacted to develop
more attentiveness and sensitivity to nonverbal behavior,
and to assess the contribution of increased sensitivity
and attentiveness to empathy, level of regard, congruence,
and unconditionality of regard. Graduate students in
guidance counseling were subjects. The results were that
microcounseling did not create more sensitivity to

nonverbal cues than no microcounseling. Furthermore, microcounseling in conjunction with practicum training did not enhance sensitivity to nonverbal cues. However, greater attentiveness did develop from exposure to micro-counseling.

365. Pliner, P., Krames, L., and Alloway, T. (Eds.). Advances in the study of communication and affect: Vol. 2. Nonverbal communication of aggression. New York: Plenum Press, 1975.

Pliner et al. collected articles on nonverbal communication in humans and animals. The book contained eight chapters; however, Chapters 1 through 3 pertained to human behavior. The topics covered in these chapters included visual behavior and power, visual behavior and aggression, and language.

366. Polefka, D. A. Expressive behavior and durability of social impressions. Dissertation Abstracts International, 1976(Nov), Vol. 37(5-B), 2575.

Subjects observed videotapes of female students who were either very successful or unsuccessful at distinguishing between fake and genuine suicide notes. Congruency of the actor's performance feedback and her expressive behavior in regard to that feedback were manipulated by dubbing failure feedback over successful actors and successful feedback over unsuccessful actors. Polefka hypothesized that subjects would persevere in maintaining their impressions of the actor (even after being told the performances were prearranged) in congruent conditions. However, the results showed a tendency for all subjects to devalue the actor's "actual" performance. Impressions did not persevere. A second study was done to control for certain artifacts and to check the reliability of the devaluation response. It replicated the findings from the first study.

367. Porier, G. W. and Lott, A. J. Galvanic skin responses and prejudice. Journal of Personality and Social Psychology, 1967, 5, 253-259.

The researchers replicated the Rankin and Campbell (1955) study which found greater galvanic skin responses to incidental hand contact by a Black assistant than by a White assistant with White male subjects. Porier and Lott had each assistant make two adjustment contacts instead of one each. They used White male subjects. Self-report measures of prejudice were also taken. They did not replicate the Rankin and Campbell results when all subjects were combined. However, scores from the California E Scale correlated with the GSRs, while scores from Rokeach's Opinionation Scale did not. The lack of replication of the Rankin and Campbell study was discussed.

368. Porter, E., Argyle, M., and Satter, V.   What is sig-
nalled by proximity?   Perceptual and Motor Skills, 1970,
30(1), 39-42.

    Porter et al. attempted to determine how proximity is
    perceived as a cue in dyadic interaction with teen-age
    boys.   Subjects had conversations with confederates at
    three distances and completed rating scales on the con-
    federates.   Proximity did not count for any significant
    amount of the variance in any of the scales.   The exper-
    imenters concluded that while proximity has certain de-
    terminants such as liking and emotional adjustment, these
    are not reflected in the way proxmity is perceived.

369. Puk, G.   Reinforcement processes and the group-induced
shift: The effects of nonverbal behavior within a group discussion.   Dissertation Abstracts International, 1977(Jan),
Vol. 37(7-B), 3653-3654.

    Puk compared three models of group-induced shift and the
    effects of nonverbal behavior within a group discussion.
    Assistants were trained to display certain nonverbal be-
    haviors which induced positive affect, negative affect,
    or were affectively neutral during a group discussion
    with a subject.   Subjects also filled out the Interper-
    sonal Judgment Scale.   The results showed that the non-
    verbal behaviors of the assistants were successful in
    inducing the appropriate affect and also affected the
    attractiveness of the assistants.   Puk also presented
    results concerning the various discussion-manipulation
    conditions he had used.

370. Raiche, B. M.   The effects of touch in counselor portrayal of empathy and regard, and in the promotion of child
self-disclosure, as measured by video-tape simulation.
Dissertation Abstracts International, 1977(Oct), Vol. 38
(4-A), 1902-1903.

    Raiche examined the effects of a counselor's touching
    the hand, shoulder, back, or knee of a young child in
    helping the child disclose more information and also in
    communicating empathy with and regard for the child.
    Young children were shown videotapes three times of a
    six-year-old child who was purportedly being counseled
    by an adult who engaged in or did not engage in the
    touching behavior.   The viewer child was asked which
    grown-up cared most for the child, which could best
    understand problems the viewer might have, and which
    grown-up would be the easiest to talk with.   Results
    showed that the child chose the adult who used touching
    more than the other adults.   The proportion of children
    choosing touch generally increased with age; however,
    it decreased at certain ages depending upon the ques-
    tion.   The sex of the counselor affected responses to
    certain questions.

371. Ramsey, S. J. A method of validating selected nonverbal behaviors in small groups. Dissertation Abstracts
International, 1977(Jul), Vol. 38(1-A), 25-26.

   Ramsey looked at the co-occurrence of certain nonverbal
   behaviors with certain verbal themes within a small group
   setting. Twelve nonverbal variables were rated from
   still photographs. She found that, for example, movement
   of arms and body orientation were indications of dissonance since they tended to co-occur, and no nonverbal
   behavior seemed to be indicative of consonance. She
   also noted that nonverbal displays which co-occurred
   during verbal dissonance varied according to the intensity of the dissonance.

372. Rankin, P. P. Looking at change in the area of body
image and self-concept in adolescent females after exposure
to two types of small group counseling experiences. Dissertation Abstracts International, 1975(Mar), Vol. 35(9-A),
5828-5829.

   The study was done to examine the change in the body
   images of subjects who had been exposed to ones of two
   types of group counseling experiences. Subjects in counseling groups using verbal communication were compared to
   those using verbal communication and body language, movement exercises, and awareness techniques. Two counselors
   met with the two groups composed of five adolescent girls
   each. A control group of subjects was also used. The
   results showed that there was a significant difference
   between the subjects exposed to the different experiences
   on an attitude, an anxiety, and a body awareness scale.
   Additionally, subjects exposed to the nonverbal experience became more willing to partake in school activities
   and generally more outgoing.

373. Rankin, R. E. and Campbell, D. T. Galvanic skin response to Negro and White experimenters. Journal of Abnormal
and Social Psychology, 1955, 51, 30-33.

   Rankin and Campbell measured galvanic skin responses
   among male college students as a result of incidental
   contacts (touching) by a Black and a White assistant.
   The contact occurred when the experimenter adjusted a
   dummy GSR apparatus on the subject's left hand. The
   actual recording was being taken on the right hand. The
   researchers found differential responses to the two assistants, with a greater response being made to the Black
   assistant. Rankin and Campbell noted that although race
   may have been the prime factor in the responses, differences in physical attributes other than race for the two
   assistants may have been effective.

374. Rawls, J. R., Trego, R. E., McGaffey, C. N., and Rawls,
D. J. Personal space as a predictor of performance under
close working conditions. Journal of Social Psychology,
1972, 86, 261-267.

The authors compared persons desiring greater distance
between themselves and others (high PS scorers) with
those desiring less distance between themselves and
others (low PS scorers) as to their performance as psychomotor and arithmetic tasks under different degrees of
closeness. It had been hypothesized that the performance
of high PS scorers would deteriorate under conditions of
increased closeness, while the performance of low PS
scorers would be unaffected. Results from two experiments with male undergraduates lent some support to the
hypothesis.

375. Raymond, B. J. and Unger, R. K.   'The apparel oft pro-
claims the man': Cooperation with deviant and conventional
youths. Journal of Social Psychology, 1972, 87, 75-82.

The study was designed to determine whether people would
react differently to others because of style of dress or
hair. Two male college students (one White, one Black)
dressed either conventionally or nonconventionally. The
White confederate dressed hippie style for his nonconventional condition, and the Black confederate dressed in
"Afro" style clothing and hairdo for his nonconventional
condition. Subjects were approached for change in various shopping centers. It was found that more people complied with the request for change when the confederates
were conventionally dressed. In a second experiment the
race of the subject was considered, and it was found that
more Blacks complied with the request with the deviant
Black condition and the conventional White condition than
with the other two conditions. In a third experiment no
difference in cooperation due to ages of subjects was
found.

376. Reece, M. M. and Whitman, R. N.   Expressive movements,
warmth, and verbal reinforcements. Journal of Abnormal and
Social Psychology, 1962, 64, 234-236.

Reece and Whitman wanted to determine the effects of an
experimenter's warmth or coldness on verbal conditioning
in a free association task. College students were subjects and were randomly assigned to four groups: warm-
reinforced, warm-nonreinforced, cold-reinforced, and
cold-nonreinforced. The following nonverbal behaviors
were used as expressions of warm behavior: leaning
toward the subject, looking directly, smiling, and keep-
ing hands still. The following behaviors were used as
expressions of cold behavior: leaning away from the
subject, looking around the room, not smiling, and drum-
ming fingers. Plural nouns were reinforced by the experimenter's saying "mm-hmm." The results showed that
the interaction of verbal reinforcement and warm expressive behaviors produced the greatest amount of verbal-
izations from the subjects.

377. Rekers, G. A. and Amaro-Plotkin, H. D. Sex-typed man-
nerisms in normal boys and girls as a function of sex and
age. Child Development, 1977, 48, 275-278.

   The study was done to investigate the occurrence of eight
   gestures (which had been found for gender-disturbed males)
   in young males and females. The subjects were 48 White
   elementary school children. They were observed through
   a one-way mirror as they performed a standardized play
   task. Some of the observed and rated gestures were hand
   clasp, limp wrist, palming, and flexed elbow. Each of
   these gestures and the four others were defined by the
   investigators. The results showed that there was a sex
   difference for the total gesture score, with females per-
   forming the "feminine" gestures more than males. There
   was no significant difference between ages of subjects
   and no significant interaction for age by sex. For the
   hands-on-hips gesture, males and females were found to
   use somewhat different approaches. Lastly, only three
   of the eight gestures previously reported for disturbed
   boys discriminated between the present normal boys and
   girls. The investigators noted the need for further
   research into this area.

378. Rekers, G. A. and Yates, C. E. Sex-typed play in feminoid boys vs. normal boys and girls. Journal of Abnormal
Child Psychology, 1976, 4, 1-8.

   The investigators developed a method for assessing children's sex-type play. One hundred and twenty normal boys
   and girls and 15 known feminoid boys were subjects. The
   children were observed from behind a one-way mirror while
   they played. It was found that the sex-typed behavior
   of the feminoid boys was significantly different from
   the play behavior of the normal boys, but was not significantly different from the behavior of the normal
   girls. The results also showed that there were clear
   differences between the sex-typed behavior of normal
   males and females and that these differences could be
   identified as early as age three. They also seemed to
   remain stable at least through age eight.

379. Robson, K. S. The role of eye-to-eye contact in mater-
nal-infant attachment. Journal of Child Psychology and Psychiatry, 1967, 8, 13-27.

380. Rodgers, J. A. Relationship between sociability and
personal space preference at two different times of day.
Perceptual and Motor Skills, 1972, 35, 519-526.

   Degrees of sociability and emotional adjustment were determined for a group of undergraduates by the Heron Two-
   Part Personality Inventory. Three measures of personal
   space preference--maximum, optimum, and minimum distance
   for comfortable standing conversation--were obtained for
   each subject between the hours of 8:30 to 9:30 A.M. and

2:30 to 3:30 P.M. Contrary to earlier studies, there was
no relationship between degree of sociability and preference for personal space. However, there were differences
in preference depending upon time of day--greater distance was preferred in the morning than afternoon. Low-
sociability subjects showed more variability in the amount
of preferred personal space than did high-sociability subjects in four of the six trials.

381. Rosenfeld, H. M. Approval-seeking and approval-inducing
functions of verbal and nonverbal responses in the dyad.
Journal of Personality and Social Psychology, 1966, 4, 597-
605.

As part of a project to identify instrumental affiliative
functions of acts expressed in free interaction, several
nonverbal and verbal categories of behavior of same-sex
members of ad hoc dyads were recorded under two condi-
tions--an approval-seeking condition and an approval-
avoiding condition. Twenty-six and 20 dyads were formed
for the two conditions, respectively. One member of each
dyad was secretly instructed to gain or avoid the approval
of the other member. It was found that approval-seeking
subjects were significantly higher than approval-avoiding
subjects in nonverbal and verbal responsiveness and in
the percentage of smiles, positive head nods (for males
only), gesticulations (for females only), and recognitions
(a class of brief verbal reinforcers). Approval from the
other member of the dyad in the approval-avoiding condition was positively correlated with the subject's positive
head nods, recognitions, and references to the other member, and negatively correlated with the subject's self-
manipulations and self-references.

382. Rosenfeld, H. M. Classroom area per pupil and discipline problems: An experimental exploration of the relationship of classroom size to pupil deviant behavior and its
management by teachers. Dissertation Abstracts International,
1968, 29(5-A), 1406-1407.

Rosenfeld wanted to discover whether or not there was a
relationship between classroom area per pupil and the frequency of deviant behavior and time spent by teachers in
controlling the behavior. Third- and fifth-grade children
were subjects. The conclusions were that, in conjunction
with the hypothesis, there was no relationship between
frequency of deviant behavior and classroom area per pupil
except for the instance in which for the fifth grade the
area per pupil was reduced to 15 square feet. No relationship was found between frequency of behavior and area
per pupil for the third grade, and no relationship between
duration of behavior and area per pupil was found in
either grade.

383. Rosenfeld, H. M. Effect of an approval-seeking induction
on interpersonal proximity. Psychological Reports, 1965, 17,
120-122.

To determine whether interpersonal proximity is used as an instrumental act for the attainment of social approval, female college students were assigned either approval-seeking or approval-avoiding roles, and their proxemic behavior in relation to a female confederate in an un-structured social situation was observed. The subject was to take a chair into a room where another "girl" (the confederate) was already seated and waiting. The subject's placement of the chair in relation to the con-federate was observed through a one-way mirror as well as being noted by chalk marks left on the floor from the legs of the chair. Differences were found between the two conditions on the distance measure, but not on angle of placement. Greater distances were used in the approval-avoiding condition than in the approval-seeking condition.

384. Rosenfeld, H. M. Nonverbal reciprocation of approval: An experimental analysis. Journal of Experimental Psychology, 1967, 3, 102-111.

Rosenfeld did an experiment to provide a demonstration of the reciprocation of common approval-related responses. Each of 48 ninth graders was given a standard interview by an adult. The interviewer followed each answer given by the subject with approval responses (positive head nods, smiles, verbal acknowledgment, and gesticulations), disapproval responses (head shakes, frowns, and verbal disparagements), or no response. Subjects smiled and nodded their heads significantly more in response to approval than to disapproval or no response. Also, sub-jects responded with their lowest percentages of self-manipulatory responses and speech disturbances in the approval situation. The results supported the idea of a reinforcement-feedback system which may be a major determinant of the social interaction process.

385. Rosenthal, D. A. and Lines, R. Handwriting as a corre-late of extraversion. Journal of Personality Assessment, 1978, 42, 45-48.

The investigators wanted to determine whether or not there was a correlation between handwriting and extra-version. The handwriting of male and female college students was examined. They were also given the Eysenck Personality Inventory. The results were that there were no significant differences between males and females other than for letter slant. Males used a greater slant to the right than females. For the personality measure, there was no significant correlation between extraversion scores and the various handwriting measures.

386. Ruesch, J. and Kees, W. Nonverbal communication: Notes on the visual perception of human relations. Berkeley: Uni-versity of California Press, 1970.

The book explored the ways in which people communicate
with each other nonverbally. It included numerous photographs of interactions and forms of communication. The
authors noted that they realized still pictures created
a kind of distortion of the behavior under consideration;
however, they hoped the book would be used as a step
toward investigating nonverbal communication further.
The book included such topics as the role of biology
and culture in nonverbal communication, movement and
its informative value, and language and psychopathology.

387. Russo, N. Connotation of seating arrangements. In
R. Sommer (Ed.). Personal space: The behavioral basis for
design. Englewood Cliffs, N. J.: Prentice-Hall, 1969.

Russo asked college students to rate diagrammed seating
arrangements along dimensions of intimacy, talkativeness,
friendliness, and equality. Friendliness, talkativeness,
and intimacy correlated with increasing physical distance
which indicated less acquaintance, less friendliness, and
less talkativeness, except where increased eye contact
countered the effects of increased distance. Cultural
norms influenced the head position on the equality dimension so that if one member of a pair was at the head
position, the pair was rated as being more unequal than
if both members were at the side of the table or at the
end.

388. St. Martin, G. McA. Male/female differential encoding
an intercultural differential decoding of nonverbal affective
communication. Dissertation Abstracts International, 1976
(Nov), Vol. 37(5-A), 2499-2500.

St. Martin investigated the nonverbal communication of
emotions within a simulated intercultural context. A
White male and a White female responded to spoken emotion-
evoking paragraphs for each of six affects: sadness, disgust, anger, surprise, happiness, and fear. The best
portrayal of each affect by the male and female was selected by three judges. The portrayals were edited onto
a videotape. The respondents in the study were male and
female White, Black, Latin American, and Malaysian individuals. They rated the senders from the videotape. St.
Martin found that the male and female senders' abilities
were rated differently. Male and female respondents made
similar ratings. Culture had an effect such that people
from different cultures rated the senders differently.
Black Americans and White respondents differed most.
Finally, the mode of communication made a difference
such that responses differed for the visual, audio, and
audiovisual modes.

389. Saitz, R. L. and Cervenka, E. J. A handbook of gestures:
Colombia and the United States. The Hague: Mouton Publishers, 1972.

390. Samuel, W. Response to bill of rights paraphrases as influenced by the hip or straight attire of the opinion solicitor. Journal of Applied Social Psychology, 1972, 2, 47-62.

Samuel investigated Bill of Rights-type preferences among a sample of White middle-class suburban residents as influenced by the type of dress of an opinion solicitor. Three experimental conditions of exposure to paraphrases of the Bill of Rights were used. Thirteen White male and female confederates solicited the signatures. Some were dressed in hip fashion, others were straight. Samuel found differential signings due to dress and tone of the paraphrase. A straight solicitor got more signatures with the negative paraphrase than with the "real" or "wishy-washy" paraphrases. There was no differential signing with the hip solicitor. In general, straight solicitors got more signatures than hip solicitors. Other results were discussed in regard to the various types of paraphrases and time of solicitation.

391. Satthouse, T. A. Nonverbal visual stimuli are remembered nonverbally. Dissertation Abstracts International, 1975(Jan), Vol. 35(7-B), 3626.

Satthouse conducted three experiments to determine whether nonverbal visual stimuli were represented in memory in a symbolic or verbal mode or an image or spatial mode. Schematic faces or airplane-photograph stimuli were used for the main trails, and numerical or letters were used in the subtrails in each experiment. The subjects were required to remember the positioning of the target items for a spatial-information condition and to remember the identities of the items for a verbal-information condition. Satthouse concluded that visual stimuli, which are not composed of numerical or alpha characters, have an image mode of representation. Furthermore, he concluded that the results indicated that image and symbolic information are processed and stored in different systems.

392. Scherer, S. E. Proxemic behavior of primary school children as a function of their socioeconomic class and structure. Journal of Personality and Social Psychology, 1974, 29, 800-805.

In Study I, the experimenter hypothesized that pairs of lower-class White children would stand farther apart while conversing than pairs of lower-class Black children. Same-sex, same-race dyads of elementary school children in grades one through four were observed during morning recess and lunch-hour breaks over a three-day period. Results showed no significant difference between the groups in terms of interaction distance, although means were in the predicted direction: White children stood further apart than Black children. Study II was conducted in order to examine the affects of

social class and subculture on dyadic conversation interaction distances. Subjects were lower-class and middle-
class children. Similar observation techniques were used.
Results for Study II indicated a significant main effect
for class such that middle-class dyads stood farther
apart than lower-class pairs. The main effect for subculture was not significant. The culture by class interaction was significant in that middle-class Whites stood
farther apart than lower-class Whites; however, no significant difference was found between middle-class and
lower-class Blacks.

393. Scherer, S. E. and Schiff, M. R.   Perceived intimacy,
physical distance and eye contact.   Perceptual and Motor
Skills, 1973, 36, 835-841.

Thirty male undergraduates rated photographic slides on
the degree of intimacy of two males shown seated at a
cafeteria table. Another 10 subjects rated the slides
on both intimacy and eye contact. Fifty-four different
seating arrangements were used. Side and corner arrangements were varied by body and head position through five
angles (0, 30, 45, 60, and 90 degrees) and three distances (3, 4, 5, and 6 feet). Results supported the
main hypothesis that intimacy varies inversely with distance and that intimacy ratings are directly related to
ratings of eye contact. Corner seating was judged more
intimate than side seating.

394. Schiffenbauer, A. When will people use facial information to attribute emotion? The effect of judges' emotional
state and intensity of facial expression on attribution of
emotion.   Representative Research in Social Psychology, 1974,
5, 47-53.

395. Schiffenbauer, A. and Babineau, A. Sex role stereotypes
and the spontaneous attribution of emotion. Journal of Research in Personality, 1976, 10, 137-145.

The researchers hypothesized that high-intensity expressions would evoke more emotional labels than low-intensity
expressions since the former are more rare within this
society. They also predicted a difference in emotion
labeling due to the sex of the expressor and expression
intensity. Two experiments were conducted. In Experiment I, 60 subjects were used (33 females, 27 males).
Slides of the faces of males and females whose gender
had been judged to be ambiguous or unambiguous were used.
The slides depicted different emotional and intensities
of emotions. While viewing the slides, the subjects were
required to describe each one using one word or a brief
phrase. After viewing the slides, the subjects filled
out questionnaires about sex stereotyping the expressions.
Sex differences among the judges were found and the hypothesis concerning high- and low-intensity expressions
was supported. In Experiment II, the researchers

replicated the three-way interaction for sex of judge by
sex of expressor by intensity of expression. Male and
female high school students were subjects. The unambiguous male and female slides were used. A similar procedure
to that used in Experiment I was employed for Experiment
II except that the subjects did not complete the stereotype questionnaire. The main effect for sex of expressor
was significant. In addition, the interactions for sex
of judge by sex of expressor and sex of expressor by
expression intensity were significant.

396. Schiffrin, D. Handwork as ceremony: The case of the
handshake. Semiotica, 1974, 12, 189-202.

Schiffrin looked at the use of the handshake as a ritual
ceremony. She suggested that a great deal of social information is conveyed in this single gesture and that as
a result it is protected by various norms. She also discussed the various functions of the handshake and concluded that the meaning of handwork cannot be determined
outside of the context in which it occurs.

397. Schlachter, L. C. The relation between anxiety, perceived body and personal space, and actual body space among
young female adults. Dissertation Abstracts International,
1971(Dec), Vol. 32(6-B), 3458.

Schlachter noted that perceived body space (PBS) and perceived personal space (PPS) were theorized to act as a
protection zone against threats to one's emotional well
being. The author predicted that as anxiety level increased, the differences between PBS and actual body
space (ABS), PPS and actual personal space (APS), and
PPS and PBS would increase. Female college students were
subjects. Each was given the IPAT Anxiety Scale Quest-
tionnaire. Additionally, each subject reported her PBS
and PPS by identifying the areas of a topographic device.
The width of each subject's shoulder girdle was the measure of ABS. The results showed a significant correlation between anxiety and PBS and ABS. There was no significant correlation between anxiety and PPS and ABS.
However, a partial correlation was significant. Lastly,
no significant correlation was found between PPS and PBS,
although, again, a partial correlation was significant.

398. Schlosberg, H. A scale for the judgment of facial expressions. Journal of Experimental Psychology, 1941, 29,
497-510.

Schlosberg wanted to investigate Woodworth's scale of
facial expressions further. Subjects were required to
sort 216 pictures into seven bins. The bins were in one
row and were labeled Love, Happiness, Mirth, Surprise,
Fear, Suffering, Anger, Determination, Disgust, Contempt, and a residual category Scatter. Male and female subjects were used and worked on the sorting

individually. Schlosberg found that the scale was continuous rather than a collection of six categories. He
also suggested that the scale was circular. This was
indicated by the spread of the subjects' judgments across
the gap between categories six and one. Another suggestion was that the scale was like an ellipse with a
Pleasant-Unpleasant axis covering the long side and an
Attention-Rejection along the short side. Schlosberg
indicated that further investigation was needed on the
scale.

399. Schlosberg, H. The description of facial expressions in
terms of two dimensions. Journal of Experimental Psychology,
1952, 44, 229-237.

Schlosberg conducted three experiments using eight, nine,
and 18 subjects, respectively. The subjects were required to rate 72 pictures of facial expressions on two
nine-point scales: Pleasantness-Unpleasantness and
Attention-Rejection. A fourth experiment was conducted
using 20 subjects who rated 32 facial expression pictures
from a different source. Schlosberg plotted the position
of the pictures on the circumference of a circle and
attempted to predict the values received by each picture on an elliptical six-category scale, similar to
that used by Woodworth. He concluded that both sets
of pictures could be described by an oval scale and
that the axes would be Pleasantness-Unpleasantness and
Attention-Rejection.

400. Schoeberle, E. A. and Craddick, R. A. Human figure
drawings by freshman and senior student nurses. Perceptual
and Motor Skills, 1968, pp. 11-14.

Female freshman and senior nursing students drew the
"ideal" nurse and the most "undesirable" nurse, and also
rated themselves on a five-point scale measuring whether
or not they felt they were least like the ideal nurse or
not. The subjects were tested in groups. The experimenters found that significantly more seniors drew themselves in uniform than did freshmen. In addition, senior
nursing students rated themselves closer to the ideal
nurse and drew larger figures of the undesirable nurse
than did freshmen students.

401. Schonbuch, S. S. and Schell, R. E. Judgments of body
appearance by fat and skinny male college students. Perceptual and Motor Skills, 1967, 24, 999-1002.

The experimenters were interested in the responses overweight, underweight, and normal subjects would give to
estimates of their own body appearance. Sixty male subjects were required to choose from among 10 photographs
of nude male adults the one they felt most like him in
terms of body appearance. After making his choice, four
judges chose the picture they felt depicted the subjects'

body appearance. The researchers found that overweight
and underweight subjects made more inaccurate choices
than did normal subjects. In addition, members of the
extreme groups tended to overestimate their body size
and shape. Further research was suggested to explore
this finding more fully.

402. Schulz, R. and Barefoot, J. Non-verbal responses and
affiliative conflict theory. British Journal of Social and
Clinical Psychology, 1974, 13, 237-243.

Schulz and Barefoot manipulated interpersonal distance
and topic intimacy in an interview setting and monitored
eye-contact behavior and smiling among male college students. Their aim was to extend the studies on the affiliative conflict theory by Argyle and Dean (1965). The
subjects were videotaped while they engaged in an interview with an experimenter whose looking behavior was held
constant. The distance between the subject and the experimenter varied from three to 5½ feet. Topic intimacy
was also voiced. It was found that topic intimacy did
not affect looking while listening; however, as topic
intimacy increased, looking while talking decreased.
For distances, increased looking while listening occurred
for the greater distances. Another finding was that mean
smile ratios were higher at the close than at the far
distance.

403. Semaj, L. Race and sex effects on spatial behavior in
a naturalistic setting. Unpublished master's thesis, Rutgers
University, 1976.

Semaj investigated differences between Black and White
male and female interaction patterns in same sex-other
sex and same race-other race pairs. He observed the subjects during lunch and dinner at a college dining hall
during a two-week period. He found that people generally
preferred to sit across the table from each other rather
than side-by-side. White same-sex pairs preferred across
the table patterns, while Black same-sex pairs showed no
preference. During both meals, an across-the-table pattern was preferred.

404. Sensening, J., Reed, T. E., and Miller, J. S. Cooperation in the prisoner's dilemma game as a function of interpersonal distance. Psychonomic Science, 1972, 26, 105-106.

Twenty dyads of male subjects played 50 trials of the
Prisoner's Dilemma Game. Personal distance was varied
by seating two subjects either at the same table (close
condition) or at widely separated tables (far condition).
Players sat at right angles with no barriers. Results
were that at the greatest distance there were significantly fewer mutual cooperative choices, smaller earn-
ings, and greater differences in outcome between the
pair. Mutual cooperation among subjects in the far

condition extinguished completely in later trials.
Greater cooperation was found in the near condition.

405. Sewell, A. F. and Heisler, J. T.   Personality correlates
of proximity preferences. Journal of Psychology, 1973, 85,
151-155.

Male subjects entered a room individually in which a male
interviewer was seated at the opposite end. Distance between the interviewer's chair and the subject's chair was
correlated with scales of the Personality Research Form.
The major findings of the study was that subjects who
scored high on an "Exhibition" scale tended to position
themselves close to the interviewer. Subjects scoring
high on the "Impulsivity" scale showed similar behavior.
Not significant, but interesting, was the fact that subjects who had scored high on the "Cognitive Structure"
scale sat farther from the interviewer. The findings
supported those by Leipold (1963) and Patterson and
Holmes (1966) who reported that extroverts would approach an interviewer more closely than introverts.

406. Sheldon, W. H.   The varieties of human physique.   New
York: Harper & Bros. Publishers, 1940.

Sheldon suggested that personality may be understood as
the dynamic organization of affective, cognitive, cona-
tive, morphological, and physiological factors of a human
being. His book presented a study of these aspects of
individuals as they are important to personality and
clinical problems. He conducted a study designed to
classify physiques. Three basic body types were determined: the endomorph, the mesomorph, and the ectomorph.
Descriptions and illustrations of each type were presented. Finally, Sheldon discussed the types of temperament which seemed to correlate with the various body
types.

407. Shrout, P. E.   Impression formation and nonverbal behaviors as a function of sex of observer and of target. Dissertation Abstracts International, 1976(Dec), Vol. 37(6-B),
3054-3055.

Videotapes of dyadic interactions between unacquainted
individuals were made. Four male and four female observers rated them. Shrout wanted to determine which behaviors were used in forming impressions. A favorableness
checklist was filled out by the observers for each target.
Shrout found that behavioral activity was positively related to favorableness scores. Sex of observer and sex
of target differences were found for various behaviors.
A sex of target finding showed that males' smiles were
more related to favorableness than females' smiles. The
results were discussed in terms of male-female stereotypes.

408. Siegman, A. W. and Feldstein, S. (Eds.). Nonverbal
behavior and communication. Hillsdale, N. J.: Lawrence
Erlbaum Associates, 1978.

This book was prompted by the authors' perception of the
need for a comprehensive text written for advanced undergraduates and graduate students. They felt that much of
the existing literature was either too restricted or too
specialized. Their book is divided into four basic parts.
Some of the articles discuss gestural, visual, and facial
behaviors in humans; the role of space and time in social
interactions; and vocal expressions.

409. Slatterie, E. F. A comparative study of selected
effects of alcohol and marihuana on verbal and nonverbal
behaviors. Dissertation Abstracts International, 1976(Apr),
Vol. 36(10-B), 5284.

Two groups of subjects consisting of five individuals
each were videotaped under two experimental situations.
One group had free access to alcohol, and the other group
had free access to marihuana. Verbal and nonverbal behaviors were observed. It was found that significantly
more positive verbal behavior occurred with marihuana and
more negative verbal behavior occurred with alcohol. For
nonverbal behaviors, it was found that significantly more
backward body positioning occurred with alcohol.

410. Sleet, D. A. Physique and social image. Perceptual and
Motor Skills, 1969, 28, 295-299.

Sleet tested the presence of stereotypes about various
physiques. White males in an adult fitness program were
subjects. The subjects were shown photographs of men
representing Sheldon's (1954) three somatotypes. The
subjects were required to rank the photos on seven personality traits in order from the physique most suited
to that least suited to each trait. Sleet found that
the endomorph physique was ranked lowest on all of the
traits. Mesomorphs were ranked highest, and ectomorphs
were next highest. Sleet's results were similar to those
found by Kiker and Miller (1967) in a study with college-
age males.

411. Smith, B. J., Sandford, F., and Goldman, M. Norm violations, sex, and the 'blank stare.' Journal of Social Psychology, 1977, 103, 49-55.

Smith et al. assessed the differential reactions of males
and females when they were stared at blankly by a male
and female assistant. The study took place in a library.
White male and female college students were subjects.
White males and females served as assistants. The assistants placed themselves at a table across from the subject and maintained an expressionless stare directed at
the subject for 15 minutes or until the subject left.

Female subjects left sooner than male subjects. When
males were staring, females left after shorter periods
of time than did male subjects. When females were staring, there was no difference in departure time for male
and female subjects. Another result was that fewer
glances were given to the assistant by female subjects
than by male subjects.

412. Smith, G. H. Personality scores and the personal distance effect. Journal of Social Psychology, 1954, 39, 57-62.

Smith looked at the personal distance effect in a controlled, nonverbal setting and related this behavior to
scores on two personality inventories. Male undergraduates were required to look at four slides of male faces
--two pleasant and two unpleasant--and to adjust the size
of the pictures to their liking. They were then asked
to indicate whether or not they liked the face and if
they felt it was interesting. Results were that for the
two pleasant faces, subjects who made the faces larger or
brought them closer were better adjusted, according to
scores on the Bell Inventory, than those who made the
faces smaller or farther away. On the Knutson Inventory,
the difference suggested more personal security for the
subjects who brought the faces closer. Similar results
were true for unpleasant faces and the Bell Inventory
results.

413. Smith, W. J., Chase, J., and Lieblich, A. K. Tongue
showing: A facial display of humans and other primate spe-
cies. Semiotica, 1974, 11, 201-246.

The researchers analyzed human tongue-showing behavior
and its meaning. They also discussed this behavior among
gorillas and other primates and suggested it may share
evolutionary origins with human behavior. Observations
were made of nursery school children in the United States
and of people in the Canal Zone, Panama, and Mulatupo.
Observations of the gorillas were made at the Philadelphia Zoo. They found that for the school children,
tongue showing usually occurred during activities re-
quiring concentration or situations which had negative
content for the participant. In some instances, tongue
showing occurred when the individual gave up physical
control. Similar findings were found for the other subjects of the study. The researchers discussed various
other usages of tongue showing and also presented a section on the ontogeny of human tongue showing.

414. Snodgrass, L. L. Patterns of transgression via nonverbal communication: A cross-cultural study. Dissertation
Abstracts International, 1977(Sep), Vol. 38(3-A), 1311.

Snodgrass examined the use of bio-electric measures to
examine violations of nonverbal communication patterns
between Asians and Westerners and the effect of certain

variables on the affective response to cultural trans-
gressions transmitted through nonverbal communication.
Male Westerners and Asians from three socioeconomic
groups were used as subjects. They were individually
shown movies of Asian and Western cultural transgres-
sions and neutral scenes of Asian life. Muscle tension
fluctuations were recorded. Asians experienced more
emotion to the stimuli than did Westerners. Lower-socioeconomic groups showed higher emotional responses than
upper-socioeconomic groups.

415. Snyder, M. Self-monitoring of expressive behavior.
Journal of Personality and Social Psychology, 1974, 30, 526-
537.

The investigator constructed a measure called the Self-
Monitoring Scale initially using 16 fraternity members.
The scale was further validated using a group of actors
and psychiatric ward patients. The measure was then used
on male and female college students. From their scores
on the scale, they were divided into a high self-monitoring and a low self-monitoring group. The subjects' facial
and upper-body expressions were videotaped as they read
aloud a three-sentence emotionally neutral paragraph.
Other individuals who were also either high or low in
self-monitoring judged and rated the expressions. One
result was that judges were more accurate in judging the
expressions of high self-monitoring subjects than low
self-monitoring subjects. Furthermore, high self-monitoring judges tended to be better judges of emotion than were
low self-monitoring judges. Further validation and other
results were reported.

416. Sommer, R. Classroom ecology. Journal of Applied Behavioral Science, 1967, 3, 489-502.

Male and female college students switched their class-
rooms in midsemester in order to determine the effects
of participation on seating arrangement. It was found
that in a seminar-style arrangement, those subjects who
sat directly opposite the instructor participated more
than those who sat to the sides. In straight-row situations, subjects who sat in the front participated more
than those who sat at the sides. Sommer concluded that
his results supported the hypothesis relating direct
visual contact to increased interaction. (Summary of
abstract summary.)

417. Sommer, R. Intimacy ratings in five countries. International Journal of Psychology, 1968, 3, 109-114.

In judging closeness of seating arrangements, American,
English, and Swedish college subjects were alike, while
Pakistani and Dutch subjects deviated somewhat. Paki-
stanis saw opposite seating as more distant than did the
other groups, and Dutch subjects rated corner seating to

be less intimate. All groups judged arrangements from
greatest to least intimacy to be side-by-side, corner-
to-corner, opposite at square tables or the short side
of a rectangular table, and distant or diagonal arrangements. Ambiguous words and the possibility that sitting
at a table may have different meanings in different cultures created interpretative problems. Information on
spatial arrangements could nevertheless be valuable for
fostering or impeding social intercourse.

418. Sommer, R. Leadership and group geography. Sociometry,
1961, 24, 99-110.

Sommer conducted a study in a natural setting of the ways
in which individuals in small groups (three to six people)
arranged themselves vis-à-vis leaders who occupied certain
positions. Rectangular tables were used in the experiment with eight chairs around them. Subjects were hospital visitors, nonprofessional employees, student nurses,
and volunteer workers. Same-sex groups of subjects elected a leader for a brief discussion. In Experiment II,
groups in which leaders were not elected were used. Experiment III was conducted in order to determine the distance for comfortable conversation under conditions in
which the individuals knew each other fairly well and discussed nonpersonal material. In this experiment same-sex
pairs of subjects were asked to enter a lounge to discuss
certain topics. Sofas placed at various distances from
one another served as the basis of judgment for distance
preferences. Some of the results were as follows: (1)
in Experiment I, with groups of three, leaders showed no
preference for seating choices; however, with groups of
four, five, and six, the leader usually sat at an end
position; (2) when the leader sat in an end chair, the
corner chairs were used most often with the other end
chairs rarely being used; and (3) when the leader sat at
a corner (in groups of three and four), subjects sat
corner-to-corner or opposite the leader. For Experiment
II, seating in leaderless groups was similar to that in
groups with leaders with subjects using ends of the
tables; and although symmetrical seating around one end
predominated in small groups, it became less frequent in
groups of five and six. For Experiment III, when couches
were from one to three feet apart, subjects sat opposite
each other. When they were from 3½ to six feet apart,
subjects sat side-by-side.

419. Sommer, R. Man's proximate environment. Journal of
Social Issues, 1966, 22, 59-70.

Sommer attempted to summarize the behavioral studies of
human spatial relations. He discussed such areas as territory and density and suggested the need for more research into the dynamics of man's need for space or a
certain kind of space.

420. Sommer, R. Personal space: The behavioral basis for
design. Englewood Cliffs, N. J.: Prentice-Hall, 1969.

   Sommer studied the characteristics of personal space and
   presented a number of interesting examples of the ways
   in which people behave according to the dynamics of this
   phenomenon.

421. Sommer, R. Small groups ecology. Psychological Bulletin, 1967, 67, 145-152.

   Results of the study of the arrangement of individuals
   in small groups have shown that spatial arrangement is
   a function of group task, degree of the relationship between individuals, the personalities of the individuals,
   and the amount and kind of available space. Knowledge
   of small groups ecology can help in developing a theory
   of social relationships which includes the environment
   in which the interaction takes place as well as principles for design functional environments from the stand-
   point of human relations.

422. Sommer, R. Studies in personal space. Sociometry,
1959, 22, 247-260.

   Sommer was concerned with how pairs of people in small
   groups arranged themselves. He conducted several studies of personal distance within small groups. His results showed that people in neighboring chairs interacted
   more than people in distant chairs; those in corner positions interacted more than those side-by-side or facing
   each other; people generally preferred corner positions
   when taking seats in a cafeteria to discuss various
   topics; females sat closer to female decoys than to
   male decoys, while males sat farther; and schizophenics
   had a different conception of personal space than did
   normal subjects.

423. Sommer, R. The ecology of privacy. Library Quarterly,
1966, 36, 234-248.

424. Sommer, R. and Becker, F. D. Territorial defense and
the good neighbor. Journal of Personality and Social Psychology, 1969, 11, 85-92.

   Sommer and Becker conducted several studies to try to
   understand how markers (other persons or impersonal artifacts) are used to reserve space and how they receive
   legitimacy from other people, including "neighbors"
   (those sitting next to the individual) and potential
   intruders. The studies were conducted at soda fountains
   and at university libraries. In general, they found that
   people were willing to honor the markers left by others
   and to also protect the markers left by others in cases
   of potential intrusion.

425. Spence, D. P. and Feinberg, C.   Forms of defensive looking: A naturalistic experiment. Journal of Nervous and
Mental Disease, 1967, 145, 261-271.

    Spence and Feinberg wanted to examine defensive looking
in a naturalistic setting. College undergraduates were
subjects. They were given several tests: social desirability, repression, and mood. From the mood scale, 18
traits which a majority of the subjects felt did not
apply to them were used in the manipulation. A booklet
with the subject's name was left on a table, visible to
him. The booklet had a note attached indicating that
the experimenters felt certain of the enclosed traits
applied to him. The subject was observed through a one-
way mirror as to whether or not he looked at the booklet
and read through it. Some of the results were that
avoidance of looking was related to need to show socially
desirable traits. Those subjects who had low scores on
the social desirability scale engaged in active looking.
Another finding was that avoiders drew elaborate and de-
tailed pictures when asked to draw a figure at the table
while waiting for the experimenter to return.

426. Starkweather, C. W.   Disorders of nonverbal communication. Journal of Speech and Hearing Disorders, 1977, 42,
535-546.

    Starkweather discussed the phenomenon of nonverbal com-
munication including some points on the individual's
inability to communicate his affect state adequately.
He referred to this inability as a disorder of nonverbal communication. His article presented some of
the types of nonverbal communication disorders as well
as therapies for these disorders.

427. Stass, J. W. and Willis, F. N., Jr.   Eye contact, pupil
dilation, and personal preference. Psychonomic Science,
1967, 7, 375-376.

    Male and female subjects were asked to choose partners
for experiments. The available choices differed in eye
contact or pupil dilation. Subjects of both sexes were
more likely to choose partners with whom they had had
eye contact during an introduction. Males were more
likely to choose females who had dilated pupils, and
females made similar choices.

428. Stein, S. A.   Selected teacher verbal and nonverbal behaviors as related to grade level and student classroom performance. Dissertation Abstracts International, 1977(Jan),
Vol. 37(7-A), 4246-4247.

    Stein attempted to answer the following questions: (1)
are teachers' verbal and nonverbal behaviors influenced
by the class performance of their students? (2) are
teachers' verbal and nonverbal behaviors influenced by

the grade levels they teach? and (3) do these behaviors differ according to preference for a high- or low-ability group of students? Twenty-seven teachers and 341 students from elementary schools were used. Results showed through multivariate analysis of variance and certain univariate analyses that some of the verbal and nonverbal variables were significantly different. A discriminant analysis found no significant results for the factor concerning teacher preference for high- or low-ability students.

429. Steinzor, B. The spatial factor in face-to-face discussion groups. Journal of Abnormal and Social Psychology, 1950, 45, 552-555.

Steinzor hypothesized that seating arrangement in a small face-to-face group would help to determine the individuals with whom one was likely to interact. People sitting in a position which would allow them to observe more of each other's behavior would follow one another in verbal behavior more often than people whose view of each other was limited due to the fact that they sat closer. Two groups were studied, one with and one without a leader. The results were in the general direction of the hypothesis and were that people sitting opposite each other in a circle interacted significantly more with each other than did those who were neighbors.

430. Stephenson, G. and Rutter, D. Eye contact, distance, and affiliation: A re-evaluation. British Journal of Psychology, 1970, 61, 385-393.

The authors discussed Argyle and Dean's (1965) test of the affiliative-conflict theory of eye contact and the intimacy model which stemmed from it and which found that as the distance between subjects in a dyadic discussion increased, recorded eye contact increased. The hypothesis, that with increasing distance gaze directed at the ear and shoulder was increasingly recorded as eye contact by observers in the Argyle and Dean experiment, was tested using 21 and 32 undergraduates and observers, respectively. Results showing that recorded eye contact increased with distance but as a function of observer performance, not subject performance, strongly confirmed Stephenson and Rutter's hypothesis. It was suggested that Argyle and Dean's results may have been an artifact of observer behavior, not subject behavior.

431. Sternbach, R. A. and Tursky, B. Ethnic differences among housewives in psychophysical and skin potential responses to electric shock. Psychophysiology, 1965, 1, 241-246.

The experimenters were concerned with the skin potential reactivity of three ethnic groups and a comparison between their psychophysical performances. Housewives with one school-age child and who were Protestant-

American, Jewish, and Roman Catholic Irish and Italian
were subjects. Each subject was subjected to electric
shocks, and skin potential and threshold for pain were
measured. It was found that there were significant differences between the groups in terms of upper thresholds
and in the adaptation of diphasic palmar skin potentials.
These differences were also consistent with attitude differences. Other specific results were reported.

432. Stewart, D. J. and Patterson, M. L. Eliciting effects
of verbal and nonverbal cues on projective test responses.
Journal of Consulting and Clinical Psychology, 1973, 41, 74-
77.

Stewart and Patterson investigated the role of verbal and
nonverbal cues (the word "good," eye contact, and body
lean) by an experimenter upon thematic responses to the
TAT. Male and female undergraduates were subjects. During the TAT administration, an experimenter gave the verbal response only when subject showed clear development
of a theme. During this condition the experimenter re-
frained from looking at the subject. In the eye-contact
condition the experimenter gazed directly toward the subject after each theme response for about five seconds or
until the return of the gaze by the subject. In the body-
lean condition the experimenter leaned forward at a 45-
degree angle for a few seconds after the subject's response. Tape recordings were made of the subject's responses and were later rated by an independent judge.
Results showed that thematic responses were greater with
verbal reinforcement than with eye contact or body lean.
Responses also increased for verbal reinforcement at both
distances (three and six feet) and for eye contact at the
far distance. Additionally, the difference between the
eye contact conditions at the two distances became greater
over trials. The importance of these forms of communication during experimentation was noted.

433. Storms, M. D. and Thomas, G. C. Reactions to physical
closeness. Journal of Personality and Social Psychology,
1977, 35, 412-418.

Storms and Thomas conducted three experiments in order to
determine the effects of physical closeness on the ratings
of male subjects about other males. In Experiment I, subjects responded to a male confederate who supposedly had
similar or dissimilar attitudes to their's and who also
either sat at a close distance or a normal distance from
them. In Experiments II and III, the confederate acted
in a friendly or hostile way while sitting close to or at
a normal distance from the subject. A result for all of
the studies showed that there was an interaction between
the distance the confederate sat from the subject and cues
about the confederate (similar-dissimilar attitudes or
hostile-friendly manner). The confederate was liked more
when he sat close to the subject, had similar attitudes,

and was friendly. The researchers also discussed the implications of their results for theories of physical closeness.

434. Streeter, L. A., Kraus, R. M., Geller, V., Olson, C., and Apple, W. Pitch changes during attempted deception. Journal of Personality and Social Psychology, 1977, 35, 345-350.

The experimenters conducted two studies on pitch changes in subjects' voices during attempts at deception. Male college students were subjects in the first study. In Experiment I, pairs of subjects were formed. One person played the role of an interviewer, the other an interviewee. Predetermined questions were asked by the interviewer, and the interviewee was supposed to give false responses to two of the questions. The interviewer was informed that the interviewee would be lying on two topics, but he was not told which two. Videotapes were made of the interviews. Subjects in this experiment were also "aroused" by increasing their motivation to deceive on the two topics. It was found that higher voice pitch was associated with deceptive replies. In addition, arousal or stress influenced pitch. In Experiment II, the audiotapes were shown to male and female subjects who rated the truthfulness of the responses. One tape had the semantic content unintelligible, the other did not. The results were that pitch was used as a clue to deception when semantic content was unintelligible.

435. Sweeney, D. R., Tinling, D. C., Eby, L. A., and Schmale, A. H., Jr. Factor analytic studies of four expressive modes of emotion. Proceedings of the 76th Annual Convention of the American Psychological Association, 1968, 3, 169-170.

The researchers were interested in analyzing four modes of expression and comparing their dimensional structure across verbal and nonverbal modes. Males and females of varying ages responded to the Barker Scale of Suggestibility. Twenty with high scores were used as subjects. In one of two states--relaxed-nonhypnotic and hypnotic-- the subjects were cued with an emotion word. They were asked to express the emotion facially and posturally, to draw a picture, and to give continuous free verbal association to the word. Their activity was recorded on film. Forty raters evaluated each expressive mode on the semantic differential. Results showed four factors (from a factor analysis) which were consistent across the four modes.

436. Sweeney, M. A. Nonverbal communication: A study of selected characteristics of an individual in relation to his ability to identify information about human emotional states. Dissertation Abstracts International, 1975(Oct), Vol. 36 (4-A), 2036.

The study investigated the relationship between the sex, graduate school major, linguistic interests, and psychological mindedness of 100 students in regard to their ability to identify nonverbal information about emotions. Fifteen pictures of males and 15 pictures of females expressing various emotions were used as stimuli. The pictures were grouped according to the part or parts of the body which were involved in the expression of the emotion. The results showed that female subjects were more accurate than males at identifying the pictured emotions. No significant difference was found due to the subjects' major field of study. Additionally, regardless of the sex of the subject, the emotions of female stimuli were more easily identified than those of males.

437. Tankard, J. W. Effects of eye position on person perception. Perceptual and Motor Skills, 1970, 31, 883-893.

Tankard attempted to measure awareness of the eye position changes of models by interviewing subjects immediately after they had seen the stimulus pictures. Black and white photographs of three White male and three White female models each posing in three eye positions, looking straight forward, looking off to the side, and looking down, were used as stimuli. Each subject was required to respond to the pictures separately on semantic differential scales and other questions. Results showed that the subjects' impressions of the models were influenced by changes in the position of their eyes from eye-contact to noneye-contact positions. Additionally, the amount of movement of the eye necessary to produce significant differences in ratings was small. The experimenter noted that the study also showed a larger number of differences in ratings for straight and downward comparisons than for straight and sideways comparisons.

438. Tankard, J. W. The connotative meaning of the eye contact cue to a perceiver. Dissertation Abstracts International, 1970(Oct), Vol. 31(4-B), 2330-2331.

The author asserted that there was not much previous research on what eye contact communicates to receivers. His hypothesis that eye contact would be perceived as communicating attention was supported for comparison of straight and downward gaze positions in photographs, but not for comparison of straight and sideways gaze positions among male and female subjects. The hypothesis that the downward gaze would be perceived as communicating an unpleasant affect was supported. The expected meanings of eye position for different dyads were not found. On one semantic differential scale (Pleasant-Unpleasant), models with straight gazes were seen as less pleasant than those with sideways gazes. The experimenter concluded that eye position could influence subjects' responses to persons in photographs whether or not subjects were aware they were being influenced by the eyes.

439. Thayer, S. and Schiff, W. Eye contact, facial expression, and the experience of time. Journal of Social Psychology, 1975, 95, 117-124.

Thayer and Schiff investigated the impact of eye contact
and facial expression on the experience of time. Female
college students were subjects. Only females were used
because there was evidence that they were more visually
responsive than males to variations in affective quality
of social interactions. Each subject was exposed to two
conditions and were asked to reproduce the time for these
on a masked stopwatch. In one condition the subject
waited for a particular period of time to pass. In the
other condition, which was identical in length to the
first, she was to maintain eye contact with a male or
female confederate. The confederates maintained either
a scowling-angry facial expression or a smiling-friendly
one. The results for the effects of facial expression
showed that greater time was judged for the negative expression. An interaction for sex of confederate by
facial expression showed that greater time was judged
for the female-angry situation. Other findings were
discussed as well as suggestions for further research.

440. Thayer, S. and Schiff, W. Gazing patterns and attribution of sexual involvement. Journal of Social Psychology,
1977, 101, 235-246.

Thayer and Schiff investigated how certain stimulus dimensions of eye contact related to an individual's impressions of the presence and the degree of sexual involvement between himself and the person he is observing.
Two eye-contact durations were used and the gazes were
either returned or not returned. Male and female college
students saw films of same- and opposite-sex dyads seated
across from each other in a library. The two on film
engaged in the various eye-contact patterns. The subjects were to indicate whether there was evidence of
sexual interest between the pair. Thayer and Schiff
found that longer and reciprocated eye contact was attributed to greater sexual involvement. Gaze variations
for opposite- as opposed to same-sex dyads also resulted
in attributions of sexual involvement.

441. Thompson, D. F. and Meltzer, L. Communication of emotional intent by facial expression. Journal of Abnormal and
Social Psychology, 1964, 68, 129-135.

The investigators conducted their study to determine the
ability of college students to convey their emotions to
others through facial expressions and to determine possible personality, intellectual, and demographic correlates of this ability. Fifty students were subjects.
Each subject was to communicate the emotions given to him
on cards by the experimenter to a judge who sat facing
him. The judge was to indicate the expression he felt

was being communicated from a list of 10 emotions. Scho-
lastic aptitude scores and scores from a personality inventory were obtained for each subject. The investigators
found that all of the subjects were able to communicate
the emotions to some extent but that certain emotions
produced more accuracy among the judges than others.
Finally, there were no personality correlates of communication ability.

442. Thompson, J. Development of facial expression of emotion in blind and seeing children. Archives of Psychology,
1941, 37, 264.

Thompson studied various facial expressions of emotion
among blind and sighted young children. The children
were photographed in naturally occurring situations.
Her purpose was to answer questions about the innateness
of the expressions, the effect of maturation on the expressions, and the role of social mimicry in modifying
the expressions. She found that facial activity was almost equal for both groups of subjects and that for both
the mouth was more active than the eyes in expressing the
emotions. Some other results were, for example, that for
crying, facial activity increased at the older age levels
at which it occurred for both groups. Responses showing
anger, annoyance, sadness, and sulkiness were found for
sighted children as well as for blind and deaf-blind
children. Mimicry seemed to affect expressions for the
sighted children. Various other findings were presented.

443. Thornton, G. R. The effect of wearing glasses on judgments of persons seen briefly. Journal of Applied Psychology,
1944, 28, 203-207.

Thornton partially replicated an earlier study by him
which had shown that people shown in photographs wearing
glasses were rated as more dependable, industrious, intelligent, and honest than those without glasses. In his
second study male and female college students were shown
in photographs, as well as in person, wearing or not wearing glasses. Other students rated them on six personality
traits. It was found that the results for photographs
supported the findings from the previous study. For in-
person presentations, it was found that people wearing
glasses were felt to be more intelligent and industrious
than those not wearing glasses. The differences for the
remaining four traits were not significant.

444. Thornton, G. R. The effect upon judgments of personality
traits of varying a single factor in a photograph. Journal of
Social Psychology, 1943, 18, 127-148.

Thornton conducted two experiments to determine the effects of wearing or not wearing glasses, smiling versus
appearing serious, and a light photographic print versus
a dark print on personality trait ratings. Two groups

of judges (college students) saw slides of individuals
varying in the three ways. The judges rated the individuals on six personality traits presented in an 11-point
scale. Results in terms of the average rating given each
target as a result of the variations showed that more
positive ratings were given when there were glasses, a
smile, and a darker print. The second experiment used
a different group of college student judges. They rated
the photographs twice, with the variations made. The
results were essentially the same as for the first
experiment.

445. Tofalo, R. J. Body, head and limb cues, physical distance and sex of dyad as factors in the nonverbal communication of a disposition to form or avoid forming a friendship.
Dissertation Abstracts International, 1977(Jan), Vol. 37
(7-B), 3684-3685.

The study was done to determine how certain nonverbal behaviors and sex of a dyad would interact to communicate a
desire to form or avoid a friendship. The nonverbal behaviors considered were amount of gazing, time spent sitting forward in a chair, openness or closedness of arms,
number of smiles, and number of discrete glances. Each
of these was observed at three interaction distances.
Tofalo also looked at the role of compensation toward
equilibrium and sex differences among his subjects. He
found that gaze, reclining and discrete glances differentiated the form-avoid conditions. There was no significant result for compensation to achieve equilibrium for
eye contact and distance. Lastly, sex differences were
found.

446. Tolor, A. and Salafia, W. R. The social schemata technique as a projective device. Psychological Reports, 1971,
28, 423-429.

The study evaluated the affects of experimental-induced
sets and the sex of the stimuli on the constructed space
between social stimuli when the subject organized the
figures on a field. It also examined the merits of the
free placement as compared with the replacement technique.
It was predicted that (1) when ambiguous silhouette figures were perceived as having a variety of socially ap-
proved attributes, there would be less distance between
the members of the dyad than when the same figures were
perceived to have negative characteristics; and (2) on
the basis of the greater anticipated identification of
male subjects with same-sex silhouettes, the former hypothesized differences in construction distances would
be greater for same-sex stimuli than for mixed-sex stimuli. The subjects were male college students. For the
free-placement task, subjects were asked to place figures
on a board in any way they wished. Each figure was described in one of 10 ways. For the second task each subject was asked to look at each pair of figures displayed

for five seconds. The same 10 descriptions were used.
Some of the results were that positive sets combined resulted in a closer placement than negative sets combined.
Mixed-sex stimuli were placed closer together than same-
sex figures. Analogous results were not found for the
replacement technique in that none of the main factors
was a significant source of variation. Lastly, with
opposite-sex stimuli a low-support description yielded
greater separation than a low-prestigiousness description, and the low-support description yielded greater
separation than the low-intelligence description.

447. Tomkins, S. S. and Izard, C. (Eds.). Affect, cognition, and personality. New York: Springer, 1965.

448. Tomkins, S. S. and McCarter, R. What and where are the
primary affects? Some evidence for a theory. Perceptual
and Motor Skills, 1964, 18, 119-158.

A group of firemen was shown facial photos of individuals
simulating neutral poses of the following affects: en-
joyment, distress, anger, contempt, fear, surprise, interest, and shame. The subjects met in groups of four to
six people. They were seated around a table and judged
the affects they were shown. It was found that the subjects were able to identify the affects with better than
chance accuracy. Some affects were comprised in a systematic way. Finally, individual differences in judgments were found.

449. Traweek, A. C. A comparison of two procedures for training graduate student counselors and psychotherapists in the
use of nonverbal behaviors. Dissertation Abstracts International, 1977(Apr), Vol. 37(10-B), 5384.

Traweek studied two training methods (a programmed manual
on nonverbal behavior and rating of videotaped nonverbal
behavior) and their effectiveness for increasing the
awareness and understanding of nonverbal behaviors among
graduate student trainees. Traweek found that students
trained in nonverbal behavior displayed more positive
postural, eye contact, and self-manipulative behavior
than those who were untrained. In addition, the programmed method was more effective than the videotaped
method in changing self-manipulation, eye contact, and
use of posture.

450. Valins, S. Emotionality and information concerning
internal reactions. Journal of Personality and Social Psychology, 1967, 6, 458-463.

Valins hypothesized that unemotional and emotional people
would differ in regard to their use of internal cues or
sensations as sources of information when evaluating emotional stimuli. The subjects were 1,800 male undergraduates. Emotionality was defined by Lykken's (1957)

questionnaire and the anxiety factor of the MMPI. Ten
color slides of seminude females were shown to the subjects. Simultaneously, they heard recordings of what
they thought were their own heartbeats. The subjects
heard a marked change to five of the bogus heartbeats
but not to the other five. The results confirmed the
investigator's theoretical expectations. The ratings
the subjects gave to the females were dependent upon the
bogus heartbeat and whether or not they were emotional.

451. Veeser, W. R. The development of a measure of the verbal, contextual, and nonverbal vocal components of empathy.
Dissertation Abstracts International, 1975(Jan), Vol. 35
(7-B), 3602.

Veeser developed an instrument which measured an individual's ability to be sensitive to nonverbal and verbal
cues related to empathy. College students (graduates
and undergraduates) were tested using this instrument.
Veeser found that the ability to be sensitive to nonverbal cues, which are available in the empathy process,
is independent of and unrelated to the ability to be sensitive to verbal cues. Another finding was that females
were more adept than males at picking up nonverbal cues.
Finally, graduate psychology students were better than
engineering on both the nonverbal and verbal cues.

452. Villa-Lovoz, T. R. The effects of counselor eye contact, fluency, and addressing on client preference. Dissertation Abstracts International, 1975(Oct), Vol. 36(4-A),
2038-2039.

The purpose of the study was to investigate the effects
of counselor eye contact, counselor speech fluency, and
the form of the address which was directed toward the
client by the counselor on preference for a counselor
among college students. Eight groups of subjects saw
one of eight tapes of individuals playing the role of
counselor but directing their presentation to the television viewer. Each subject was to pretend he was a
counselee. Semantic differential scales were used to
measure counselor preference. The results showed significant differences between subject groups due to the
level of eye contact, fluency, and form of address, with
the latter two producing significant interaction effects.
No differences were found between male and female
subjects.

453. vonCranach, M. The role of orienting behavior in human
interaction. In A. H. Esser (Ed.), Behavior and environment:
The use of space by animals and men. New York: Plenum
Press, 1971.

The author presented a discussion of some of the articles
concerned with the communicative value and affects of
gaze behavior on sender and receiver. The discussion

was divided into sections concerned with the gaze in interaction, the assessment of gaze components by the receiver, the function of the gaze in the behavior systems
of the receiver, and the function of the gaze in the behavior system of the sender. Some of the results of one
of these studies were that individuals have good discrimination for the line of gaze of another person with respect to whether or not they are being looked at; however,
in another study, points outside the face were misjudged
by a receiver of these glances as being directed at the
face. Results from studies reporting the correlation
between looking behavior and talking were that a subject
looked at his partner more when he was talking than when
the subject himself was talking.

454. vonCranach, M. and Vine, I. (Eds.). Social communication and movement. New York: Academic Press, 1973.

vonCranach compiled papers about nonverbal expression
and communication. The book was divided into three parts
concerning nonverbal behavior patterns, analysis of
facial expressions, and methods for analyzing nonverbal
behavior. Ten papers were included in all.

455. Wahlers, K. J. An investigation of the effects of
selected inconsistent verbal/nonverbal messages on channel
preference. Dissertation Abstracts International, 1977(Oct),
Vol. 38(4-A), 1739.

Wahlers manipulated vocal intonation, facial expression,
emblems, and illustrators in an effort to determine the
relationship between inconsistent communication and preference for a particular channel. The four categories
were manipulated on two videotapes. Wahlers found that
with inconsistent vocal intonation and verbal communication, the verbal channel was not relied upon less often
to infer intended meaning as had been expected. This
finding was in contradiction to other research, and
Wahlers suggested it may have been due to methodological problems. Another finding was that when facial expressions and verbal behavior conflicted, facial expressions were relied upon more to infer meaning. Various
other significant results were determined for hand
gestures and eye behavior.

456. Walker, D. Openness to touching: A study of strangers
in nonverbal interaction. Dissertation Abstracts International, 1971(Jul), Vol. 32(1-B), 574.

Walker assessed the effect of nonverbal touching activities used in encounter groups and developed a measure of
openness to touching which would allow the exploration
of the relationship between the ideas of the Third Force
writers and empirical data. It was found that, as predicted, males in male-male groups were least open in the
touching interaction. Females in female-female groups

were most open. Pre- and posttest scores indicated that nonverbal touching was a very threatening task and made the subjects anxious and uncomfortable. Suggestions for further research pertaining to encounter groups were made.

457. Walster, E., Aronson, E., and Abrahams, P. On increasing the persuasiveness of a low prestige communicator. Journal of Experimental Social Psychology, 1966, 2, 325-342.

458. Ward, C. D. Seating arrangement and leadership emergence in small discussion groups. Journal of Social Psychology, 1968, 74, 83-90.

Ward determined to provide further evidence relating to the possible relationship between seating arrangement, interaction, and leadership emergence in a small group. Male college students served in 24 five-man discussion groups. The seating arrangement was circular, and evenly spaced around the circle's circumference were eight chairs on each of which was a small writing arm. Three members of each group always sat adjacent to each other, with the other two members opposite them. As the subjects arrived for the session, they were assigned a seat by means of a card drawn from a lottery table. At the beginning of each session the subjects filled out a questionnaire and read a case history which they were to discuss. Results showed that individuals facing the largest number of members did the most talking and were the most likely to be judged as leaders of the groups.

459. Watson, S. G. Judgment of emotion from facial and contextual cue combinations. Journal of Personality and Social Psychology, 1972, 24, 334-342.

The study was done to examine the relationship between verbal context and facial expression in the judgment of emotion. Watson hoped to demonstrate that the clarity of the source, distinct source-associated emotions, and concordant and discordant pairing of emotion sources would be important variables for judging cue combinations. One hundred and seventy-two college students were used as subjects. The faces of two males expressing various emotions (including neutral expressions) were used as stimuli in addition to various statements explaining the situational context of the stimulus. Watson found that the subjects responded to facial cues when faces and statements of equal clarity were paired contradicting three of her predictions. A fourth hypothesis, predicting that when the stated context was neutral or ambiguous and the face showed a clear affect, the facial cue was selected most often, was supported.

460. Waxer, P. H. Nonverbal cues for anxiety: An examination of emotional leakage. Journal of Abnormal Psychology, 1977, 86, 306-314.

Waxer was interested in determining the nonverbal cues
which identify anxiety. Raters looked at videotapes of
interviews with patients at a psychiatric hospital. They
rated the patients on a scale containing questions about
nonverbal cues. The cue areas were forehead, eyebrows,
eyelids, eyes, angle of head, mouth, hands, arm position,
shoulder position, and torso position. There was a significant relationship between the results of the cue ratings and responses on the A-State Scale of the State-
Trait Anxiety Inventory and the Present Affect Reactions
Questionnaire. Differences were found in terms of the
nonverbal behaviors for high- and low-anxious patients
and also between the various behaviors. Examples of the
differences were discussed.

461. Waxwood, V. C. Intercultural and intracultural communication: A study of relationship cues in an interpersonal
setting. Dissertation Abstracts International, 1976(Nov),
Vol. 37(5-A), 2501.

Waxwood wanted to determine how people from five cultures
defined and interpreted nonverbal and verbal behaviors
which constituted acceptance or rejection. Fifteen subjects were used. Each interacted in a situation with
two members of her own culture and in a situation with
two members of other cultures. The discussions were
videotaped. The subjects were interviewed during which
time they defined what they perceived were cues of acceptance and rejection. In general, the subjects defined
cues similarly in both situations. Waxwood noted that
the study was limited by the number of subjects but suggested that the results indicated how a communicator in
an intercultural setting may become aware of rejection
cues and may communicate acceptance.

462. Webb, W. W., Matheny, A., and Larson, G. Eye movements
as a paradign of approach and avoidance behavior. Perceptual
and Motor Skills, 1963, 16, 341-347.

In three exploratory studies with normal and schizophrenic
subjects, eye movements were recorded while they looked
at items consisting of four horizontally arranged pictures. The pictures were small line drawings. The pictures on each end were presumed to be affectively (positively or negatively) important, while those in the middle
were neutral. An approach-avoidance gradient of behavior
was suggested for the time spent looking in that, in general, more time was spent in looking at the neutral pictures than at the affectively charged pictures.

463. Weber, J. W. The effects of physical proximity and body
boundary size on the self-disclosure interview. Dissertation
Abstracts International, 1973(Jan), Vol. 33(7-B), 3327.

Weber conducted her study to determine how self-disclosure
is influenced by an individual's body boundary size,

physical proximity with another during an interview, and the interaction of these two factors. Forty-eight female high school students were subjects. Large and small body boundary subjects (as determined by an approach technique) were included in the study. Three interview distance conditions were used: close, normal, and distant. An interview was conducted during which the confederate interviewer maintained eye contact during the subject's responses but did not respond to the subject. Following the interview, the subjects filled out questionnaires concerning their reactions to the interview and the interviewer. Results showed no significant effects for body boundary size, distance, or their interaction. Further analysis showed that fewer words were spoken during the distant interview. Responses on the questionnaire indicated that subjects were less comfortable in the distant condition than in the others. Explanations for the lack of significant findings were given.

464. Weinstein, J., Averill, J. R., Opton, E. M., Jr., and Lazarus, R. S. Defensive style and discrepancy between self-report and physiological indexes of stress. Journal of Personality and Social Psychology, 1968, 10, 406-413.

The experimenters investigated the influences of defense styles on the discrepancies between self-report and autonomic measures of stress in re-analyzing six experiments. Defense styles were measured by various paper-and-pencil measures and stress was induced by a film about puberty rites among an Australian aborigine tribe. Physiological measures were used to determine the levels of the stress responses. The results of the re-analyses showed that the defensive disposition of the subject must be taken into account when considering self-reported emotions. It is not enough to consider the physiological and self-report indexes.

465. Weinstein, L. Social experience and social schemata. Journal of Personality and Social Psychology, 1967, 6, 429-434.

It was hypothesized that acceptance by parents and peers would be associated with positive social schemata as measured by Kuethe's felt figure-placement technique. Elementary school boys were asked to reproduce accurately from memory distances between pairs of figures. Those who underestimated distances between human pairs felt more accepted by their parents. Similar relationships were perceived or actual acceptance by classmates did not hold. An additional finding that first borns are more attracted than later borns to children having positive schemata suggested that attributes of the chooser may interact with schema of the chosen in determining sociometric choice.

466. Weinstein, L. The mother-child schema, anxiety, and academic achievement in elementary school boys. Child Development, 1968, 39, 257-263.

Weinstein investigated the mother-child schema held by White fourth- and fifth-grade boys using Kuethe's figure-placement technique. Each subject was tested individually and was asked to place two pairs of felt figures any way they wished. One pair was of an adult female and a male child, and the other was of an adult male and a male child. Each group was given an anxiety measure about one week after the figure-placement task, and academic achievement scores were obtained for each subject. As hypothesized, the correlation between the mother-child schema and anxiety was negative, but reached significance for the fifth-grade boys. However, the mother-child schemata were positive and significantly related to achievement test scores for both groups. Another hypothesis, which had predicted that the relationship between the mother-child schema and achievement would be eliminated if anxiety were held constant, was not supported.

467. Weitz, S. (Ed.). Nonverbal communication: Readings with commentary. New York: Oxford University Press, 1974.

Weitz asserted that research on nonverbal communication was and will continue to be an integral part of social psychological theories about person perception, emotional expression, and interpersonal communication. He edited 22 articles on various aspects of nonverbal expression. Some of the broad topics covered included spatial behavior, gestures and body movements, paralanguage, and visual behavior and facial expressions.

468. Welkowitz, J. and Kuc, M. Interrelationships among warmth, genuineness, empathy, and temporal speech patterns in interpersonal interaction. Journal of Consulting and Clinical Psychology, 1973, 41, 472-473.

The investigators wanted to examine interrelationships among ratings of empathy, genuineness, and warmth by conversation of partners and independent observers. Thirty-two male and 32 female college students were subjects. They were put into same-sex dyads and their unrestricted conversations were taped. Later, each member of the pair rated the other on the three traits. Independent observers also made these ratings. Three vocal parameters were analyzed: average duration of pauses, switching pauses, and vocalizations. The investigators found that none of the correlations between the subjects' ratings and those of the observers was significant. However, they did find that switching pauses (defined in the article) related significantly to ratings of warmth by the observers. Implications of the results for psychotherapy were presented.

469. Westie, F. R. and DeFleur, M. L. Autonomic responses and their relationship to racial attitudes. Journal of Abnormal and Social Psychology, 1959, 58, 340-347.

Westie and DeFleur wanted to determine whether or not autonomic responses were associated with exposure to objects for which people have scale-measured attitudes. White college students were chosen as subjects based upon their responses on an attitude scale. One-half of the subjects were categorized as prejudiced, the other half as unprejudiced. Galvanic skin response and finger pulse volume were measured for each subject as he watched slides showing Blacks and Whites in various settings. A post-experimental interview was also conducted. Prejudiced males and females gave smaller finger pulse volumes to slides of Blacks than to slides of Whites. Unprejudiced males and females showed a higher level of finger pulse activity toward slides of Blacks. The responses, however, were complicated by different levels of activity occurring within sex of subject. For GSRs, greater levels were determined for slides of Blacks by the prejudiced subjects than by the unprejudiced subjects. Further results were reported.

470. White, M. J. Interpersonal distance as affected by room size, status, and sex. Journal of Social Psychology, 1975, 95, 241-249.

White investigated the relation between room size and interpersonal distance during a seated conversation. He also examined the effects of sex and status of the speakers on interpersonal distance. The subjects were college students. They were required to meet with one of 12 confederates who was defined as a student or as a nationally known research professor in the area of student attitudes. The subjects' placement of a seat in relation to the confederate was noted. Interpersonal distance was measured by the horizontal nose-to-nose distance between the subject and confederate. The results showed that the size of the room affected interpersonal distance such that distances in the large room were shorter than those in the small room. White also found that subjects sat much farther from the unequal-status female confederate than from the equal-status female; however, they sat closer to the unequal-status male confederate than to the equal-status male. Personality differences between the male and female unequal-status confederates were suggested as explanations. Lastly, sex of confederate was not a significant main effect.

471. Wiener, M., Devoe, S., Rubinow, S., and Geller, J. Nonverbal behavior and nonverbal communication. Psychological Review, 1972, 79, 185-214.

Wiener et al. presented a discussion of some of the conceptual approaches used in studying nonverbal behavior.

They also discussed and reemphasized a conceptual distinction between nonverbal behaviors which could be called
communications and other nonverbal behaviors. Finally,
they proposed an approach to studying nonverbal behavior
as communication which emphasized encoding rather than
decoding. They hoped their proposal would prompt other
researchers to suggest alternatives to the study of the
phenomenon.

472. Willett, T. H. A descriptive analysis of nonverbal behaviors of college teachers. Dissertation Abstracts International, 1977(Aug), Vol. 38(2-A), 742.

Willett wanted to determine the relationship between the
general level of a teacher's nonverbal activity and his
or her effectiveness and the relationship between specific
nonverbal moves and teaching effectiveness. Ten college
level teachers were subjects. Five were classified as
effective teachers and five as average teachers by a student rating procedure. Student impressions of the teachers' nonverbal behaviors as well as videotapes of their
activity were used. Willett found through factor analysis that five factors described the teachers. The two
groups of teachers were dissimilar on all but two factors,
according to an analysis of variance. Willett also compared the teachers' own evaluations of their nonverbal
behavior with the students' evaluations and found differences. Effective teachers evaluated themselves more
positively and average teachers evaluated themselves less
positively than did the students. The two groups of
teachers were also found to differ in the types of nonverbal behaviors in which they engaged.

473. Williams, E. Effects of intergroup discussion on social
distance and personal space of Black and White students.
Dissertation Abstracts International, 1973(Mar), Vol. 33
(9-A), 4959.

Williams investigated the effects of participation in a
group discussion program about social distance and personal space on racial attitudes. Black and White males
and females were subjects. All of the subjects were
given a racial attitude measure which contained a social
distance questionnaire and a personal space projective
test. Control subjects did not participate in the six-
week discussion group. A retest of all subjects was made
using the racial attitude measure. Results showed changes
in the experimental subjects who had initially scored low
on the social distance measure and high on the personal
space measure. Suggestions for the use of such programs
with schools were discussed.

474. Williams, E. Experimental comparisons of face-to-face
and mediated communication: A review. Psychological Bulletin, 1977, 84, 963-976.

Williams reviewed a number of studies on the affects of the telecommunications media on human communication. He divided the studies into groups based upon the type of task used, the type of setting, and those studies concerned with interpersonal perception. Williams pointed out that because of the research that has been done, it is possible to test theories of mediated communication and to advance the understanding of nonverbal communication.

475. Williams, J. L. Personal space and its relation to extraversion-introversion. In R. Sommer (Ed.), Personal space: The behavioral basis of design. Englewood Cliffs, N. J.: Prentice-Hall, 1969.

In an attempt to determine how different people would react to excessive closeness, Williams classified students as introverts or extroverts on the basis of their scores on a personality test. He put each subject in an experimental room and then walked toward him telling him to speak out as soon as he came too close. Later, Williams used the reverse condition, beginning at a point very close and moving away until the subject reported that he was too far away for comfortable conversation. The results showed that introverts kept him at a greater conversational distance than extroverts.

476. Willis, F. N., Jr. Initial speaking distance as a function of the speaker's relationship. Psychonomic Science, 1966, 5, 221-222.

An incidental sample of 755 subjects from homes, places of business, and halls in a university were studied. Initial speaking distance was measured in inches and recorded at the moment the conversation began between the experimenter and the subject. The relationships were categorized as stranger, acquaintance, friend, close friend (same sex or dates, spouses and fiancées), age groups older than the experimenter, age groups younger than the experimenter, and peers. Distances were then related to the relationship between the individuals and to their sex, age, and race. It was found that women experimenters were approached more closely than male experimenters. Women were found to stand closer to close friends than to friends. Men approached closer when they were friends and slightly less for close friends. Peers stood closer than persons older than the experimenter. Strangers began conversations at farther distances than acquaintances. There was some evidence that both Blacks and Whites tended to stand farther from Blacks than from Whites. And, surprisingly, parents who were expected to approach their own children in a manner similar to the approach of the children's friends approached according to the distance used by strangers.

477. Wolfgang, J. and Wolfgang, A. Personal space: An unobtrusive measure of attitudes toward the physically handicapped. Proceedings of the 76th Annual Convention of the
American Psychological Association, 1968, 3, 653-654.

The purpose of the study was to examine the attitudes of
normal individuals toward physically handicapped individuals using physical interaction distance as a measure.
Male and female college students were subjects. The subjects were asked to draw a figure representing themselves
in relation to five figures presented in test booklets.
They were requested to draw the figure at a distance from
the other person which was comfortable. The other figures were described as people whose names they knew but
who were not their very close friends. Some of the results were that normal subjects maintained a greater distance from the handicapped person than from other normal
persons. The distance between the figures was a function
of the handicap of the object figure. Lastly, males
placed themselves closer to females than other males,
while females made no such differentiation.

478. Wood, B. S. Children and communication: Verbal and
nonverbal language development. Englewood Cliffs, N. J.:
Prentice-Hall, 1976.

Wood's book took a broad look at how children learn to
communicate with words, body language, voice, and touch.
Her book is divided into four parts and 15 chapters.
Part I concerned the forces that affect communication
development. Part II discussed the development of words,
sentences, and meanings. Part III concerned how children communicate nonverbally. Finally, Part IV presented
a model suggesting how communication strategies can be
used by children to deal with critical communication
situations.

479. Woodard, A. W. The relationship between perceived nonverbal behavior of principals and organizational climate of
elementary schools. Dissertation Abstracts International,
1975(Apr), Vol. 35(10-A), 6420-6421.

Woodard investigated whether or not there was a relationship between perceived congruence of nonverbal and
verbal behavior of a principal and organizational climate.
Two measures were used: the Nonverbal Reaction Sheet and
the Organizational Climate Description. Four hundred and
fourteen teachers and 20 principals from elementary
schools in Oklahoma County were used. Woodard found
that in schools where a principal's verbal and nonverbal
behaviors were congruent, the organizational climate was
more open. Another finding was the relationship between
a principal's age and years of experience in education
and the congruency between his nonverbal and verbal behaviors. Other results were also reported.

480. Woolfolk, A. E., Garlinsky, K. S., and Nicolich, M. J.
The impact of teacher behavior, teacher sex, and student sex
upon student self-disclosure. Contemporary Educational Psychology, 1977, 2, 124-132.

Two male and two female teachers varied verbal and nonverbal evaluative behaviors during a vocabulary lesson
with sixth graders. Various combinations of positive
and negative verbal and nonverbal behaviors were employed.
The results showed that the verbal behavior influenced
self-disclosure in that positive verbal evaluations elicited more disclosure. Nonverbal behavior interacted with
the sex of the subject to influence self-disclosure.
(Summary of abstract reference.)

481. Word, C. O., Zanna, M. P., and Cooper, J. The nonverbal
mediation of self-fulfilling prophecies in interracial interaction. Journal of Experimental Social Psychology, 1974, 10,
109-120.

Two experiments were designed to demonstrate the existence
of a self-fulfilling prophecy mediated by nonverbal behavior in an interracial interaction. The results of
Experiment I, which used naive White job interviewers
and trained White and Black job applicants, demonstrated
that Black applicants received less immediacy, higher
rates of speech errors, and shorter amounts of interview
time. Experiment II used naive White applicants and
trained White interviewers. In this experiment, subject
applicants received behavior that approximated that given
either the Black or White applicants in Experiment I.
The main results indicated that subjects treated like
the Blacks of Experiment I were judged to perform less
adequately and to be more nervous in the interview situation than subjects treated like the Whites of that experiment. The former subjects also reciprocated with
less proximate positions and rated the interviewers as
being less adequate and friendly. All of this behavior
was recorded by two judges placed behind one-way mirrors.

482. Young, D. M. Nonverbal communication in the employment
interview: Creating the climate to hire. Dissertation Abstracts International, 1977(Jan), Vol. 37(7-B), 3639.

Young suggested that the amount of eye contact, smiling,
and head movement would influence hiring responses among
judges observing films of simulated employment interviews.
He also hypothesized that attractiveness would influence
hiring decisions. Female college students were subjects.
Attractiveness was determined by having each applicant
videotaped while reading a standardized simple sentence.
The subjects were then randomly assigned to one of four
nonverbal cue conditions. They were given instructions
concerning how to use the nonverbal behaviors. Subse-
quently, they were videotaped as they role played an
interview. Young found that all of the nonverbal

behaviors influenced hiring. Young suggested that training situations for nonverbal behavior may be helpful in
regard to creating a favorable environment for hiring.

483. Zaidel, S. F. and Mehrabian, A. The ability to communicate and infer positive and negative attitudes facially and
vocally. Journal of Experimental Research in Personality,
1969, 3, 233-241.

Zaidel and Mehrabian were concerned with the relationships between encoding and decoding abilities in the
facial and vocal systems of individuals differing in
approval-seeking tendencies. Four hypotheses were presented. They conducted two experiments. The subjects
were male and female college students. They were tested
individually and for two sessions, one week apart. Six
photographs of facial expressions of males and females
which had been judged to express strong, positive, neutral, or strong negative attitudes were used as stimuli.
Six vocal communications were also used in Experiment I.
Twelve subjects were required to act as encoders and decoders of vocal and facial communications. These subjects were divided according to whether or not they were
high or low on social desirability according to a social
desirability scale. In Experiment II, the subjects were
divided into high and low groups and were exposed to the
encoded communications of the 12 subjects in the first
experiment. Some of the results were that there was no
significant correlation between encoding and decoding
abilities (for vocal and facial channels) in Experiment
I. Data from Experiment II showed that there was greater
variability in attitudes expressed facially than vocally.
Finally, low social approval-seeking encoders communicated
a more discriminable set of attitudes than did high social
approval-seeking encoders as was predicted.

484. Zamora, G. A comparison of the nonverbal communication
patterns of bilingual early childhood teachers. Dissertation
Abstracts International, 1975(Feb), Vol. 35(8-A), 5208.

Zamora conducted the study to compare the nonverbal behaviors of teachers on a Spanish-English program. Early
childhood teachers and teaching assistants were subjects.
The nonverbal behaviors of the subjects were recorded during two lessons in each language. A significant difference was found between the behavior of teachers and teacher assistants. One difference was the use of more positive behavior by teachers and more negative behavior by
assistants. Another finding was that teachers with more
experience used more positive touching and fewer "void"
behaviors than less experienced teachers. The comparison
by age of subject and preferred language of instruction
did not produce a significant interaction. Finally, none
of the four trials (Spanish and English instruction) produced statistically significant differences.

485. Zuckerman, M., DeFrank, R. S., Hall, J. A., and Rosenthal, R. Encoding and decoding of spontaneous and posed facial expressions. Journal of Personality and Social Psychology, 1976, 34, 966-977.

The study was done to investigate the relationship between an individual's posed and spontaneous nonverbal cues. The transmission of posed cues was compared with the transmission of spontaneous cues, and the decoding or interpretation of posed versus spontaneous cues was compared. In addition, the investigators examined the relationship between transmitting and interpreting abilities among their subjects as a function of sex and certain other characteristics. Thirty male and 30 female undergraduates were subjects. Two male experimenters conducted the study. The subjects were shown videotapes to which they were to respond, and an experimenter took pictures of their expressions. Some of the findings were that there was a higher level of accuracy for posed expressions than spontaneous ones. Additionally, females were more accurate decoders than males; however, they were not more accurate encoders than were males.

2

Studies with Psychiatric Subjects

486. Barbizet, J. Yawning. Journal of Neurology, Neuro-
surgery and Psychiatry, 1958, 21, 203-209.

   Barbizet discussed the physiological, pathological, and
   psychosocial aspects of yawning. In relation to the
   psychosocial aspect, he noted that it indicates a lack
   of interest and boredom. Beginning as an involuntary
   response, it can, however, be modified such that it takes
   on social connotations. He also noted that imitative
   yawning may be an indication of a suggestible individual
   who is psychologically irresponsible.

487. Blondis, M. N. and Jackson, B. E. Nonverbal communication with patients: Back to the human touch. New York:
John Wiley & Sons, 1977.

   Blondis and Jackson wrote a book about nonverbal communication to help nurses understand the importance of this
   phenomenon in dealing with patients. The book was divided
   into nine chapters and discussed the role of nonverbal
   communication in dealing with various types of patient
   situations from pediatrics to geriatrics.

488. Blumenthal, R. and Meltzoff, J. Social schemas and perceptual accuracy in schizophrenia. British Journal of Social
and Clinical Psychology, 1967, 6, 119-128.

   Thirty schizophrenic and 30 normal males estimated distances between 18 pairs of cutout figures representing
   neutral and hostile relationships and control rectangles
   at three different intervals under immediate and delay
   conditions. Schizophrenics were less accurate than normals. All subjects were less accurate under delay, but
   schizophrenics were more so. All subjects overestimated
   small intervals and underestimated large intervals, and
   delay enhanced this effect. The psychological deficit

characteristic of schizophrenics and such psychophysical determinants as interval length and delay in judgments were said to account for these results.

489. Booraem, C. D. and Flowers, J. V. Reduction of anxiety and personal space as a function of assertion training with severely disturbed neuropsychiatric inpatients. Psychological Reports, 1972, 30, 923-929.

The authors evaluated a modification of assertion training designed to be effective with severely disturbed neuropsychiatric patients and related changes in assertiveness to changes in person perception as indicated by the measurement of personal space. A matched group was compared on personal space and the Spielberger Self-Evaluation Questionnaire. Personal space was measured according to an approach technique with the confederate approaching from eight different directions. The subject was to signal the confederate when to stop. Subjects in the experimental group were given assertion training (positive and negative) by two male therapists. None of the control subjects participated in any kind of therapy. Results showed that assertion training, besides contribution to early release of subjects within the experimental group, also decreased their self-reported anxiety as well as personal space measures. The members of the control group showed no such decreases.

490. Bosanquet, C. Getting in touch. Journal of Analytical Psychology, 1970, 15, 42-48.

Bosanquet discussed the use of tactile communication in the analytical setting. She suggested that when the classical analytical technique is relaxed, touching can be used to promote the process. She also noted that touching should be stopped when the oedipal stage is reached and when the classical technique is resumed. Her paper also discussed the role of touching in regression, early development, and society in general. Bosanquet presented a case history to shed light on her remarks about touching during psychoanalysis.

491. Deutsch, F. Analysis of postural behavior. Psychoanalytic Quarterly, 1947, 16, 195-213.

Deutsch discussed various clinical examples of the behaviors and postures assumed by patients during therapeutic interviews. He reviewed works by other researchers which noted that these behaviors generally reflect underlying emotions or attitude states. Deutsch noted that every individual has a characteristic basic posture which he displays at rest and to which he returns whenever he deviates from it. He also suggested that observation of these behaviors could supply the therapist with additional information about the dynamics of the patient's problem.

492. Dittes, J. Galvanic skin response as a measure of patient's reaction to therapist's permissiveness. _Journal of Abnormal and Social Psychology_, 1957, 55, 295-303.

   Dittes measured the frequency of a patient's galvanic skin response while interacting with his therapist. He found that the response was inversely related to the judged permissiveness of the therapist during 42 hours of therapy. Dittes offered other interpretations of the relationship between the patient's GSR and the therapist's permissiveness. One explanation was that the therapist's manner and the GSR are both the consequences of some aspect of the patient's behavior. Other alternative interpretations were discussed.

493. Dittmann, A. T. The relationship between body movements and moods in interviews. _Journal of Consulting Psychology_, 1962, 26, 480.

   Dittmann studied three body areas (head, legs, and hands) within five moods in one patient. Parts of interviews which were recorded by videotape were used. He found that frequency of movements differentiated the moods reliably. For instance, when angry, the patient engaged in more head and leg movements, but few hand movements. However, during a depressed mood, there were few movements of the head and hands but many leg movements. Dittmann noted that Luria's (1932) theory of random overflow of energy across motor systems could not account for the patterns of movement found in his patient. He suggested Lacey's (1959) model of the interrelationships among patterns of autonomic responses of different modalities among different individuals might serve as a starting point.

494. Downing, R. W. and Rickels, K. Handwriting size and self-reported hostility in drug-treated neurotic outpatients: Comparison of completers and dropouts. _Perceptual and Motor Skills_, 1969, 28, 401-402.

   The investigators measured the handwriting size of 48 mildly anxious neurotic outpatients. They were also tested on the Buss-Durkee Hostility Inventory. Twenty-four of the patients had dropped out of the program by the end of treatment. The investigators found that completers and dropouts did not differ in mean handwriting size and in their mean hostility scores. A within-group showed that for the dropout group higher hostility was associated with smaller handwriting. The investigators noted that their findings give partial support to the idea that conflict about hostility expression may be reflected in the psychomotor control governing handwriting size in the present neurotic subjects.

495. Duke, M. P. and Mullens, M. C. Preferred interpersonal distance as a function of locus of control orientation in

schizophrenics, nonschizophrenic patients, and normals. Journal of Consulting and Clinical Psychology, 1973, 41, 230-234.

The investigators predicted that schizophrenics would prefer greater distances than normals. Forty female White patients diagnosed as chronic schizophrenic or as having affective disorders were subjects. Twenty female employees of a mental institution were controls. The measurement technique involved having the individuals indicate (by a mark) their own preferred interpersonal distance from various stimuli presented on a schematic representation of an imaginary round room with eight doors. It was found that schizophrenics preferred greater distances than the other group of subjects. A discussion of the concept of locus of control in normals and schizophrenics and its relation to personal space was also presented.

496. Esser, A. H., Amparo, S., Chamberlain, R. N., Chappel, E. D., and Kline, N. S. Territoriality of patients on a research ward. Recent Advances in Biological Psychiatry, 1964, 7, 37-44.

The authors examined schizophrenic patients' spatial relations (territoriality) and the establishment of dominance positions on a psychiatric ward. The importance of the findings in animal ecology for the study of institutionalized groups was discussed.

497. Fisher, R. L. Social schema of normal and disturbed school children. Journal of Educational Psychology, 1967, 58, 88-92.

Fisher conducted three studies to measure the social schema of normal White male and female elementary school children and White male elementary school children who were unable to adjust to the regular class structure. She used an adaptation of Kuethe's (1962) measure of social distance and required the children glue yellow cutout figures on sheets of paper. Group administration of the task was used. Two figures at a time were to be glued to each of eight sheets of paper. The distances between the figures were measured. Fisher found that normal boys placed the figures closer together than did the disturbed boys. There was no significant difference between figure distances for normal boys and girls. The investigator found, however, that there was a significant difference between the distances for normal girls and disturbed boys. In Studies II and III she found a relationship between mother hostility and schema distance for the disturbed boys, and that her version and Kuethe's (1962) original version seemed to tap similar dimensions, respectively.

498. Gardner, J. M. Indicators of homosexuality in the human figure drawings of heroin- and pill-using addicts. Perceptual and Motor Skills, 1969, 28, 705-706.

Gardner replicated and extended a study done by Kurtzberg et al. (1966). He wanted to determine whether or not adult male drug addicts at an out-patient center responded similarly to the subjects used in the previous study. The present subjects were divided into a heroin-using group and a pill-using group. He found that the heroin-using subjects drew a male figure first in 94% of the cases. The pill-using subjects did so in 87% of the cases. These findings were contradictory to those of the previous study. Another result was that pill users drew larger female figures than did heroin users. Additionally, pill users drew larger female than male figures. Finally, there was no significant difference between the size of the male figure for the two groups.

499. Garfinkel, H. Studies of the routine grounds of every-day activities. Social Problems, 1964, 11, 225-250.

500. Gerber, G. L. Psychological distance in the family as schematized by families of normal, disturbed, and learning-problem children. Journal of Consulting and Clinical Psychology, 1973, 40, 139-147.

A doll-placement technique was used to study psychological distance within families with a disturbed and a normal boy. Parents and the two children performed the task individually and as a group. As was hypothesized, boys who were emotionally disturbed and those with serious learning problems placed a greater distance between the doll representing the mother and the one representing themselves than did normal boys, with negative story themes. Among other results, female siblings of disturbed boys placed a greater distance between the father doll and female child doll than did female siblings of normal boys, with negative story themes. Similar differences were found when the family performed the tasks. All groups of families schematized the family as close with positive stories. Because of the unexpected female sibling finding, further research to investigate this occurrence was suggested.

501. Gladman, A. E. The role of non-verbal communication in the development and treatment of emotional illness. Psychosomatics, 1971, 12, 107-110.

Gladman discussed the influence of nonverbal communication on the development of emotional illness and also how it could be used in its treatment. He suggested that in treating patients, nonverbal communication or a positive environment may be as important as the particular choice of treatment itself.

502. Goodman, J., Downing, R. W., and Rickels, K. Temporal change in handwriting expansiveness in depressed and schizo-phrenic patients. Journal of Nervous and Mental Disease, 1964, 139, 53-61.

The researchers were interested in changes in handwriting size over time and with drug treatment. Samples of handwriting from hospitalized depressives and schizophrenics as well as normal controls were observed over a six-week period. Results showed that the three groups differed significantly in the way their handwriting changed over time. The patient groups used larger writing in the pretreatment condition than the control group. The schizophrenic group decreased in area of page usage over the six weeks, while the depressive group increased in area. Finally, the mean areas used by normal subjects and by depressives drew further apart with time, while the schizophrenics showed decreases in mean area and did not differ significantly from the normal subjects with regard to mean area by the time of the third week measurement.

503. Gottschalk, L. A. and Auerbach, A. H. (Eds.). Methods of Research in Psychotherapy. New York: Appleton-Century-Crofts, 1966.

504. Grant, E. C. An ethological description of non-verbal behavior during interviews. British Journal of Medical Psychology, 1968, 41, 177-184.

Grant's basic hypothesis was that the overt behavior which is displayed during social situations is related to the emotional state of the individual displaying the behavior. To test this hypothesis he did a sequential analysis of the ongoing behavior of three groups of subjects. One group consisted of female adults from the chronic wards of a hospital. They were observed during individual interviews with a doctor. The second group consisted of nonpsychotic female adults from a hospital ward. They were observed during individual or group psychotherapeutic interviews. The final group consisted of male and female theology students who were observed during group discussions within a teaching setting. Thirty behavior elements were recorded. They were placed into four groupings. The results showed that there were differences between the seriously ill subjects and the others in how they used behaviors from what was labeled the "Flight" group. Grant also found that there was a higher degree of predictability of behavior within the patient groups.

505. Hayes, C. S. and Koch, R. Interpersonal distance behavior of mentally retarded and nonretarded children. American Journal of Mental Deficiency, 1977, 82, 207-209.

Hayes and Koch examined and compared the interpersonal distance choices of mildly retarded and nonretarded Black and White children. Each child was required to approach an experimenter or a wall until the distance was uncomfortable. A third condition consisted of the experimenter approaching the child. The researchers found that

interpersonal distance was less for Black children than
for White children, specifically when the subject approached the experimenter. When the subjects approached
the experimenter, the difference between the retarded
and nonretarded groups was minimal. However, retarded
children maintained greater distances than nonretarded
children when the experimenter approached them. A race
by sex interaction showed that greater distances were
used by White females than White males. A reversed
trend was found for Black subjects.

506. Hayes, C. S. and Siders, C. Projective assessment of
personal space among retarded and nonretarded children.
American Journal of Mental Deficiency, 1977, 82, 72-78.

Hayes and Siders investigated the use of personal space
among mildly retarded and nonretarded Black and White
children using a projective technique. Three trials of
figure placement were used. Ten placement situations
were given to each subject who was interviewed individually by a female experimenter. Teachers also rated the
children on independence, sociability, friendships, relationship with the teacher, and degree of teacher recognition sought for classroom activity participation. Some
of the results were that interfigure distance was the
smallest for positive (friend, for example) categories,
and greatest for the negative (mean, for example) categories. Figures representing the self were placed closer
to the "smart" figure than to the "not smart" figure.
Results for various interactions and the teacher ratings
were also discussed.

507. Holahan, C. Seating patterns and patient behavior in
an experimental dayroom. Journal of Abnormal Psychology,
1972, 80(2), 115-124.

The study examined the affects of specific and controlled
manipulations in seating patterns on the behavior of psychiatric patients in an experimental hospital dayroom.
The seating patterns were varied from structured sociopetal, sociofugal, and mixed arrangements to an unstructured setting in which the patients arranged seating
themselves. It was found that seating pattern exerted
a powerful influence over the amount of quality of social
interaction among patients. Sociopetal and mixed arrangements produced a greater amount of social interaction and
more personal interaction than the sociofugal and unstructured arrangements. In contrast, seating arrangements
had no affect on nonsocial activity. Finally, an unexpected finding was that patients preferred sociopetal
seating arrangements to sociofugal ones.

508. Horowitz, M. J. Spatial behavior and psychopathology.
Journal of Nervous and Mental Diseases, 1968, 146, 24-35.

Horowitz compared 30 women patients in the schizophrenic,
depressive, or neurotic gross categories concerning their

approach to an object person at such a distance that a
closer point would have made them uncomfortable. Trails
early in their hospitalization were compared with those
just before discharge. Results supported the hypothesis
that schizophrenic patients preserve unusually great space
between themselves and others during the acute stage of
their illness.

509. Hutt, C. and Ounstead, C. The biological significance
of gaze aversion with particular reference to the syndrome
of infantile autism. Behavioral Science, 1966, 11, 346-356.

Gaze aversion by autistic children seemed to have the
function of inhibiting aggression on the part of others.
Happy model faces were encountered least frequently,
blank and animal faces more frequently, and environmental
stimuli (light switches, taps, windows) most frequently
by these children. Additionally, normal subjects visually
inspected the faces, while autistic subjects did not usually inspect. However, they did inspect environmental
stimuli.

510. Kendall, P. C., Deardorff, P. A., Finch, A. J., Jr., and
Graham, L. Proxemics, locus of control, anxiety, and type
of movement in emotionally disturbed and normal boys. Journal of Abnormal Child Psychology, 1976, 4, 9-16.

The study was done to determine the interpersonal distance requirements of emotionally disturbed and normal
children. It also investigated the relationship between
locus of control and anxiety to interpersonal space.
Twenty normal and 20 emotionally disturbed boys were
subjects. Each subject was required to approach a nine-
year-old White male and to allow him to approach each of
them until it felt uncomfortable. It was found that the
emotionally disturbed boys required more personal space
than the normal boys. In regard to locus of control, it
was found that externals required more space than inter-
nals. Finally, no effects were found for anxiety and
interpersonal distancing. The authors suggested that
the effects of personal space on emotionally disturbed
children should be considered when planning clinical
facilities.

511. Kurtz, P. D., Harrison, M., Neisworth, J. T., and Jones,
R. T. Influence of 'mentally retarded' label on teachers'
nonverbal behavior toward preschool children. American Journal of Mental Deficiency, 1977, 82, 204-206.

Kurtz et al. investigated the effect of labeling a young
child mentally retarded on the nonverbal behavior male
and female student teachers. Preschool boys and girls
were targets. All were actually normal children. Before
interacting with a child, the teacher read a brief medi-
cal-developmental description of the child. Half of the
children were described as mentally retarded. The other

half were not. Each teacher was required to read a short
story to a child. The sessions were videotaped. The
experimenters found that teachers assigned to read to the
"mentally retarded" children showed more body leans toward
the children than did the other group of teachers.

512. Lefcourt, H. M., Rotenberg, F., Buckspan, R., and Steffy,
R. A. Visual interaction and performance of process and reactive schizophrenics as a function of examiner's sex. Journal
of Personality, 1967, 35, 535-546.

   The experimenters did a continued exploration of differential sensitivity to an examiner's sex on the part of reactive and process schizophrenics. They hypothesized that
   process subjects would show a greater incidence of avoidance of eye contact than reactives. In addition, process
   subjects were predicted to display less eye contact with
   female than male examiners. Subjects were newly admitted
   patients to a psychiatric hospital. Patients and examiners sat in easy chairs opposite each other at close proximity. An observer behind a one-way mirror recorded frequency and duration of the subject's visual interaction
   during the two-minute interview. After the interview,
   two alternate forms of the Wechsler digit-span task were
   given to determine the affects of anxiety on performance.
   Results for duration did not reach significance. Results
   for frequency showed that for extreme groups, reactives
   tended to engage in more eye contact than process subjects. Sex by pathology level showed that reactives
   looked more than process subjects when both groups met
   with a female examiner, and the latter looked less at
   females than males. No significant difference was found
   between the groups for the digit-span test.

513. Lester, E. P. A two-year-old girl with 'tics': Theo-
retic and therapeutic considerations. International Journal
of Child Psychotherapy, 1973, 2, 71-79.

   Lester discussed the case of a two-year-old female child
   who displayed facial tics demonstrating underlying conflict. The tic entailed blinking the eyes. Lester noted
   that many times a tic is not brought to the attention of
   the psychiatrist unless they are exaggerated. Usually,
   mothers handle the situation themselves by removing the
   stressful stimulus. Lester further stated that rewarding
   the tic would not be a reinforcement of pathological behavior but a response to the child's device for communicating a certain need.

514. Levy, L. H., Orr, T. B., and Rosenweig, S. Judgments
of emotion from facial expressions by college students, mental
retardates, and mental hospital patients. Journal of Personality, 1960, 28, 342-349.

   Levy et al. compared normal subjects, mental defectives,
   and mental hospital patients (mainly psychotics) on their

ability to judge facial expressions of emotion. Judgments of pleasant-unpleasantness were examined. Forty-eight pictures of young women were shown to each subject individually by an experimenter. It was found that the groups agreed in their mean judgments of pleasantness-unpleasantness for the pictures. However, interquartile ranges showed differences between the groups with the mental defective and hospital patients having a greater range of judgments than the college sample.

515. Lykken, D. T.   A study of anxiety in the sociopathic personality. Journal of Abnormal and Social Psychology, 1957, 55, 6-10.

Lykken compared two groups of psychiatric patients and a group of normal male and female subjects on responses to the MMPI, and two anxiety measures and responses to anticipated shock. He hypothesized that individuals who had been diagnosed as psychopathic personalities would be less able than normal subjects to be conditioned to a state of anxiety, would show little manifest anxiety in normal life situations even when such a response was appropriate, and would be incapable of avoidance learning. Lykken found that the group labeled as primary sociopaths showed less anxiety than normals on the paper-and-pencil measures as well as on the GSRs. The group which was labeled neurotic sociopaths scored higher on two anxiety means than did normals.

516. Mahl, G. F.   Some clinical observations on nonverbal behavior in interviews. Journal of Nervous and Mental Disease, 1967, 144, 492-505.

Mahl was concerned about the nonverbal expression of idiosyncratic behaviors. He discussed what he called "nonverbal anticipation of spontaneous verbalization among clinical patients during a psychiatric interview." By this he meant the circumstance during which an individual speaks about one thing and performs a seemingly unrelated action. Later, the person mentions another thing related both to the earlier topic and the previous action. Examples of patients displaying this behavior were presented. Mahl also discussed actions related to dreams, the manifestation of the ego through various actions, and communicative gestures.

517. Mallenby, T. W.   Personal space: Projective and direct measures with institutionalized mentally retarded children. Journal of Personality Assessment, 1974, 38, 28-31.

Mallenby wanted to determine whether or not institutionalized mentally retarded children (males and females aged 7-14) were aware of their abnormality or denied it. A projective and a live interaction measure was used. For the projective measure each subject was to place a same-sex figure in relation to a referent figure. For the

live interaction the subject and a confederate conversed
for 20 seconds (standing), after which the distance between them was measured. The results showed significant
differences for sex for the subjects. There was also a
significant difference based on sex by degree of retar-
dation. For example, mildly retarded girls placed the
self-figure closer to the referent than did mildly retarded boys, while moderately retarded girls placed the
self-figure farther from the referent than did moderately
retarded boys. The opposite sex by group response occurred for the live interaction.

518. Marcus, N. A psychotherapeutic corroboration of the
meaning of the smiling response. Psychoanalytic Review,
1969, 56, 387-401.

Marcus presented case studies on two psychotherapy pa-
tients--one male, one female--in an effort to discuss
the use of smiling as a psychic organizer. His effort
was based upon findings reported on infants by Spitz
(1965). Marcus also discussed the need to look more
carefully at the smiling response in psychotherapeutic
situations--something which he asserted was not attended
to sufficiently.

519. Marcus, N. Yawning: Analytic and therapeutic considerations. International Journal of Child Psychotherapy, 1973,
2, 406-418.

Marcus presented the case history of a 13-year-old boy
whose main expressive response during psychotherapy was
yawning. He also presented some of the literature on
nonverbal expressions. Marcus suggested that only by
doing a comprehensive analysis of unitary nonverbal responses can the psychoanalyst gain a clearer picture of
the patient's underlying problem. It was found that
yawning served the boy's need to regress. A more extensive analysis of his behavior was presented.

520. Meerloo, J. Archaic behavior and the communicative act:
The meaning of stretching, yawning, rocking and other fetal
behavior in therapy. Psychiatric Quarterly, 1955, 29, 60-73.

Meerloo discussed the use of involuntary signals or nonverbal behaviors during psychotherapy which may represent
archaic or intrauterine behaviors. He observed such behaviors as rhythmic movements, head banging, and rocking
and dancing. His article also discussed various archaic
oral behaviors--yawning, smiling, thumbsucking, for example. Meerloo pointed out that these findings had importance for the elaboration of clinical observation.

521. Mintz, E. E. Touch and the psychoanalytic tradition.
Psychoanalytic Review, 1969, 56, 365-376.

Mintz discussed the psychoanalytic taboo on touching between client and therapist from a historical perspective.

She also discussed the theoretical validity of this approach, some contemporary views, and some of the meanings of physical contact between client and therapist.
Some of the meanings she presented were: (1) direct
libidinal gratification on the part of the client, (2)
a symbol of mothering, (3) showing a sense of being
accepted, and (4) showing a sense of reality.

522. Prkachin, K. M., Craig, K. D., Papageorgis, D., and
Reith, G. Nonverbal communication deficits and response to
performance feedback in depression. Journal of Abnormal
Psychology, 1977, 86, 224-234.

Depressed, psychiatric, and normal female subjects had
their facial expressions videotaped while being exposed
to a differential classical conditioning treatment.
Three trials were used: one with picture stimuli following a conditional stimulus, a second with auditory stimuli
following a second conditional stimulus, and a neutral
event following a third conditional stimulus. For a second session, these subjects were shown videotapes of other
subjects from the three diagnostic groups and judged to
type of conditioning treatment she was undergoing. Results showed that depressed subjects were the poorest
senders of affect. In addition, improvement in the ability to make judgments occurred over time. Other results
were also presented.

523. Rago, W. V., Jr. Eye gaze and dominance hierarchy in
profoundly mentally retarded males. American Journal of
Mental Deficiency, 1977, 82, 145-148.

Rago investigated the function of mutual gaze among profoundly mentally retarded males. Two groups of subjects
were studied. They were dichotomized into subordinate and
dominant members. An experimenter elicited eye contact
with each subject by gazing into his eyes as he approached
him. Rago found that subordinate subjects spent more time
engaged in steady eye contact than dominant subjects.
These results were contrary to previous research.

524. Riemer, N. Abnormalities of the gaze: A classification.
Psychiatric Quarterly, 1966, 29, 659-672.

In noting that the eyes are adapted for emotional activity
and that the gaze is an index of the affective components
of the psyche, Riemer discussed six abnormalities of the
gaze as determined by clinical data he had accumulated.
The six forms were: (a) excessive blinking which exists
when the closures of the eyelids exceed 10 per minute;
(b) the depressed look in which a sad appearance occurs;
(c) the dramatic gaze used to deceive one's self and
others; (d) the guarded gaze which represents a state of
severe psychopathology and is evident in the alert watch-
fulness of the patient's eyes, voice, face, manner, and
general attitude; (e) the absent gaze with a blank

expression in the eyes; and (f) the averted gaze with a
concomitant turning away of the body and an aversion of
the entire emotional being.

525. Ro-Trock, G. K. Family therapy versus individual therapy in a public mental health facility. Dissertation Abstracts International, 1976(May), Vol. 36(11-B), 5523.

Ro-Trock hypothesized that adolescents who experienced
family therapy would make better community adaptations
than those in short-term individual therapy. He also
hypothesized that family therapy adolescents, their
mothers, and their fathers would report or show more
improvement in nonverbal and verbal communication patterns than would the other group of adolescents. The
subjects were 28 hospitalized adolescents who received
10 sessions of family or individual therapy. A pre- and
posttest and a one-month follow-up were done. The first
hypothesis was confirmed; however, the adolescents, mothers, and fathers did not differ significantly on the measures for the other hypothesis as well as several other
predictions.

526. Sainsbury, P. Gestural movement during psychiatric interviews. Psychosomatic Medicine, 1955, 17, 458-469.

The purpose of the research was to measure the gestural
movements made by patients during a psychiatric interview
in which topics covering things which were likely and un-
likely to distort them were discussed. Speech accompanying the gestures was tape recorded as well as muscle potential. Six male and six female patients were given 16
interviews. Sainsbury found that the patients used more
gestures during the stressful portions of the interviews
(in terms of topics) than during the nonstressful portions. Gestures also increased when the patient spoke
about stressful things as opposed to when he or she spoke
of nonstressful matters. Heart rate increased during
stressful periods as well.

527. Scheflen, A. E. Communication and regulation in psychotherapy. Psychiatry, 1963, 26, 126-136.

Scheflen used content analysis to describe and discuss
the communicational sequences used between clients and
therapists during psychotherapy sessions. In addition to
speech, touch, body motion, dress, decor, and bodily noise
were observed during regular psychotherapy sessions. Four
examples of filmed therapy sessions were presented.
Scheflen also discussed the social structures which are
a part of psychotherapy and presented various clinical
implications of knowledge of the communication and regulation process during therapy.

528. Scheflen, A. E. Quasi-courtship behavior in psychotherapy. Psychiatry, 1965, 28, 245-257.

Scheflen noted that human behavior was systematic and patterned. Through extensive research he had determined that these patterns were arranged in lawful configurations. One such pattern concerned behavior which may normally be found in American courtship. Scheflen discussed various nonverbal behaviors associated with this quasi-courtship response during psychotherapy. He suggested that this behavior is used by both client and therapist to induce rapport and also to regulate and maintain the relationship.

529. Scheflen, A. E. The significance of posture in communication systems. Psychiatry, 1964, 27, 316-321.

Scheflen discussed various postural configurations found in psychotherapy and how they were reliable indicators of certain aspects of communication. These configurations show the components of individual behavior that each person contributes to the group activity, indicate how the individual contributions are related to each other, and define the steps and order in the interaction. Some of Scheflen's examples were concerned with the body positions used by the therapist. For instance, a posture with the head slightly downward, cocked to the right, and averted eyes was used while listening. The head tilted up marked the end of one point in the discussion and a transition to another. Lastly, the head erect, looking directly at the patient was used while making an interpretation. The clinical significance of such behavior (on the part of patient and therapist) was discussed.

530. Seguin, C. The individual space. International Journal of Neuropsychiatry, 1967, 3, 108-117.

Seguin postulated the existence of the individual space, a part of the environment surrounding the person and incorporated to his corporal scheme so that it becomes a part of it. Daily observations of normal subjects and psychiatric patients confirmed this. There were some individuals who, when talking, got so close that others tended to withdraw in order to maintain a certain distance. However, there were others who did not permit any kind of nearness whatsoever. This characteristic varied individually and in relation to culture, moods, and psychopathology.

531. Steingart, I., Grand, S., Margolis, R., Freedman, N., and Buchwald, C. A study of the representation of anxiety in chronic schizophrenia. Journal of Abnormal Psychology, 1976, 85, 535-542.

Steingart et al. looked at the nonverbal and verbal behavior of male schizophrenics in order to determine whether or not there was a relationship between these indices of communication and certain types of anxiety expression. Sixteen male chronic patients were used.

Audiovideo tapes were made of interviews with the patients. Hand movement behavior which accompanied speech
was examined. They reported that their data showed that
differences in the two general modes of expression were
linked to important differences in anxiety expression.

532. Tolor, A. Psychological distance in disturbed and normal children. Psychological Reports, 1968, 23, 695-701.

Tolor attempted to determine whether emotionally disturbed children experienced more distant psychological
relationships than normal children. His hypotheses were
that disturbed children would have greater distances in
social situations than normal children, and that the
former groups would place human figure pairings involving
at least one female farther apart than those involving
male figures. The disturbed group consisted of male and
female Black and White youngsters from seven to 12 years
of age. The normal group consisted of only White males
and females of the same age. A modified version of
Kuethe's (1962) replacement technique was employed. The
results showed that there was no significant difference
in replacement distances for the two groups. However,
age had an affect in that for both groups at the 11 to
12 age range, there was greater separation of figures
than at the 10-year level. Another finding was that
interracial male-female reconstructions were generally
made more distant than same-race male-female pairings.

533. Tolor, A., Warren, M., and Weinick, H. M. Relation between parental interpersonal styles and their children's
psychological distance. Psychological Reports, 1971, 29,
1263-1275.

The authors investigated the relationship between parent
past life styles of varying degrees of closeness or distance to others and their children's interpersonal distance patterns by W. Mottola's History of Interpersonal
Distance Scale and two measures based on Kuethe's Social
Schemata Technique. Two groups of children--a clinical
population and a normal population and the mothers (some-
times fathers) of each child--participated. On some measures, normal subjects showed a pattern of psychological
distance opposite to that of their parents of the same
sex. Disturbed subjects tended to have a psychological
distance that differed from that of the opposite of both
parents. There was no evidence of a greater correlation
between a subject and same-sex parent for disturbed subjects than for normals. However, there was some indication of a greater degree of social closeness in the history of parents of normal subjects. Normal and disturbed
subjects did not produce different distance patterns.

534. Trumbo, D. P. The effect of the experimenter's nonverbally communicated personal warmth and verbal praise on the
task persistence of educable mentally handicapped children.

Dissertation Abstracts International, 1977(Sep), Vol. 38
(3-A), 1335.

Trumbo studied the effects of an experimenter's nonverbally warm cues on task persistency among educable mentally handicapped children. He also looked at the effects
of this nonverbal warmth in conjunction with verbal praise
on persistency. Four conditions combining nonverbal
warmth-no warmth and verbal praise-no praise were used.
Children with a mean age of 7.9 were subjects and were
individually interviewed by a female examiner while attempting to complete a jigsaw puzzle which was insoluble.
No significant difference was found between the group
means according to an analysis of variance.

535. Weinstein, L. Social schemata of emotionally disturbed
boys. Journal of Abnormal Psychology, 1965, 70, 457-461.

Two experiments using Kuethe's schemata technique were
designed to demonstrate that children defined as emotionally disturbed differed predictably from normal children in the ways they organized social stimuli. When
emotionally disturbed and normal boys placed pairs of
felt figures on flannel boards, normals placed child figures closer to mother figures than to father or peer figures; emotionally disturbed boys did the reverse. When
disturbed and normal boys placed pairs of human and geometric figures previously set 15 inches apart, the disturbed boys placed the human figures farther apart than
the nonhuman figures significantly more often than normals. Results were interpreted as reflecting a tendency
for disturbed children to construe people, especially
females, more negatively than do normal children.

536. Winick, C. and Holt, H. Seating positions as non-verbal
communication in group analysis. Psychiatry, 1961, 24, 171-
182.

Winick and Holt looked at how patients seated themselves
during therapy sessions and analyzed certain personality
characteristics associated with seating position, choice
of particular kind of chair, and seated posture, as these
communicated things to the therapist and to other patients.
For example, when both fixed and folding chairs were provided during the therapy session, those who chose folding
chairs were likely to be, according to the authors, more
insecure and to have a greater need to control externals
than those who chose fixed chairs. Patients who sat on
the floor during group analysis, despite the presence of
chairs, were likely to be dependent and to be seeking to
make parental images of the group or to want more attention than they had been getting. When the therapist consistently sat in the same chair, a patient's choice of a
chair to the right or left of him could be significant.
This was asserted to be a carry-over of the seating arrangements used in the parents' home. Sitting to the

left of the therapist was frequently seen as feminine, while sitting on the right was seen as masculine. Women who appeared to have a need to play a mother role might sit on the therapist's left.

Subject Index

The numbers after each word refer to item numbers in the bibliography.

Author Index

Sewell, A. F., 405
Shears, L. M., 359
Sheldon, W. H., 406
Shephard, J., 122
Shrout, P. E., 407
Siders, C., 506
Siegel, H. E., 85
Siegman, A. W., 408
Sigler, E., 70
Slatterie, E. F., 409
Sleet, D. A., 410
Smallbone, A., 161
Smith, B. J., 411
Smith, G. F., 156
Smith, G. H., 412
Smith, W. J., 413
Snodgrass, L. L., 414
Snortum, J. R., 20
Snyder, M., 415
Sommer, R., 143, 301, 416,
  417, 418, 419, 420, 421,
  422, 423, 424
Spence, D. F., 425
Spratt, G., 161
Staneski, R. A., 256
Starkweather, C. W., 426
Stass, J. W., 427
Steffy, R. A., 512
Stein, S. A., 428
Steingart, I., 531
Steingart, J., 36
Steinzor, B., 429
Stephenson, G., 430
Stern, D. N., 360, 361
Sternbach, R. A., 431
Stewart, D. J., 432
Stewart, R. A., 329
Storms, M. D., 433
Streeter, L. A., 434
Stricker, G., 271
Strongman, K. T., 221
Sundstrom, E., 79
Sweeney, D. R., 435
Sweeney, M. A., 436

T

Tankard, J. W., 438
Thayer, S., 439, 440
Thibaut, J., 138
Thomas, G. C., 433
Thompson, D. F., 441
Thompson, J., 442
Thornton, G. R., 443, 444
Tinling, D. C., 435
Tofalo, R. J., 445

Tolor, A., 446, 532, 533
Tomkins, S. S., 121, 447, 448
Tracy, D. B., 75
Traweek, A. C., 449
Trego, R. E., 374
Trumbo, D. P., 534
Tursky, B., 431
Tyler, J. D., 164

U

Ulehla, Z. J., 299
Unger, R. K., 375

V

Valins, S., 450
Van DeVoort, D., 177
Vaughan, K. B., 249
Vaughan, R. C., 249
Veeser, W. R., 451
Villa-Lovoz, T. R., 452
Vine, I., 454
vonCranock, M., 453, 454
Vukcevic, D. P., 248

W

Wahlers, K. J., 455
Walker, C. A., 108
Walker, D., 456
Walkley, J., 168
Wallace, W. P., 62
Walster, E., 457
Ward, C. D., 458
Ward-Hull, C. I., 28
Warren, M., 533
Watson, S. G., 459
Wauson, M. S., 167
Waxer, P. H., 460
Waxwood, V. C., 461
Webb, W. W., 462
Weber, J. W., 463
Weingarten, N., 272
Weinick, H. M., 533
Weinstein, J., 464
Weinstein, L., 465, 466, 535
Weinstein, M. S., 25
Weise, B. C., 68
Weitz, S., 467
Welkowitz, J., 468
Westie, F. R., 469
White, M. J., 470
Whitman, R. N., 376
Wiener, M., 230, 471
Wiens, A. N., 206

ABOUT THE COMPILER

Constance E. Obudho is presently an educational/vocational counselor for the Veterans Administration at the College of Medicine and Dentistry of New Jersey. She was formerly a Predoctoral Fellow at the Institute for Research in Human Development, Educational Testing Service, Princeton, New Jersey, in 1976-1977.

Dr. Obudho is currently a member of the American Psychological Association, Society for the Psychological Study of Social Issues, and the Rutgers University College Honor Society. Her areas of interest include nonverbal communication, racial attitudes and family counseling.

She is the author of a variety of articles and book reviews. Her major publications include "Clean is Beautiful: The Effects of Race and Cleanliness on Children's Preferences" in Edward Krupat, ed., *Readings and Conversations in Social Psychology: Psychology Is Social*, *The Proxemic Behavior of Man and Animals: An Annotated Bibliography*, and *Black-White Racial Attitudes: An Annotated Bibliography* (Greenwood Press, 1976).